IMAGES
of America

WAKE FOREST

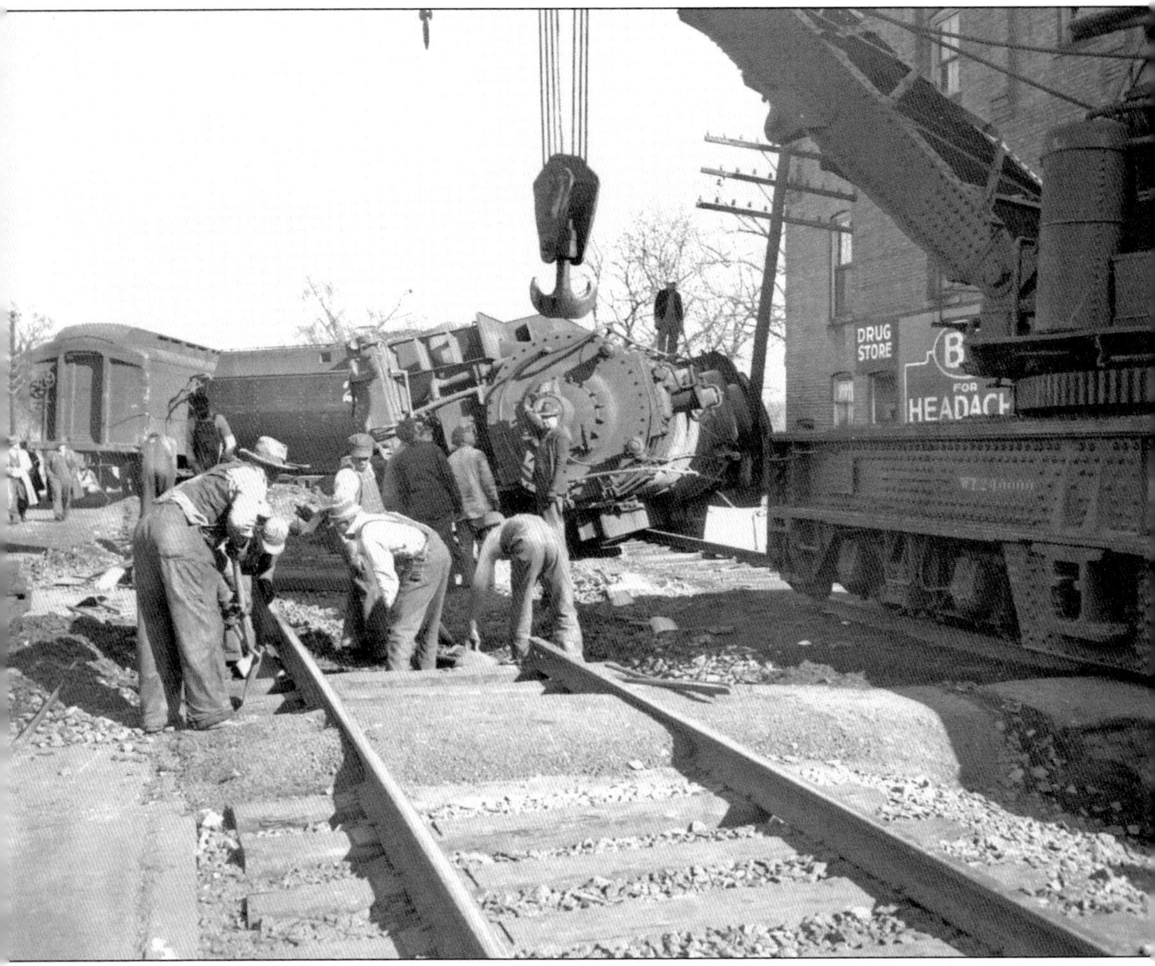

In January 1942, the New York–Florida Limited, traveling more than 50 miles an hour, slammed into a bakery truck near Wake Forest. The train dragged the truck nearly 3,000 feet before stopping near South White Street. The truck driver was killed; the train passengers were rerouted to Apex, and repair crews went to work on 500 feet of twisted track. (Courtesy of the *News and Observer* and the North Carolina State Archives NO.42.1.119-113.)

On the Cover: Wake Forest has always been a religious community. The New Light Baptist Church, founded in 1771, and Wake Union Church, built in 1789, predate the town itself. Wake Forest Baptist Church, pictured here c. 1918 soon after its construction, grew out of local revival meetings. First organized in 1835, its congregation began with Wake Forest College faculty and staff and grew to include the town's leading merchants and many other residents. (Courtesy of Southeastern Baptist Theological Seminary.)

IMAGES
of America

WAKE FOREST

Jennifer Smart

ARCADIA
PUBLISHING

ISBN 978-0-7385-5379-5

Published by Arcadia Publishing
Charleston, South Carolina

Printed in the United States of America

Library of Congress Catalog Card Number: 2007941020

For all general information contact Arcadia Publishing at:
Telephone 843-853-2070
Fax 843-853-0044
E-mail sales@arcadiapublishing.com
For customer service and orders:
Toll-Free 1-888-313-2665

Visit us on the Internet at www.arcadiapublishing.com

In honor of the Wake Forest Birthplace Museum for the memories it preserves. And for the Town of Wake Forest and the future it holds.

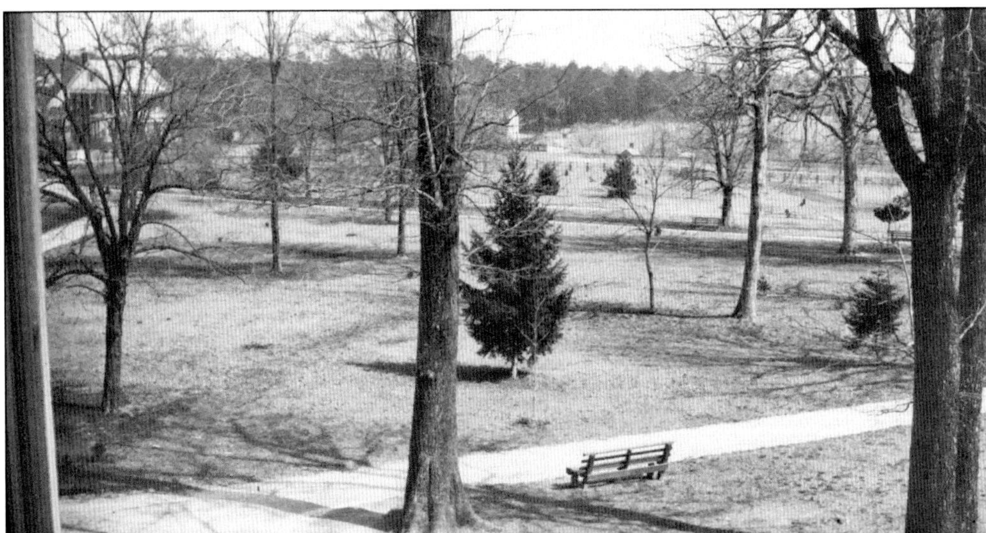

This campus view, c. 1900, looks northeast and shows commercial farm buildings beyond the 1838 North Brick House on the left. College president Charles Taylor (1884–1905) was intensely interested in transforming the campus from what he viewed as a rustic farmstead into a beautiful park. This photograph, taken from an upper window of the College Building, documents the success of his project. (Courtesy of the Wake Forest Birthplace Museum.)

Contents

ACKNOWLEDGMENTS

Wake Forest, with its unique past, has much in common with its antique homes where layers of paint have collected like historic images in the pages of an album. The Wake Forest College Birthplace Society has spent many years preserving the actual images of the town's history, and this volume attempts to match those photographs with memories.

This is the work of many—too many to list without accidental omission. But the direction and guidance offered was both necessary and appreciated. Extraordinary gratitude is due the Wake Forest Birthplace Museum and its wonderful director, Ed Morris, who, in sharing hundreds of artifacts deserving of widespread interest and support, expertly shaped this book. Susan Brinkley, who serves as president of the Wake Forest College Birthplace Society, was vitally important in editing the finished text. Beverly Whisnant, Margaret Weininger, Lawrence Perry of the National Alumni Association of the DuBois School, Betty Frankow, Rev. Enoch Holloway of Friendship Chapel Baptist Church, Hallie Arrington Hearn, and Lorenzo Jackson have been instrumental and deserve much appreciation and credit, as do Lance Michaels of Southeastern Baptist Theological Seminary, Speed and Barbara Massenburg, A. C. and Gloria Hall, Robert White of Wake Forest Federal Savings and Loan, and Jim Mackie. Kelly Lally's outstanding volume *The Historic Architecture of Wake County, North Carolina* was an invaluable resource, as was Elizabeth Reid Murray's published history of Wake County. And I owe a tremendous debt to Carol Pelosi, publisher of the *Wake Forest Gazette*. Without its reliable reporting, this book would have lacked the details that help make history come alive.

This project would never have gotten off the ground without the talented researchers of the North Carolina State Archives in Raleigh: Kay Tillotson, Steve Case, Vann Evans, and expert archivist Kim Cumber. Historic images from the *Raleigh News and Observer* come via Peggy Neal and Paul Magann.

Finally, I want to thank my editor at Arcadia Publishing, Maggie Bullwinkel, for her support, advice, and guidance. Billy and Maggie Smart—thank you for your enthusiastic research assistance. And thanks most of all to William Spencer Smart II, who makes it all happen.

INTRODUCTION

There was a time when Wake County's two largest towns were Raleigh and Wake Forest. That was not long after the early days, when Wake County farmers let their livestock roam through pasture and town. Indian corn and pork were the most popular foods, so corn-shuckings and hog-killings were the premiere social events.

But farms—large, isolated, and far-flung—were missing one essential ingredient: a central business district. The earliest mention of a more structured community in the Wake Forest area refers to a 1700s trading post at the banks of the Neuse River. Built at the Falls of Neuse more than 200 years ago, the store served northern Wake County and grew into the first of the various communities that later converged to form Wake Forest Township.

Also in the 1700s, the Crenshaw family began settling the banks of Horse Creek north of Falls of Neuse, opening a mill and store. This vaguely defined section north of the falls has an odd history all its own. Informally known as "the Harricane" for more than two centuries, the hardscrabble area was originally named for a fierce storm—a purported hurricane—that cut paths of destruction through the wooded terrain sometime in the 18th century. The name is pronounced exactly as it's spelled, though few are around to remember.

Another colloquialism, foreshadowing the eventual name of the town, also rose from the terrain. In the 1790s, a large area of northern Wake County became known as "the Forest of Neuse" or "the Forest District." Soon folks were calling it "the Wake Forest" and praising its reputation for learning and sophistication. By the early 19th century, it boasted three schools, two churches, a doctor, and a lawyer. In 1832, with growing concern over the education of Baptist ministers, the North Carolina Baptist Convention decided to establish an institute of religious learning. Prompted by local minister John Purefoy, the convention settled on 615 acres in the Forest District owned by Dr. Calvin Jones, whose newspaper advertisement stated, "The inhabitants, without I believe a single exception, are sober, moral, and thriving in their circumstances, and not a few are educated and intelligent."

The land and farmhouse sold for $2,000, and Wake Forest Institute opened on February 3, 1834, enrolling a class of 15 local boys who traded manual labor for lessons, room, and board. Some paid tuition with items such as flour, butter, beef, soap, and feathers—all of which were entered in the student account book. The first student to enroll was John Crenshaw, son of the institution's treasurer, William Crenshaw. The school's first president was Samuel Wait, a Baptist minister from upstate New York who helped shape the school's vision, curriculum, and mission. By the end of that first year, the student body had grown to 72. Construction of the first campus buildings and faculty houses had begun.

But Wake Forest soon discovered its burgeoning population needed more. Specifically, it needed a train depot. The nearest stop in Forestville, approximately a mile southwest of town, forced long walks on out-of-town students traveling by train. At that time, Forestville was a thriving community with a post office, stores, and two churches; its continued success was closely bound to the railroad line. But Wake Forest town leaders kept the pressure on until, after much wrangling, the Raleigh and Gaston Railroad agreed to move the depot in 1874. Forestville's growth eventually stalled. Its town charter was repealed in 1915, and it later became part of Wake Forest—leaving only a roadside marker on South Main Street, along with a handful of historic churches and homes.

In the meantime, the college was gathering speed. As the second institution of higher learning to open in North Carolina and the first in Wake County, it was soon educating young men from across the southeast in the Baptist tradition. The trustees began laying out plans for the surrounding town, settling on 80 one-acre plots of land on which homes would be built for faculty and staff. A sturdy commercial center sprang up around the new train depot, as businesses such as Powers and Holding Drugstore, Dickson Brothers Dry Goods, and Jones Hardware made a tidy profit in sales. The African American community, concentrated in the northeast section of town, developed its own shops and neighborhoods catering primarily to the black community. Massenburg's Store and Smith's Shoe Shop were among the best known and lasted through most of the 20th century. In 1880, the town was incorporated as Wake Forest College, changing the name to the Town of Wake Forest in 1909.

At the same time, Wake Forest stepped into industry with the founding of the Royall Cotton Mill north of Faculty Avenue. The mill was the brainchild of Robert Royall, Thomas Holding, and William Powell, all Wake Forest College graduates. The mill manufactured a variety of cotton fabrics, while W. W. Holding and Company, working from a building on South White Street, became a major supplier of raw cotton purchased from area farmers and sold to mills across the southeast. Those making up the foundation of this towering economic achievement, the mill workers, lived in the mill village; consisting of a commissary, school, churches, and network of four-room houses, the village and mill were incorporated as the Town of Royall Mills in 1907. Although the mill families often felt isolated from the rest of Wake Forest, the village itself functioned quite efficiently. However, the business eventually fell on hard times, and at the request of mill management, the village charter was repealed in 1943.

It was all going so well until residents heard a hint of the future through a radio broadcast. On March 25, 1946, a news report claimed the R. J. Reynolds Foundation was offering to give the college millions of dollars if it would move to Winston-Salem. The student newspaper compared the news to the drop of an atomic bomb, a life-changing moment that could not be undone. Ten years later, the college was gone. The town was bereft; without the faculty, students, and life it had known, it was left without a collective identity. The Southern Baptists bought the campus for a seminary, ensuring Wake Forest wouldn't become a ghost town. But there was a larger gap to fill.

After an eight-year stretch during which everyone wondered if the town would survive, an industrial boom at last delivered the missing element, not entirely filling the void but returning Wake Forest to economic stability. The Schrader plant, maker of air-control equipment, and the Athey plant, which built machines for moving heavy material, were the first to arrive. Together they brought hundreds of jobs. By the late 1960s, the community was no longer struggling, but residents still missed the excitement and bustle of the college days. It took the turn of yet another century for the town to regain a glimmer of its former glory. By 1990, the Census Bureau counted more than 15,000 people living in Wake Forest Township. By 2005, that number had grown to 25,000. With the introduction of new residents, businesses, and schools, the town—former home to Wake County's first college campus—has come to be so much more.

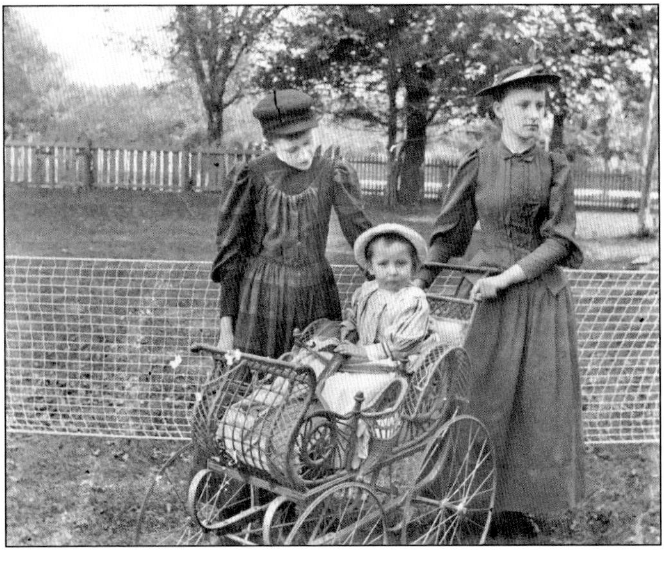

Two daughters of Wake Forest College president Charles Taylor pose on a tennis court while his young granddaughter, Virginia Gorrell, holds a racket. Tennis was an acceptable and popular sport for women in the late Victorian period. In this highly posed composition, the child's mother, Fannie Gorrell, looks away from the camera as if ignoring its presence. (Courtesy of the Wake Forest Birthplace Museum.)

One

FIVE TOWNS

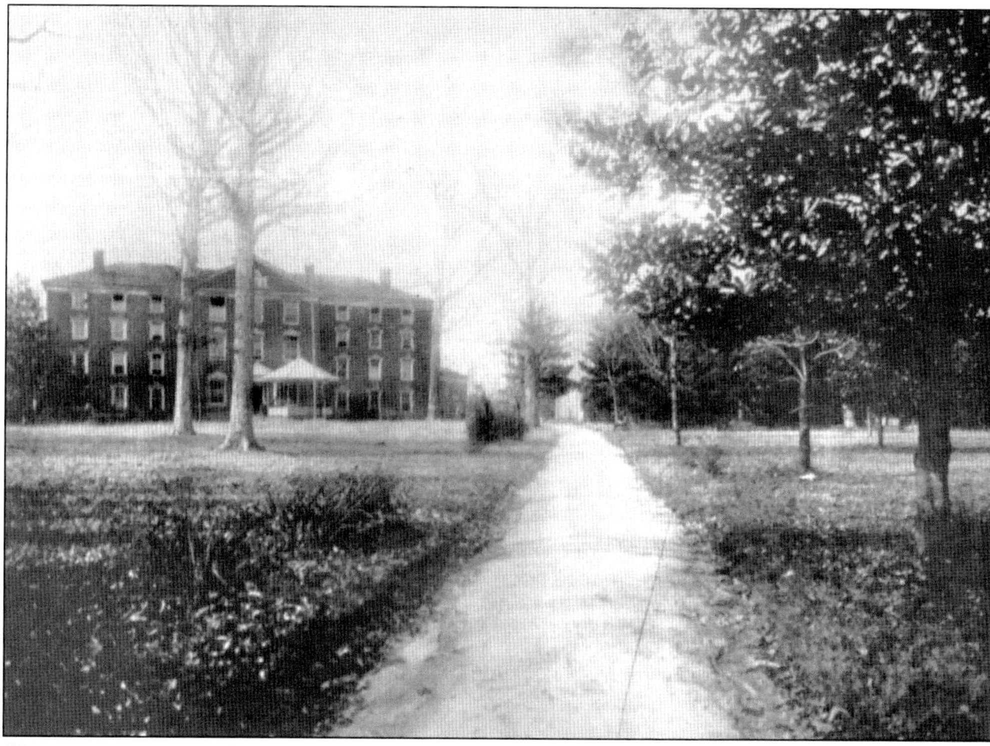

"Five towns in one" is how locals once described Wake Forest. It had the college campus, founded in 1834 and originally populated by an exclusively male faculty and student body. Then came the tiny network of streets surrounding the school, home to college professors and business owners, culminating in the fine houses along Faculty Avenue, later called North Main Street. Just past those elegant blocks, the mill village was eventually incorporated as the Town of Royall Mills, supporting its own store, churches, and school. The segregated northeast section of Wake Forest was home to the town's African American community. It operated quite independently of the rest of Wake Forest, producing many successful residents, schools, and businesses. Finally, farther from the town proper, the rural region northwest of Wake Forest was popularly known as "the Harricane." Its exact location remains a mystery as, when asked precisely where to find it, residents invariably answered with a vague, "over yonder a ways." (Courtesy of the Wake Forest Birthplace Museum.)

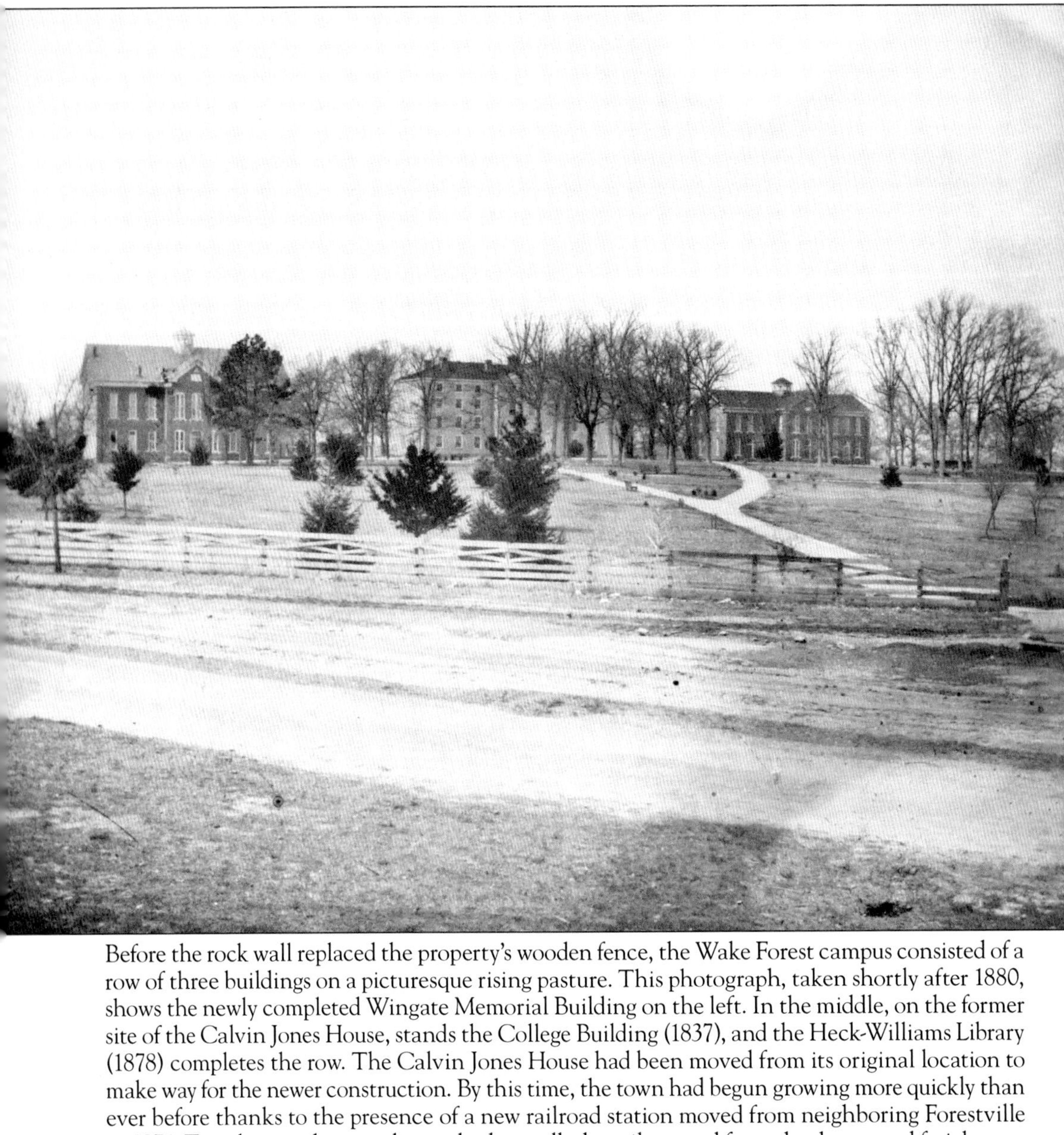

Before the rock wall replaced the property's wooden fence, the Wake Forest campus consisted of a row of three buildings on a picturesque rising pasture. This photograph, taken shortly after 1880, shows the newly completed Wingate Memorial Building on the left. In the middle, on the former site of the Calvin Jones House, stands the College Building (1837), and the Heck-Williams Library (1878) completes the row. The Calvin Jones House had been moved from its original location to make way for the newer construction. By this time, the town had begun growing more quickly than ever before thanks to the presence of a new railroad station moved from neighboring Forestville in 1874. Traveling students no longer had to walk the mile to and from the depot, and freight cars were establishing commercial trade. (Courtesy of the Wake Forest Birthplace Museum.)

The college yearbook and newspaper were popular reading material on and off campus. Though both contained occasional items of interest and news regarding the town, their content was mainly campus-based. In fact, the college was virtually a town unto itself. By 1925, it boasted a population of more than 700 young men and 31 professors. (Courtesy of the Wake Forest Birthplace Museum.)

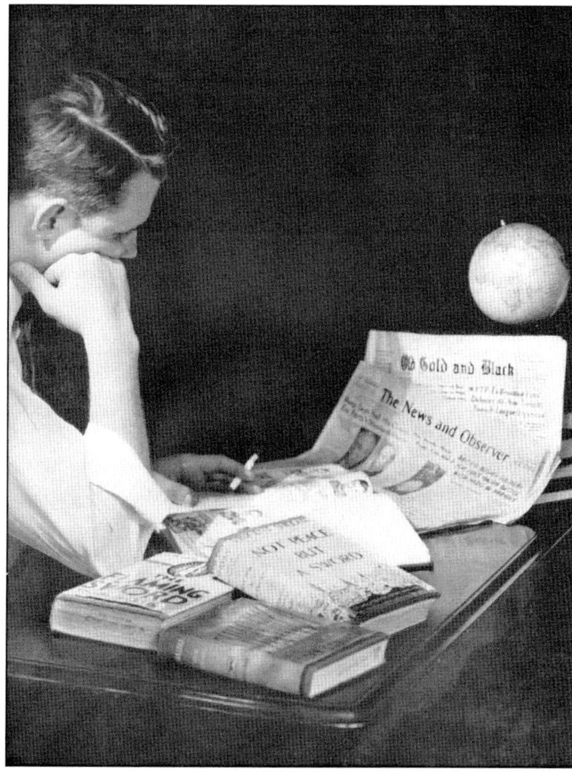

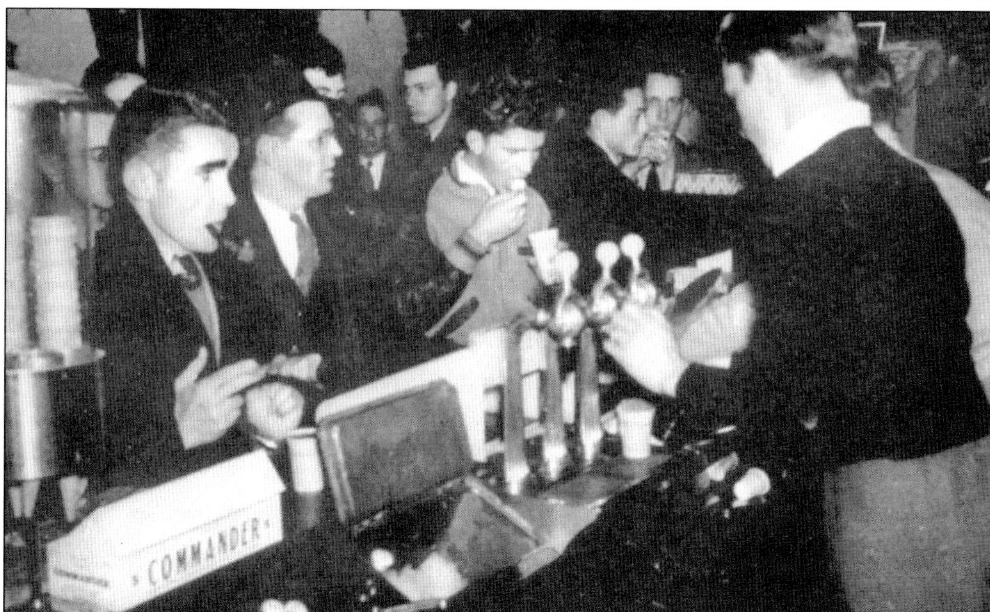

The town's restaurants prospered during the college years, as the school had no cafeteria. This 1940 photograph of the College Soda Shop, located on South White Street, shows a typical crowd. The college brought $2 million into town each year and, when it moved in May 1956, shops and stores were forced to close. The town became a much quieter and more sedate place. (Courtesy of the Wake Forest Birthplace Museum.)

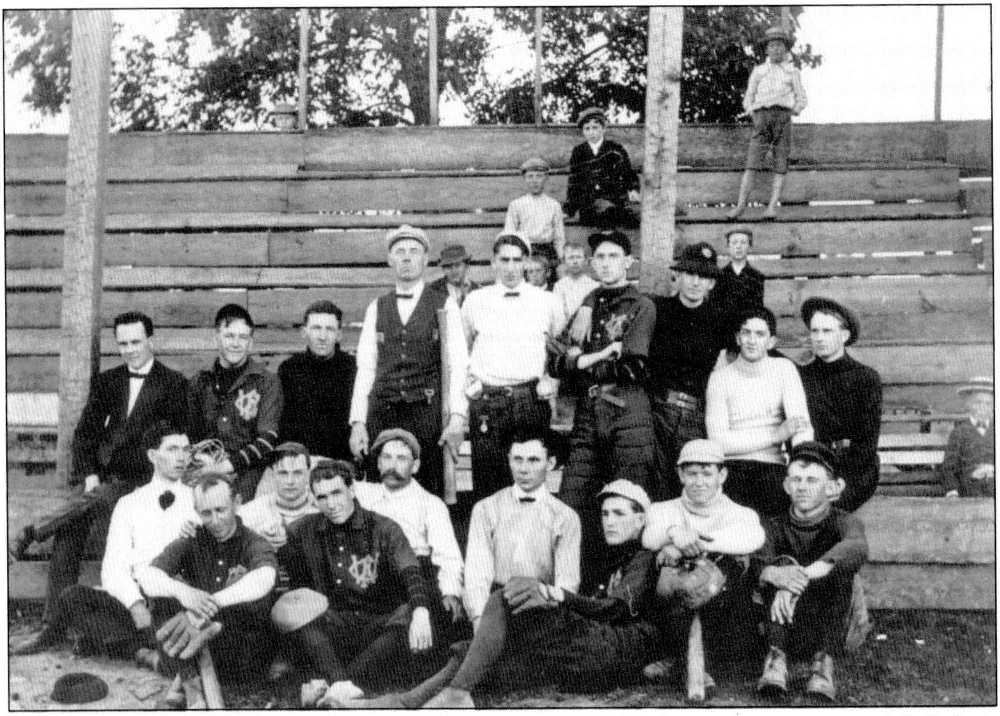

The faculty and staff of the college, living in homes surrounding campus, were a tightly knit community within the larger town. These teachers, members of the faculty baseball team, posed together at a game in 1903. (Courtesy of the Wake Forest Birthplace Museum.)

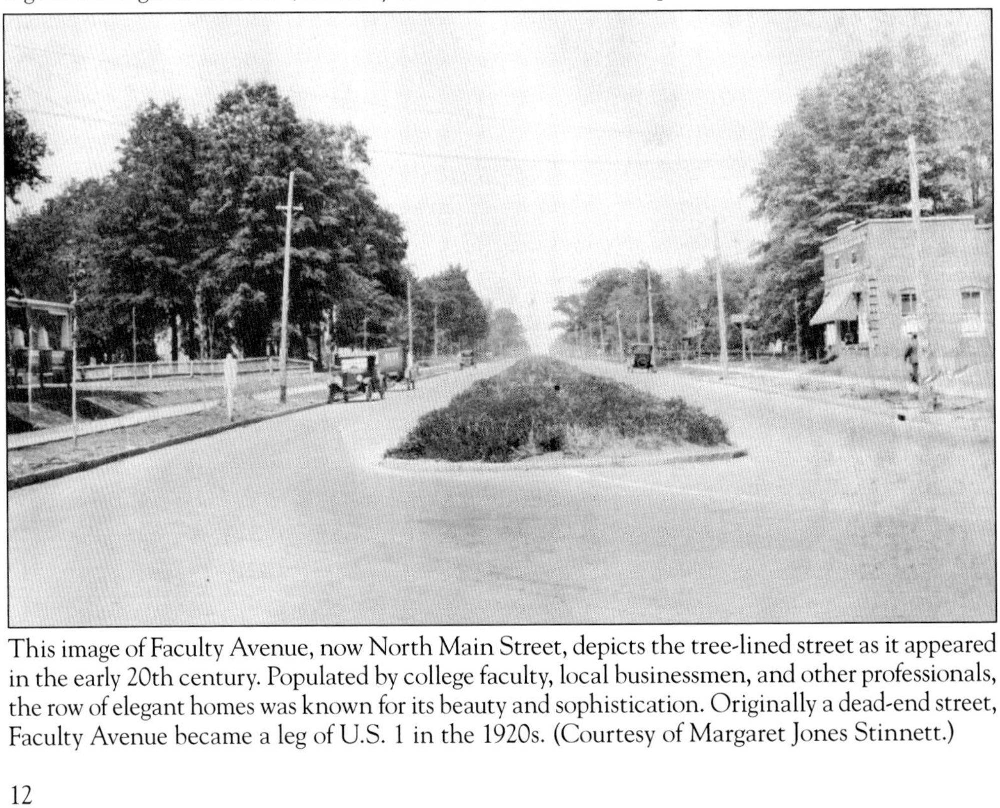

This image of Faculty Avenue, now North Main Street, depicts the tree-lined street as it appeared in the early 20th century. Populated by college faculty, local businessmen, and other professionals, the row of elegant homes was known for its beauty and sophistication. Originally a dead-end street, Faculty Avenue became a leg of U.S. 1 in the 1920s. (Courtesy of Margaret Jones Stinnett.)

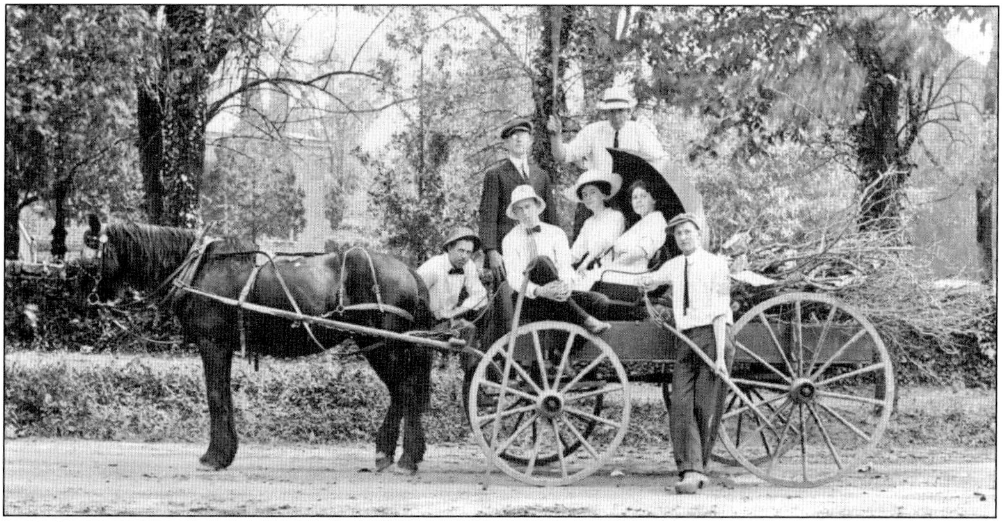

A fashionably dressed Hallie Powers Arrington, in the center of this c. 1910 photograph, was a direct descendant of the college's first president, Samuel Wait. Seated on her left is her husband, Tom Arrington II, a Wake Forest College graduate. The image appears to be posed alongside the rock wall bordering campus. Tom Arrington later served as the town's fire chief. (Courtesy of the Wake Forest Birthplace Museum.)

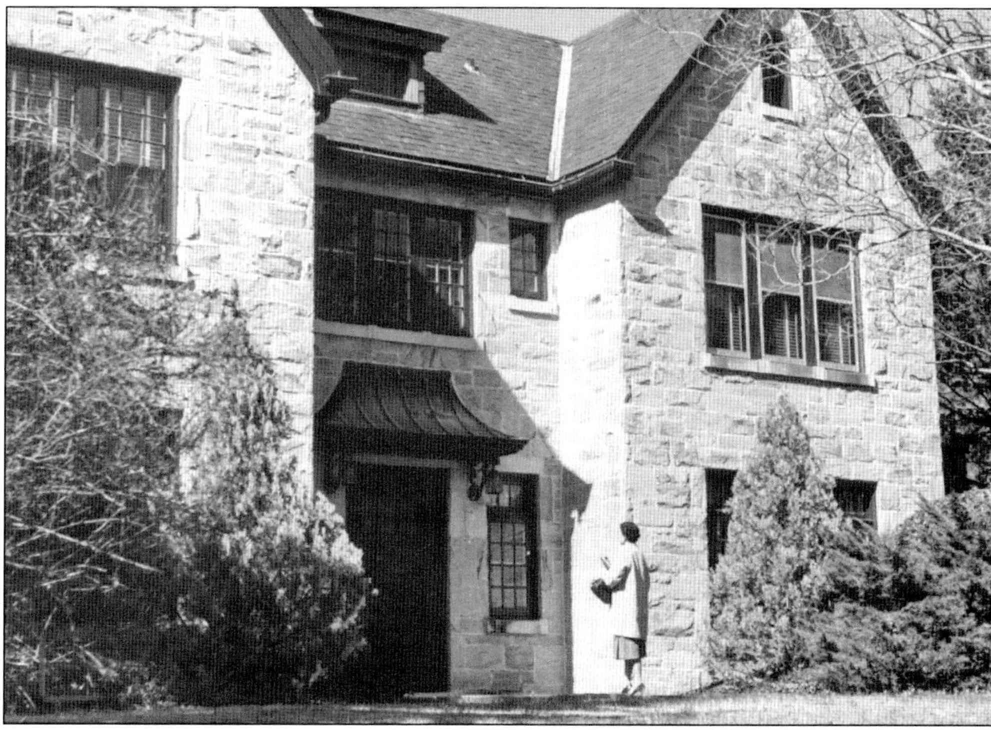

The Wake Forest College president's home was completed in 1928 at a cost of $25,000. It took six months to build and is constructed of Wake County limestone similar to that used at Duke University. On the first floor, there were five original rooms and a sun parlor. The second floor had six bedrooms and a study for the president. (Courtesy of Southeastern Baptist Theological Seminary.)

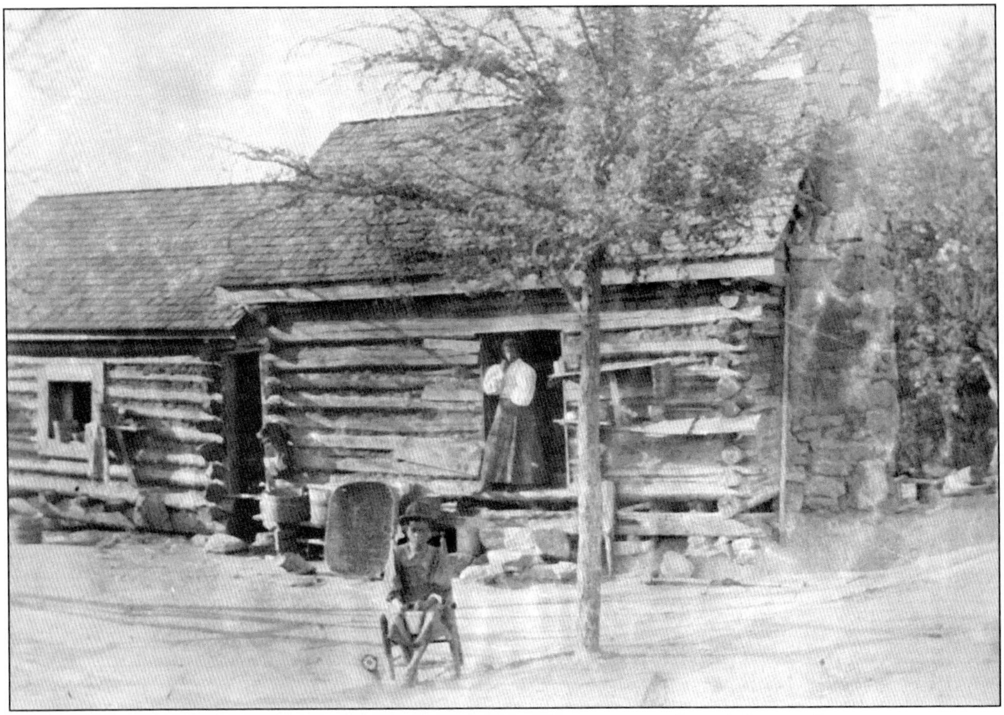

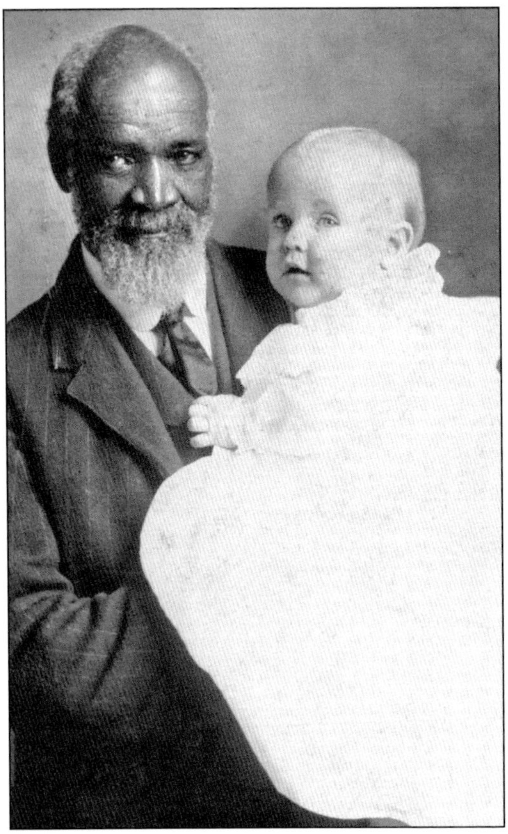

This image of an African American family at home in Wake Forest in the late 19th century provides a rare glimpse into the living conditions for many families in the decades following the Civil War. The photograph suggests concern on the part of college president Dr. Charles Taylor and his wife, both of whom wished to improve life for the town's African American residents. (Courtesy of the Wake Forest Birthplace Museum.)

Baby Henry Seawell and Harry, a family employee at Oakforest, a former plantation house in historic Forestville, posed for this photograph in August 1903. A direct descendant of original landholder Benjamin Smith, Henry was brought up in the plantation house, which has been owned by Smith's descendants for more than two centuries. (Courtesy of Speed Massenburg and family.)

Black and white residents lived together but had little social contact. Many African American men and women worked for white families and were photographed in that role. In this c. 1935 image, an unidentified cook poses with two grandchildren of Wake Forest College professor James L. Lake, patriarch of the family that has produced two justices of the North Carolina Supreme Court. (Courtesy of the Wake Forest Birthplace Museum.)

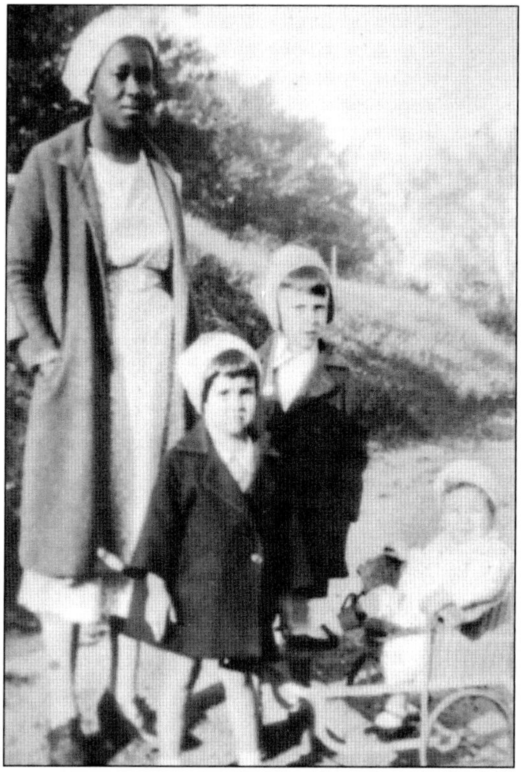

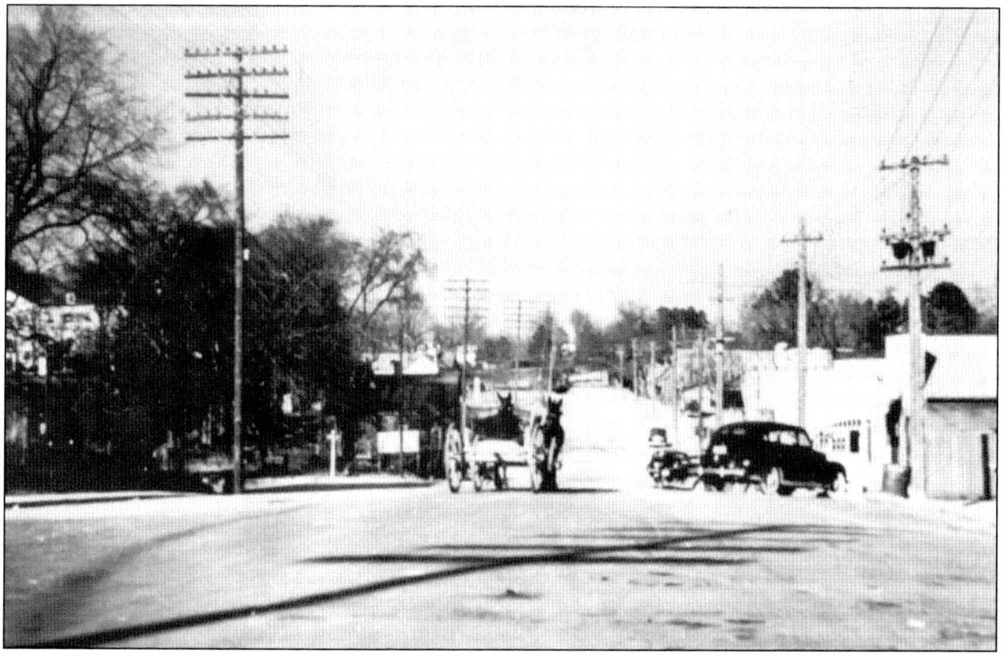

This photograph of the northeast section of town, home to most of Wake Forest's African American families, was likely taken in the 1920s. Infrastructure was relatively undeveloped in this part of town, where streets were still without lights, sewer, or adequate water lines. The streets remained unpaved until the 1980s. (Courtesy of the Wake Forest Birthplace Museum.)

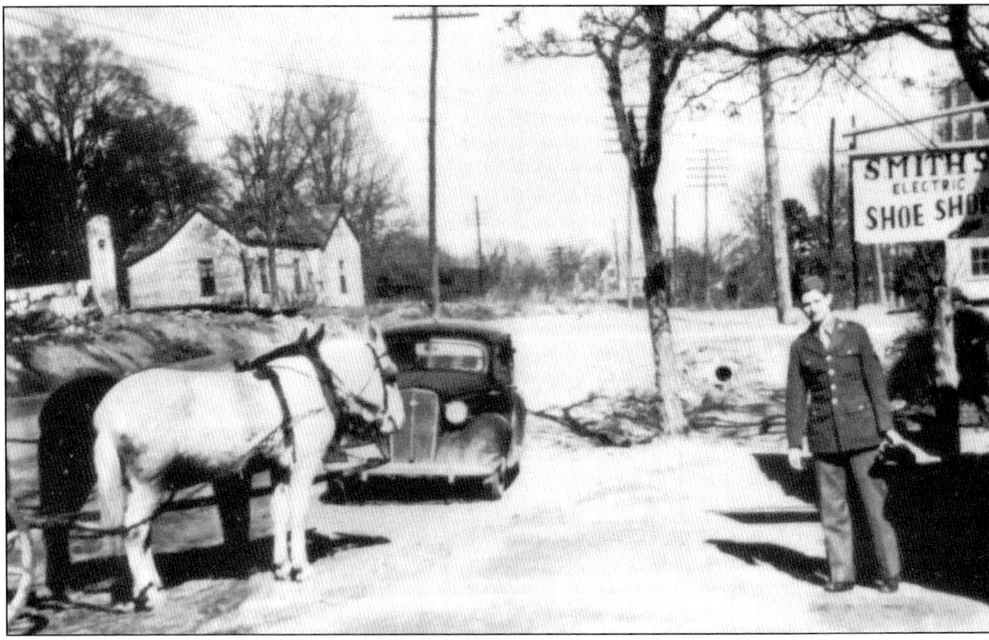

Oscar C. Smith, a prominent member of the African American community in the early and mid-20th century, owned Smith's Shoe Shop in the northeast section of town. Smith served 10 terms as president of the North Carolina Volunteer Firemen's Association, the statewide counterpart to the white association. At his shop, he taught generations of young men about shoes and business. (Courtesy of the Wake Forest Birthplace Museum.)

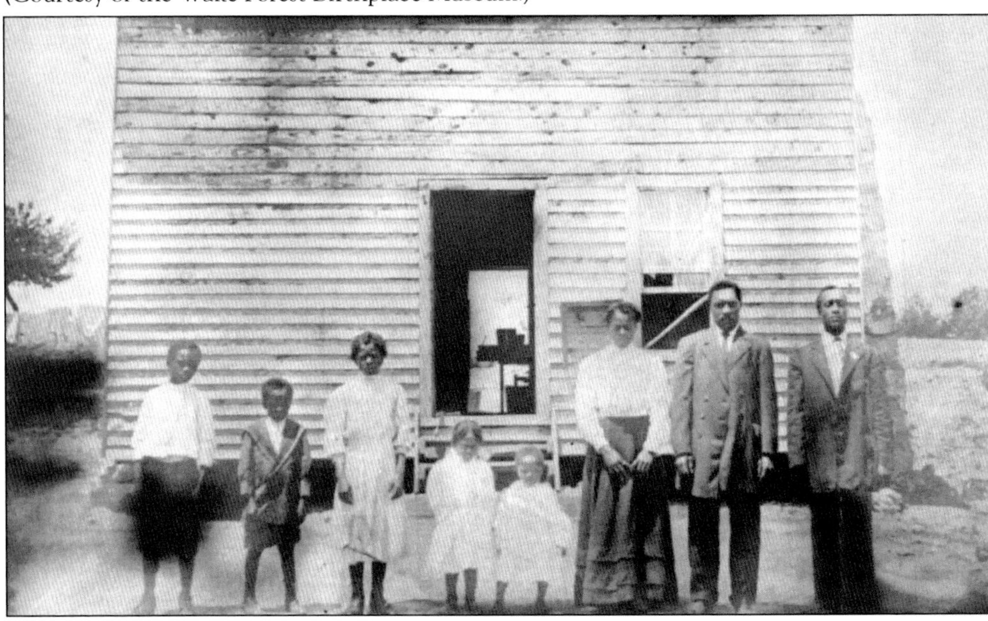

This sharecropper family tended fields on the property of J. K. Ray at Rogers Store near Old Bethel Church. Many such small communities existed in the rural areas surrounding Wake Forest. Pictured, from left to right, are Cephus Keith, John Keith, Susie Durham, Esther Keith, Hudie Keith, Viola Allen Keith, Wade Keith, and Rufe Keith. The photograph was taken in 1911. (Courtesy of the North Carolina State Archives N.91.8.20.)

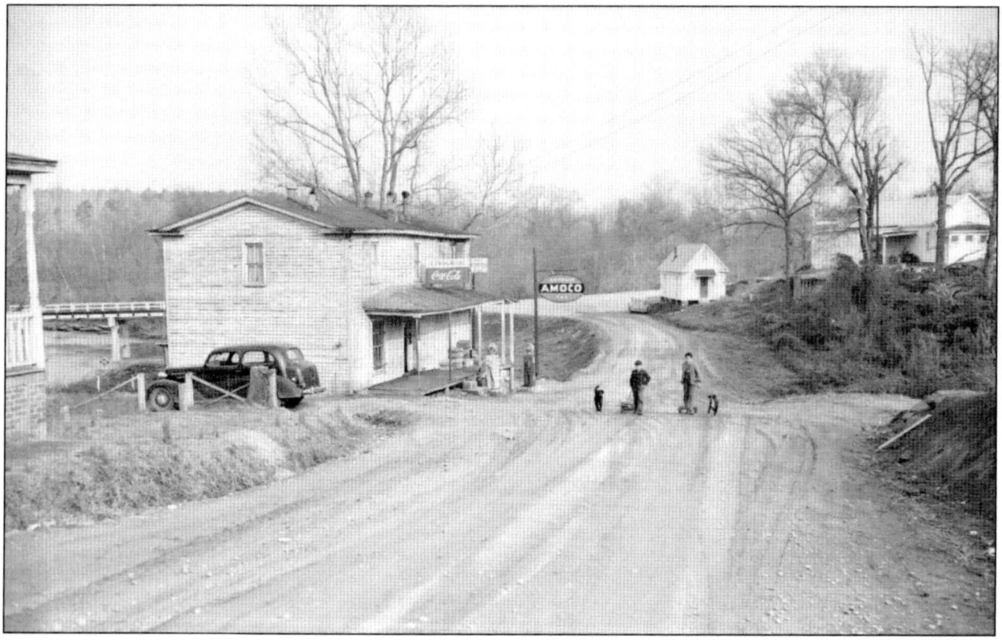

"The Harricane," spelled as commonly pronounced, was named for a storm that devastated a large section of Wake, Granville, and Franklin Counties sometime in the mid–18th century, leaving the land unsuitable for farming. The area encompasses current day Purnell Road, Thompson Mill, and the Falls of Neuse area, where this photograph was taken around 1950. (Courtesy of the *News and Observer* and the North Carolina State Archives N.2006.1.7-13.)

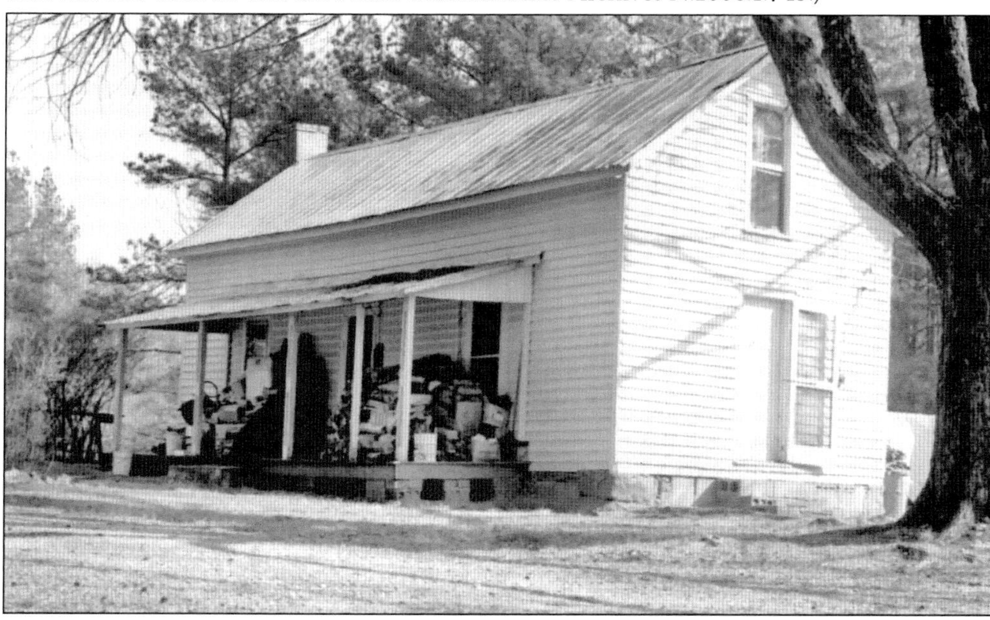

Also in the area once known as the Harricane is Rock Cliff Farm, the Stony Hill homestead founded by B. W. Wells, former head of the Department of Plant Pathology at North Carolina State University. Wells spent many years painting and researching at Rock Cliff, which is now part of the state's recreation area surrounding Falls Lake. (Courtesy of the North Carolina State Archives N.93.7.1320 and 1323.)

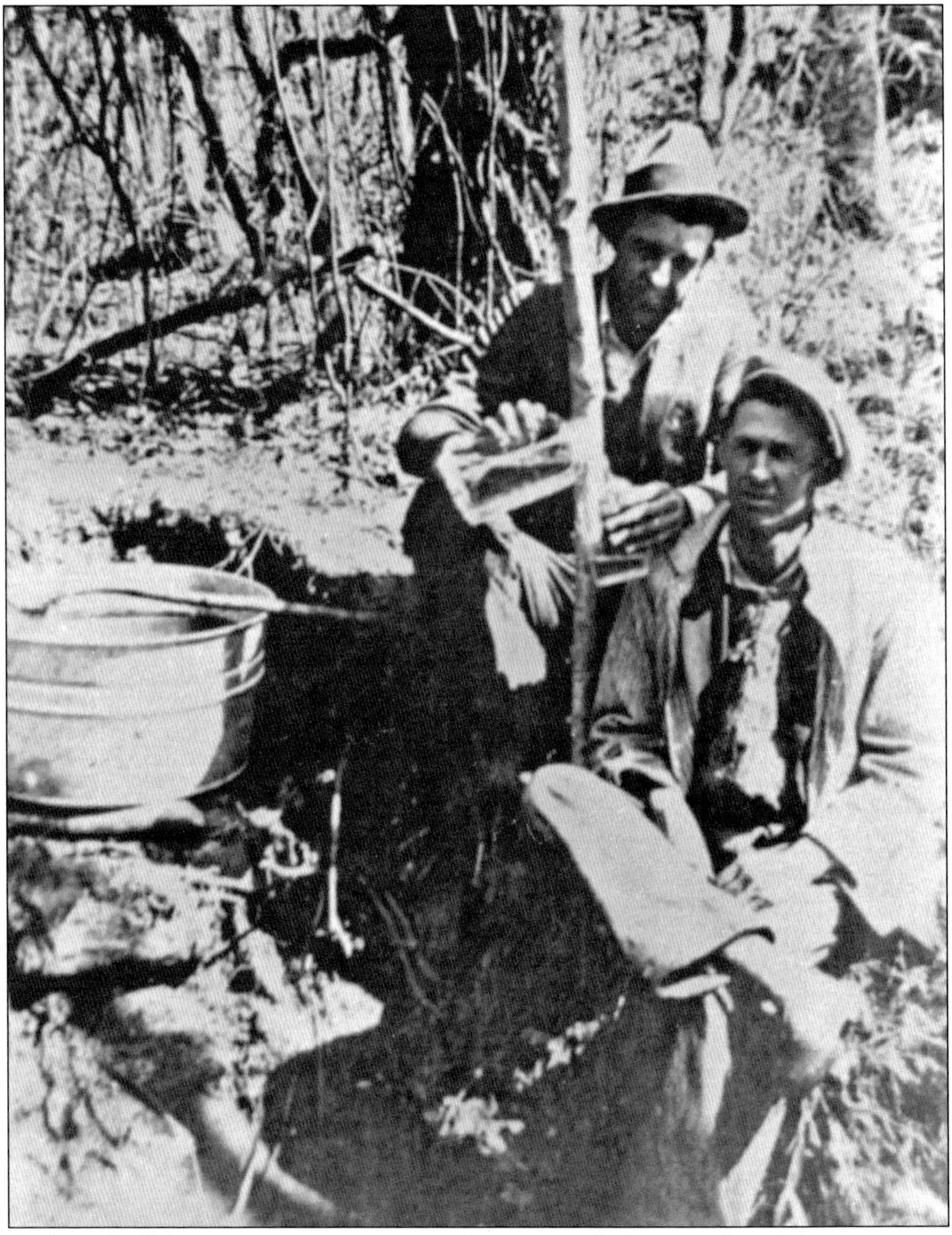

By the early 20th century, the Harricane was known mainly for moonshine. These men were among those who plied their trade with a rickety still in the overgrown, underdeveloped forested land. At least one Wake Forest resident recalls a moonshiner pushing a fruit cart through town, his illegal whiskey bottles hidden on shelves beneath more commonly accepted wares. This was only the most contemporary dubious activity based in the rocky rural area, also once known as "the Rogue's Quarter." According to legend, it made a good hideout for a Georgia prison inmate who'd escaped to North Carolina in 1794. (Courtesy of the Wake Forest Birthplace Museum.)

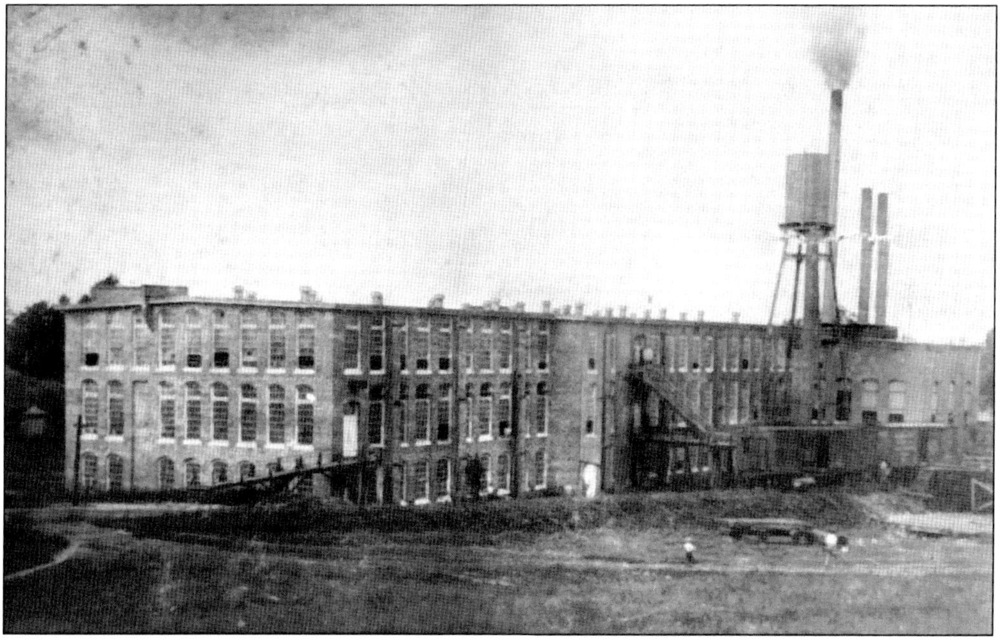

Wake Forest's oldest industry was founded when W. C. Powell, Robert E. Royall, and Thomas E. Holding, all Wake Forest College graduates, decided to build a cotton weaving mill with muslin sheeting as its principal product. They constructed their manufacturing facility north of town, surrounded it by a village of mill houses, and called it Glen Royall Cotton Mill. (Courtesy of the Wake Forest Birthplace Museum.)

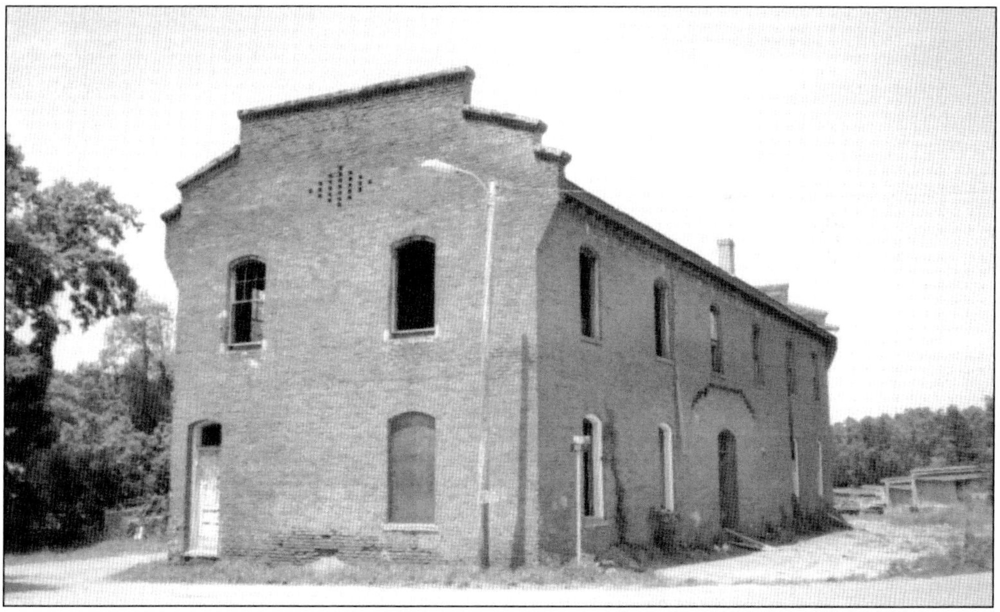

The Royall Cotton Mill Commissary, a grocery and supply store for mill workers and their families, was one of many structures comprising a town within a town. The mill village had 75 homes, two churches, and a school. The commissary, which closed in 1934, was purchased by developers Jim Adams and Steve Gould in 1990 and, now restored, houses apartments. (Courtesy of the North Carolina State Archives N.91.7.302 and 312.)

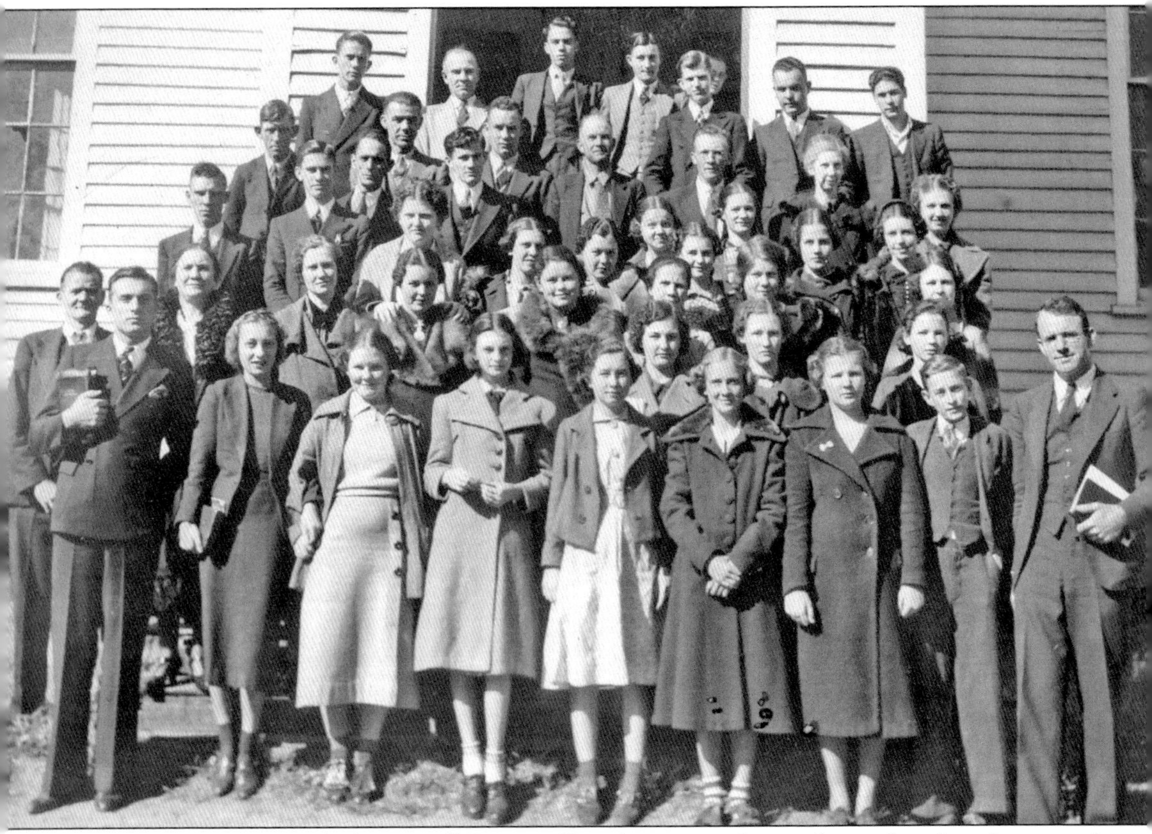

The congregation of Glen Royall Baptist Church supported one of two churches that served the mill and its village. These worshippers pose for a group photograph around 1925. Although hard feelings lessened in later years, many who grew up in the mill village felt very strongly their isolation from the larger town. Never wholly convinced of their welcome, most mill families stuck to the commissary, school, and churches provided them. The separation was no illusion. The mill town was incorporated as the Town of Royall Mills in 1907 and remained a separate, incorporated community until 1943, when the charter was repealed. Wake Forest commissioners voted to forcibly annex the Royal Mills area in 1977. (Courtesy of the Wake Forest Birthplace Museum.)

Two

Town and Gown

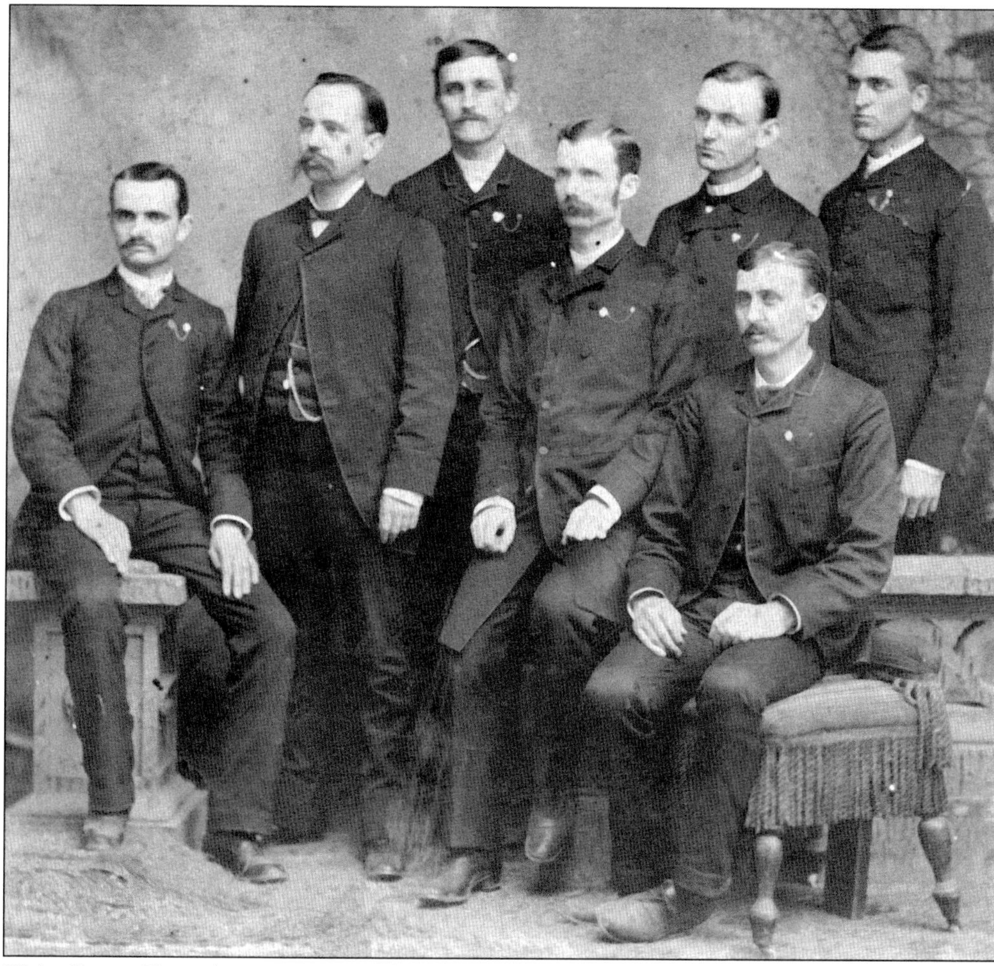

Wake Forest Township was an area known for its excellent schools long before the arrival of its college. In fact, throughout the region, it was known for its somewhat swanky reputation, prompting one 19th-century visitor to write, with more than a dash of gratitude, that they treated him "with as much respect as if I had been the son of some wealthy man." Forest Hill Academy, Wake Forest Academy, and Pleasant Grove Academy were all in operation by the mid-1820s. Each of the three schools could be reached along the highway from Raleigh to Oxford, over the river bridge crossing the Neuse, and two of the three changed focus after the opening of Wake Forest College. Forest Hill became a preparatory school, while Pleasant Grove began educating girls only. Meanwhile, the college flourished, as evidenced by the Wake Forest College graduating class, c. 1881. Second from left is William L. Poteat, who later served as one of the school's most respected presidents. (Courtesy of the Wake Forest Birthplace Museum.)

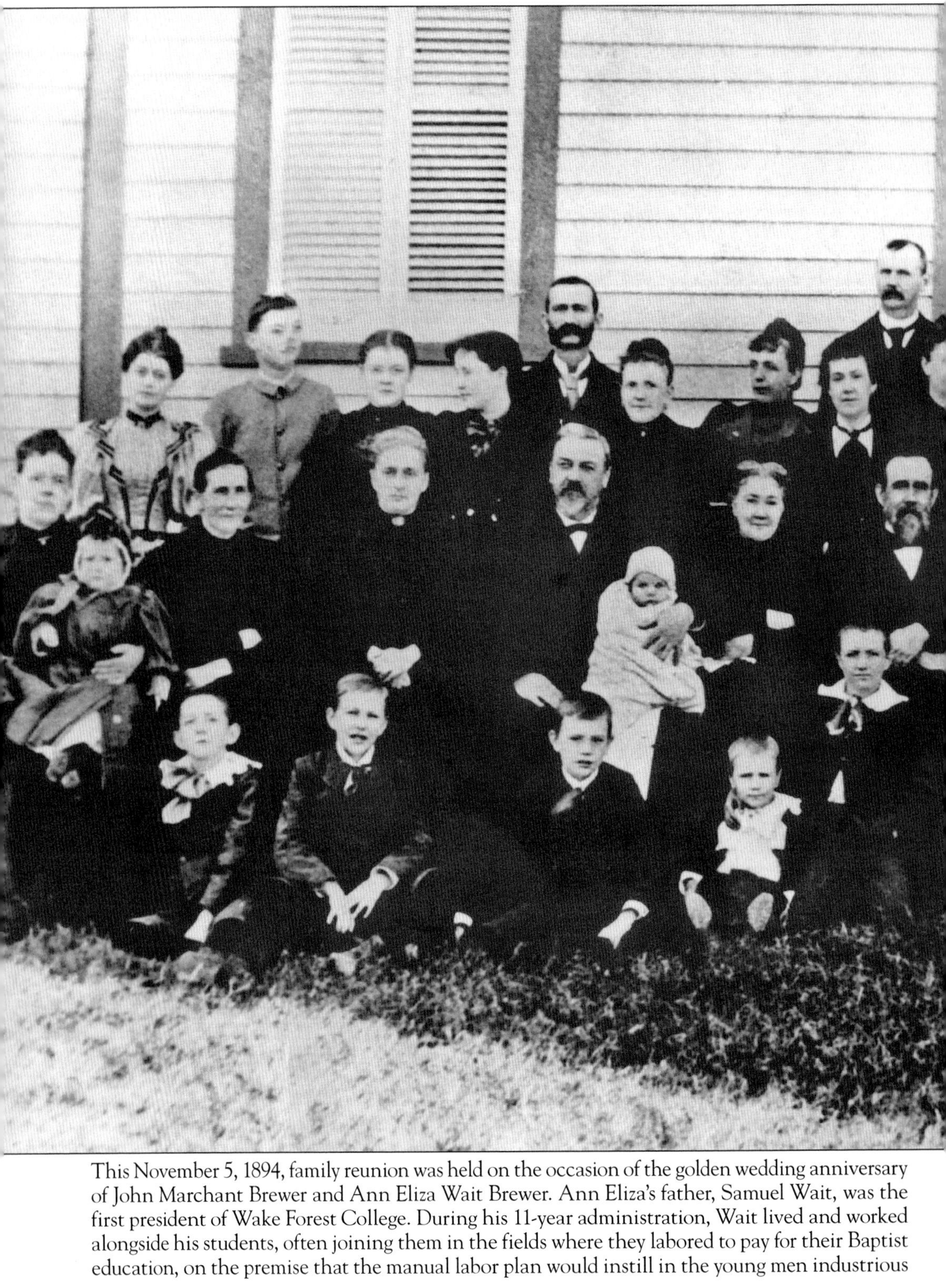

This November 5, 1894, family reunion was held on the occasion of the golden wedding anniversary of John Marchant Brewer and Ann Eliza Wait Brewer. Ann Eliza's father, Samuel Wait, was the first president of Wake Forest College. During his 11-year administration, Wait lived and worked alongside his students, often joining them in the fields where they labored to pay for their Baptist education, on the premise that the manual labor plan would instill in the young men industrious

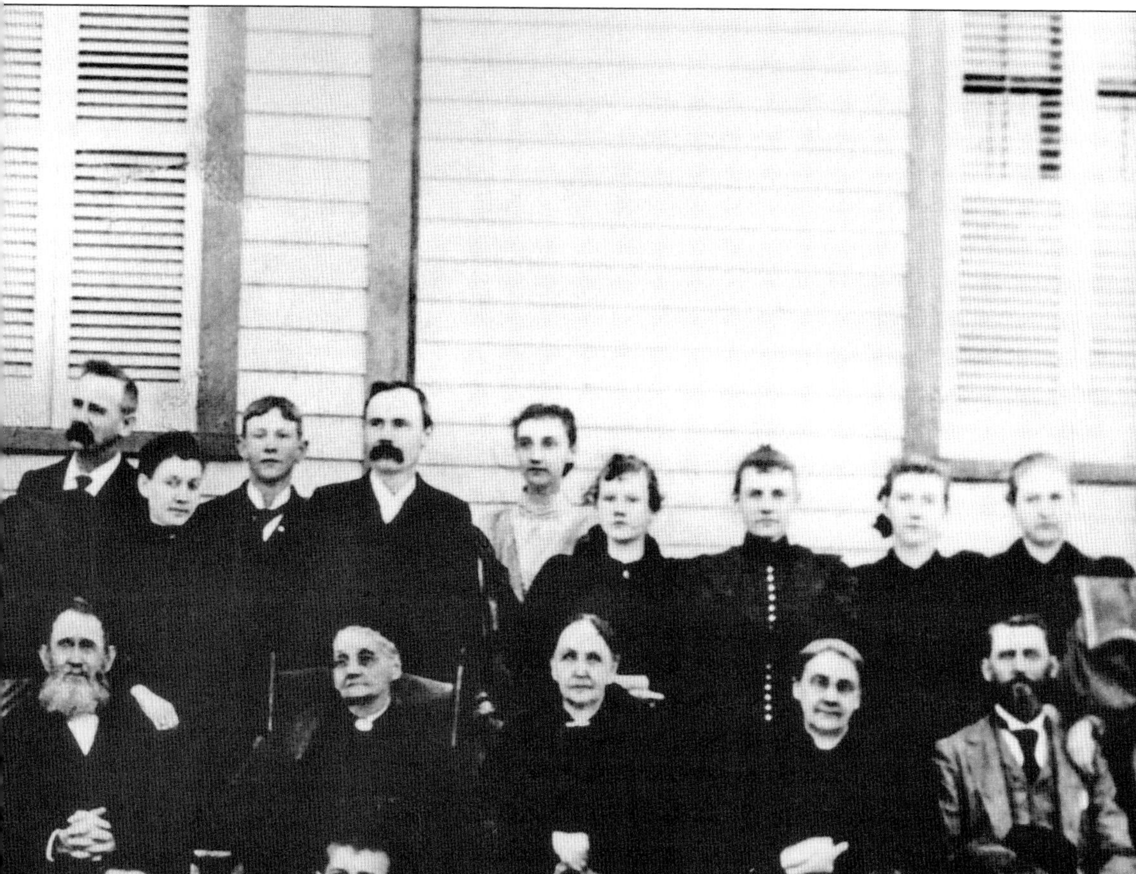

habits and good health. Wait loved the town and its campus until his death in 1871 and spent his old age quietly walking its expanded grounds. Twenty-three years after his death, four generations of Wait's descendants attended this gathering, representing many of the town's most prominent families. The anniversary couple is seated just right of center in the second row. (Courtesy of Hallie Arrington Hearn.)

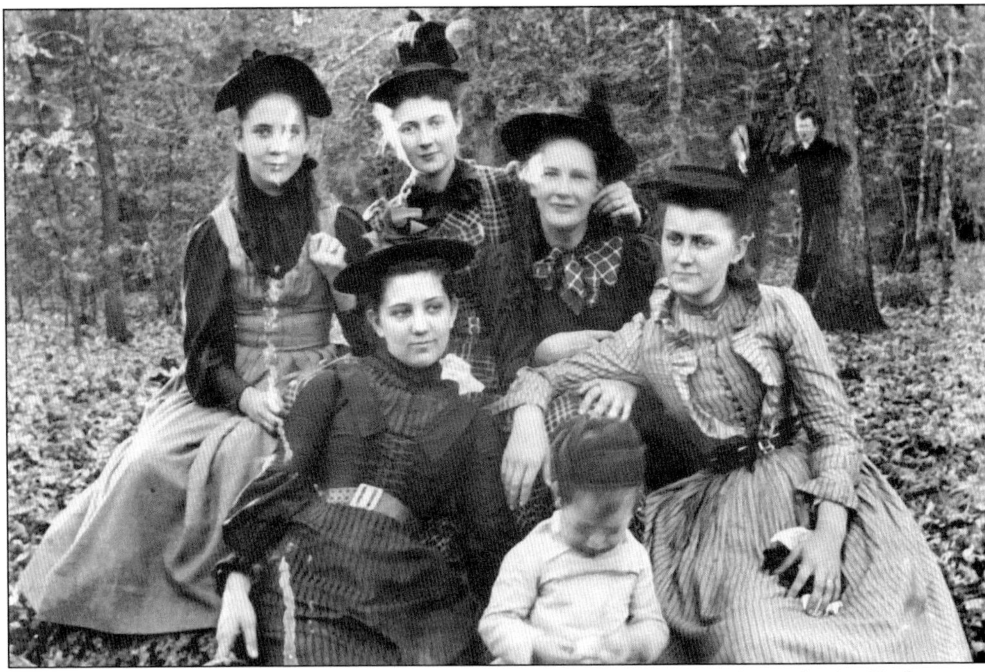

In this *c.* 1900 photograph, the daughters of Wake Forest College president Charles Taylor are in their teens and twenties. Fannie Taylor Gorrell poses with her toddler, Virginia, while her brother clowns in the background. Daughter Ethel Taylor, who lived to be 103 years old, was mother of noted historian Christopher Crittenden. Both she and her sister Edith worked at the college. (Courtesy of the Wake Forest Birthplace Museum.)

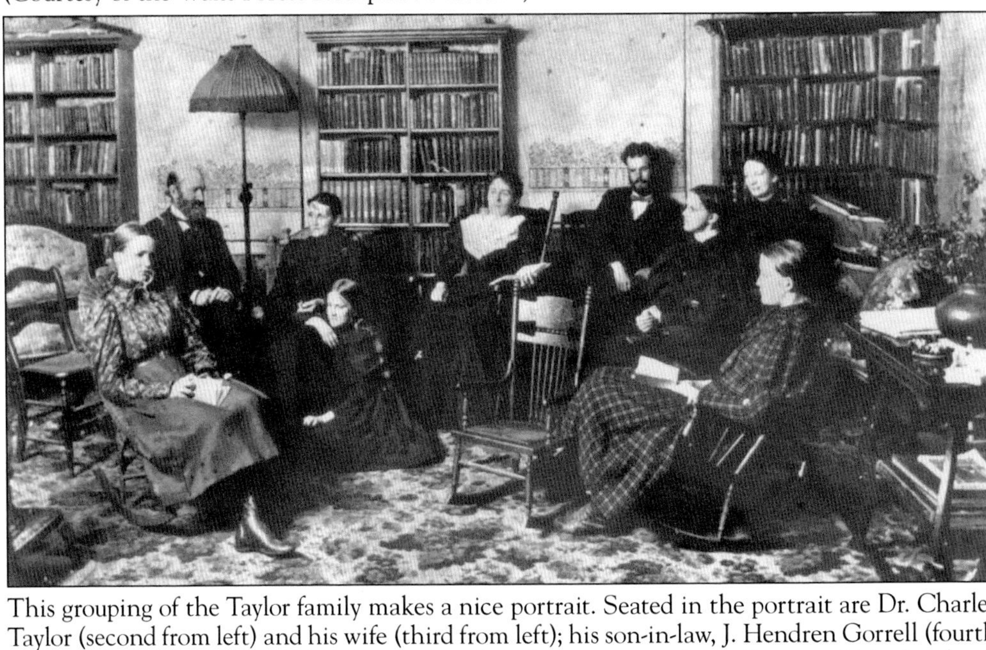

This grouping of the Taylor family makes a nice portrait. Seated in the portrait are Dr. Charles Taylor (second from left) and his wife (third from left); his son-in-law, J. Hendren Gorrell (fourth from right), who later served as head of modern languages at the college; and his daughters Agnes, Ethel, Mary, Edith, and Fanny (second from right). (Courtesy of the Wake Forest Birthplace Museum.)

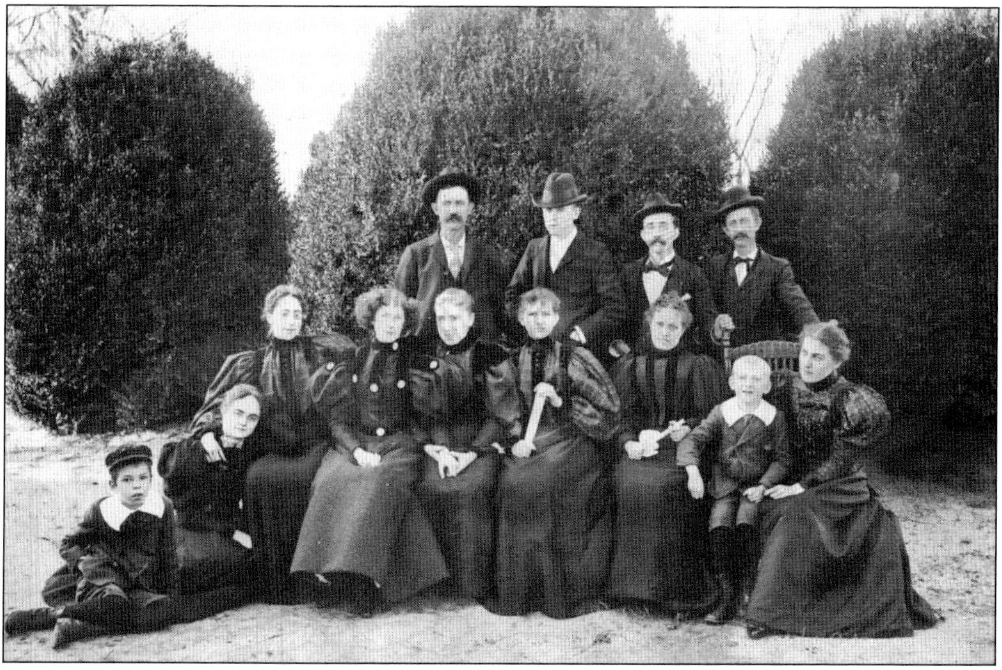

Thanksgiving at Oakforest, a notable Forestville plantation house, was a formal event in 1895 with family posing for a group portrait. Among those in the back row from left to right are John Jones and Joe Seawell. The boys are Craig and Shell Jones. The woman in the center is Pearl Carver Seawell, and the lady in the wicker chair is identified as Annie Martin. (Courtesy of the North Carolina State Archives N.97.10.15.)

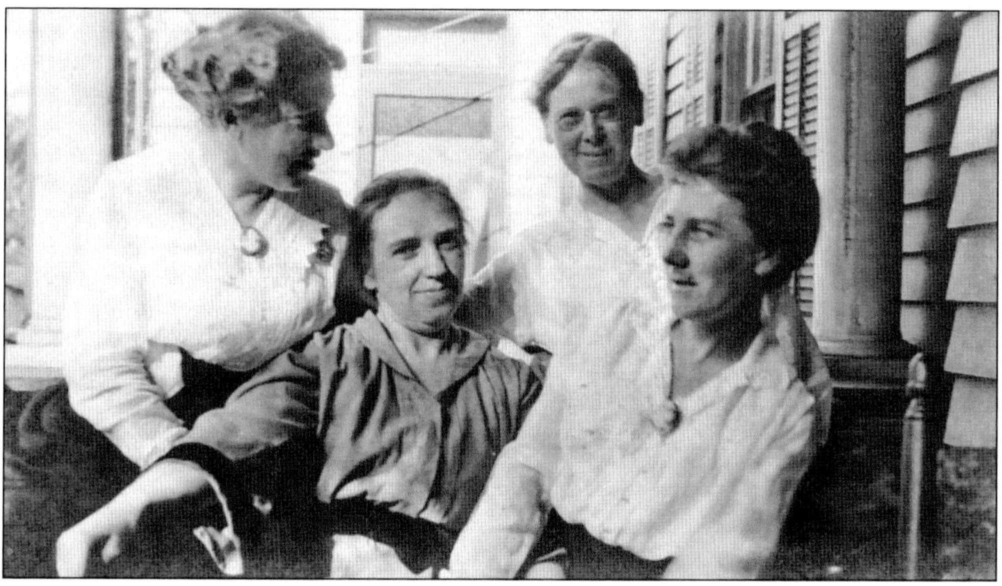

Pearl Carver Seawell (second from left) posed on the porch at Oakforest with three friends from her class at Goldsboro College, around 1900. Called by a local Raleigh newspaper "a woman of rare refinement and culture," Pearl, who went on to manage the plantation, was married to a clerk of the North Carolina Supreme Court. She had 18 college classmates in the bridal party at her magnificent wedding. (Courtesy of Speed Massenburg and family.)

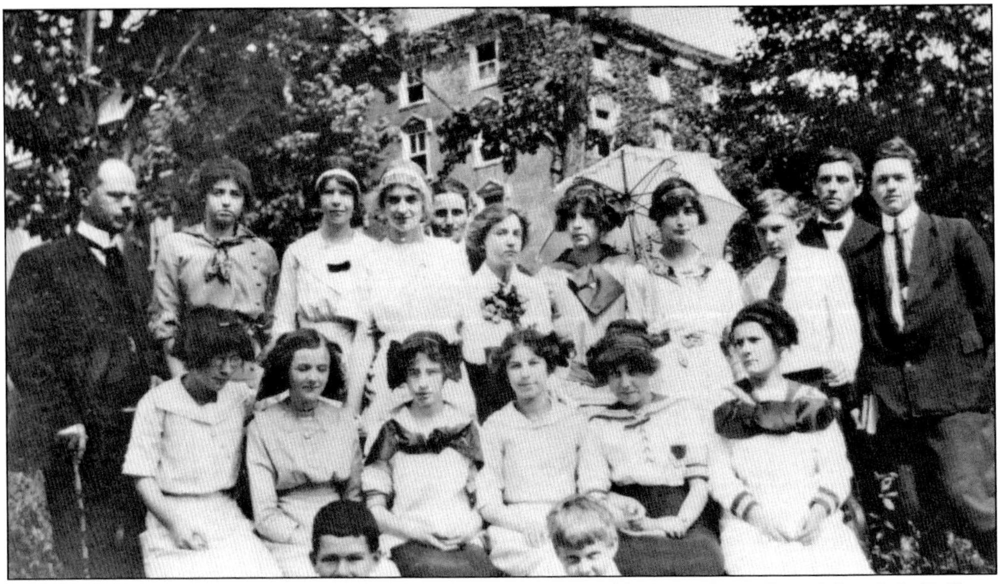

In the years before women were admitted to Wake Forest College, students from Meredith College attended summer school on the Wake Forest campus. This photograph was taken during a summer session around 1920. (Courtesy of the Wake Forest Birthplace Museum.)

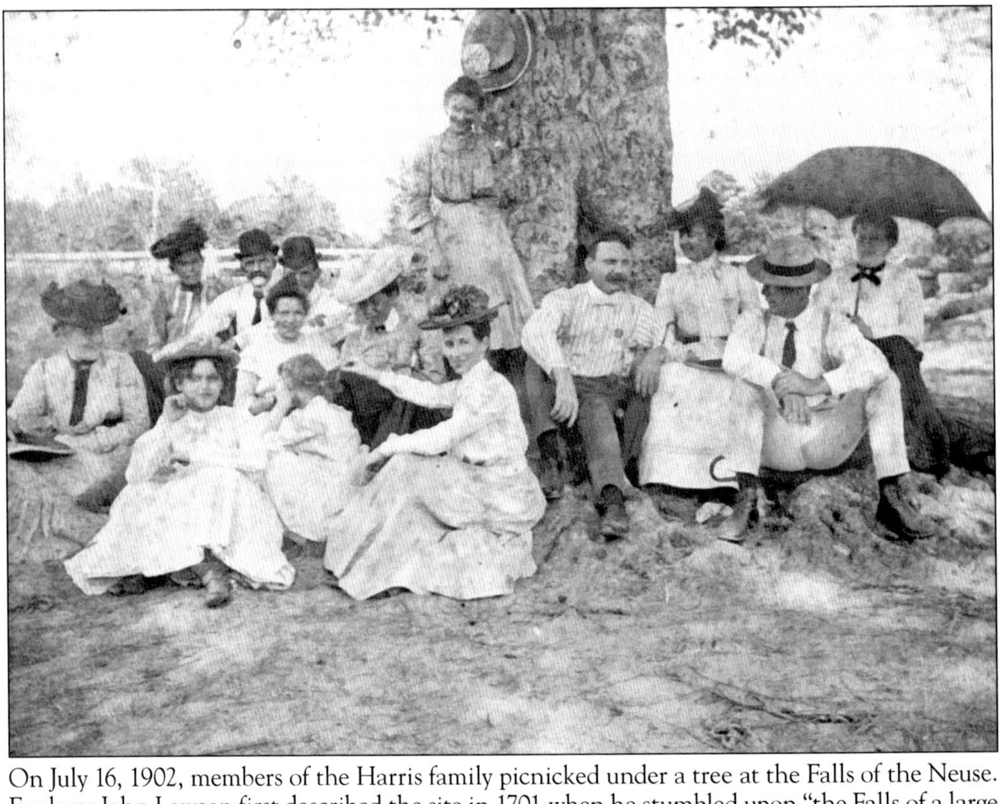

On July 16, 1902, members of the Harris family picnicked under a tree at the Falls of the Neuse. Explorer John Lawson first described the site in 1701 when he stumbled upon "the Falls of a large Creek, where lay mighty rocks, the Water making a strange noise, as if a great many Water-Mills were going at once." (Courtesy of the North Carolina State Archives N.98.4.38.)

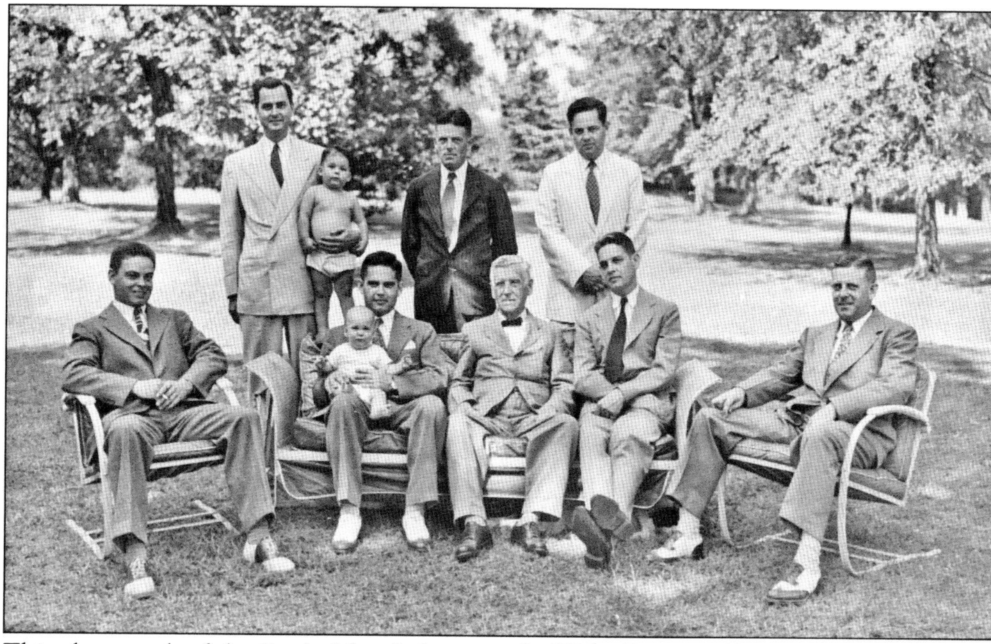

This photograph of the Paschal family boasts eight Wake Forest College graduates, including Dr. George W. Paschal, six sons, one son-in-law, and two grandsons. Dr. Paschal, a Wake Forest College professor and Baptist historian who died in 1956, wrote a definitive, three-volume history of the town and its school. (Courtesy of the Wake Forest Birthplace Museum.)

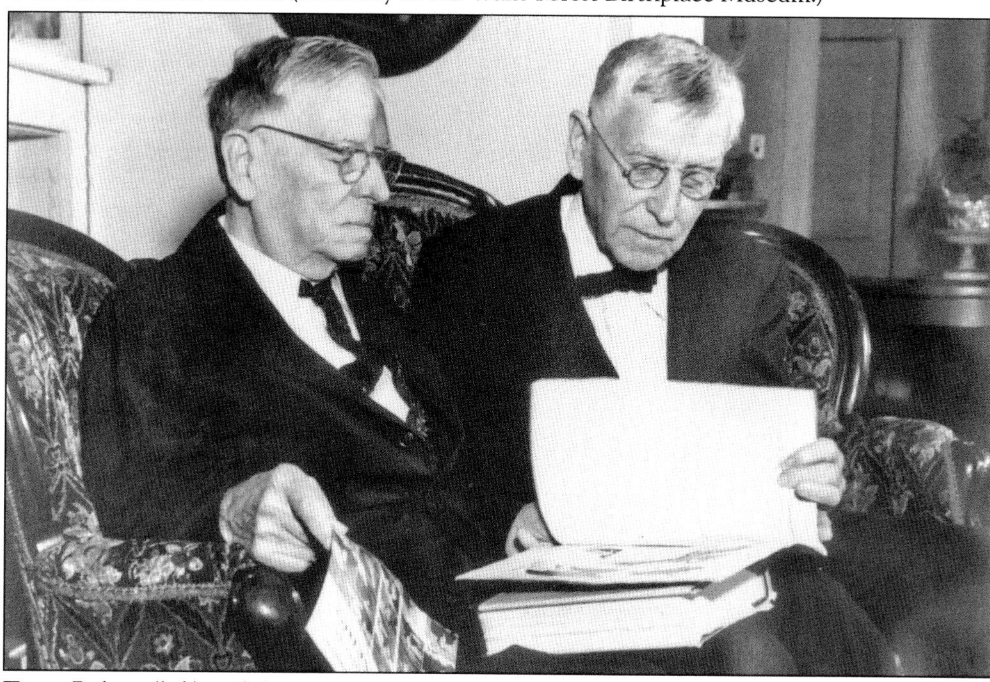

Twins Robert (left) and George Paschal graduated from Wake Forest College in 1891 and 1892, respectively. George went on to teach while Robert served as an attorney for the North Carolina State Department of Revenue. Both were well known in the town of Wake Forest. (Courtesy of the Wake Forest Birthplace Museum.)

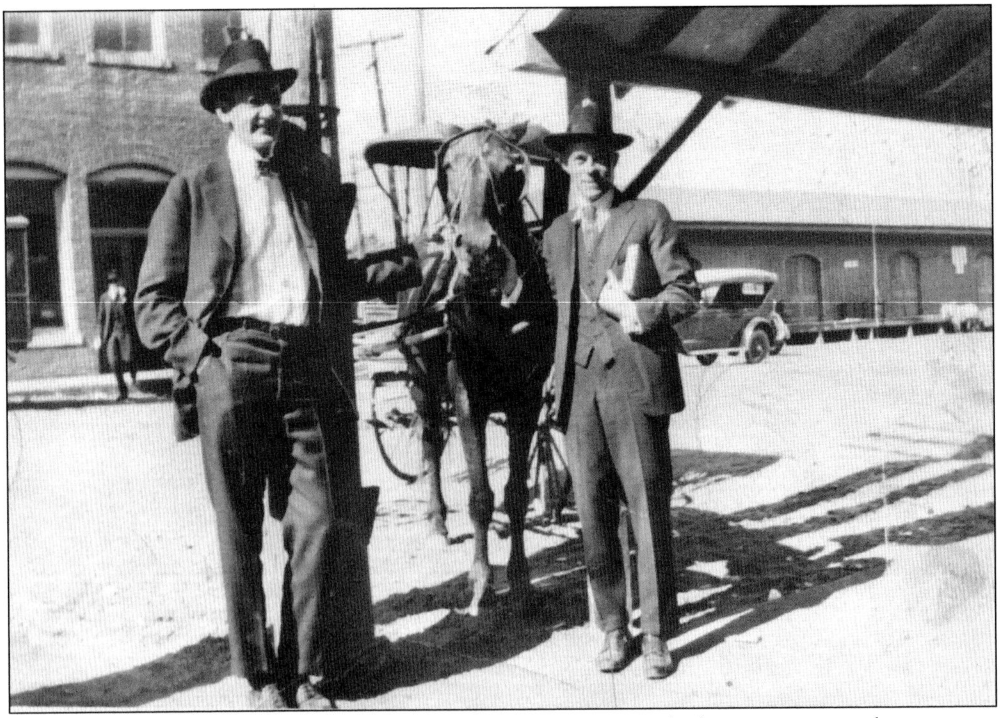

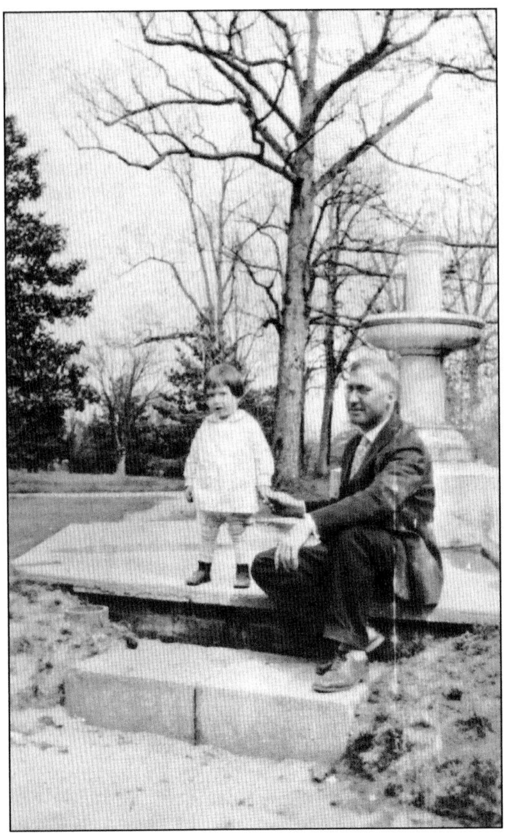

Two men and a horse pose on a dusty downtown street, *c.* 1915. By this time, the town had approximately 1,500 residents, and some of its early businesses were prospering. For instance, Jones Hardware, located on White Street where this photograph appears to have been taken, had opened in 1906 and was already well established. (Courtesy of the Wake Forest Birthplace Museum.)

The old well is a famous campus landmark that may date back to the days of the Calvin Jones House. It is thought the well may have been the property's original water source. Eventually the class of 1911 raised funds for the marble fountain to replace the old pump. (Courtesy of the Wake Forest Birthplace Museum.)

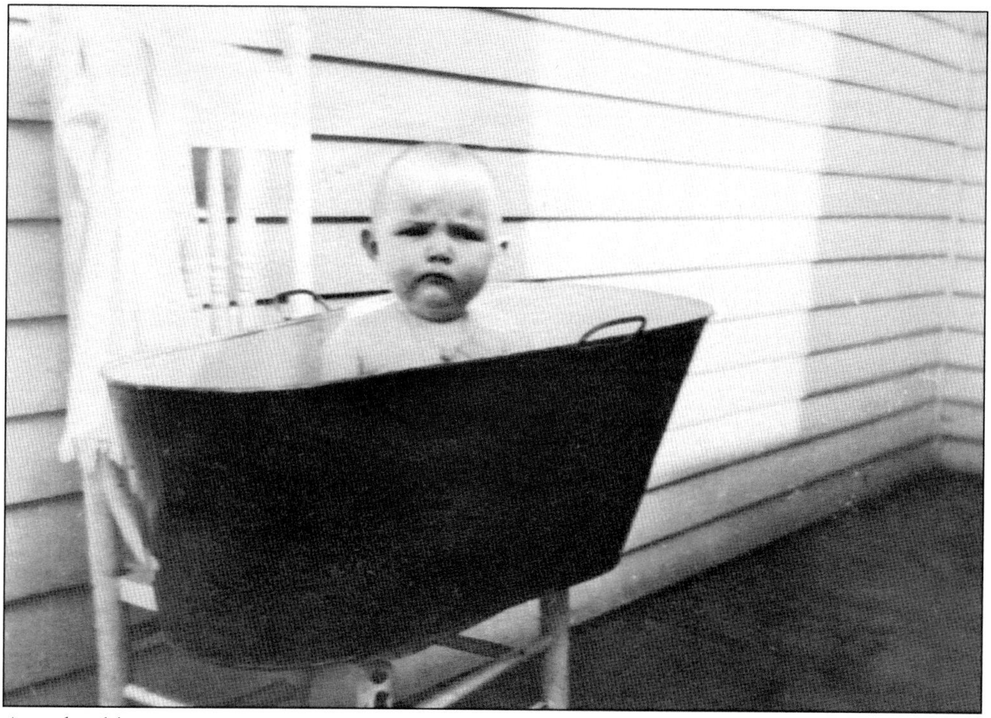

An adorable Tom Arrington III was bathed in a porch tub *c.* 1918, long before he graduated from Wake Forest College. Tom was a member of the class of 1939; a direct descendant of Samuel Wait, the college's first president; and the son of former Wake Forest fire chief Tom Arrington Jr. The historic family home is still located near campus. (Courtesy of the Wake Forest Birthplace Museum.)

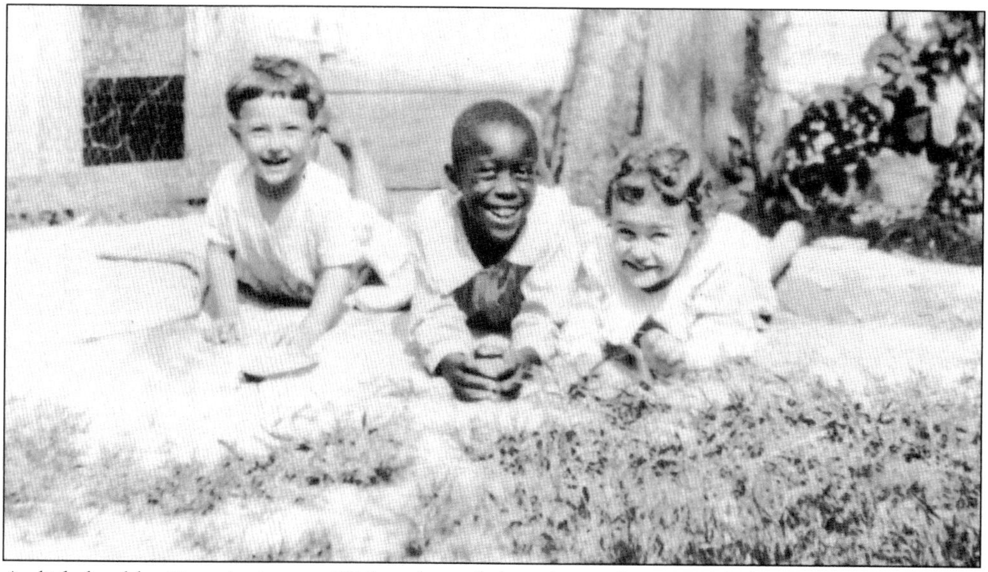

A slightly older Tom Arrington III (on the right) smiles in this *c.* 1925 photograph of boys in a row. It was unusual for a photograph of this era to depict black and white children playing together. The African American boy (unidentified) returned to town many years later to look up his old friend. (Courtesy of the Wake Forest Birthplace Museum.)

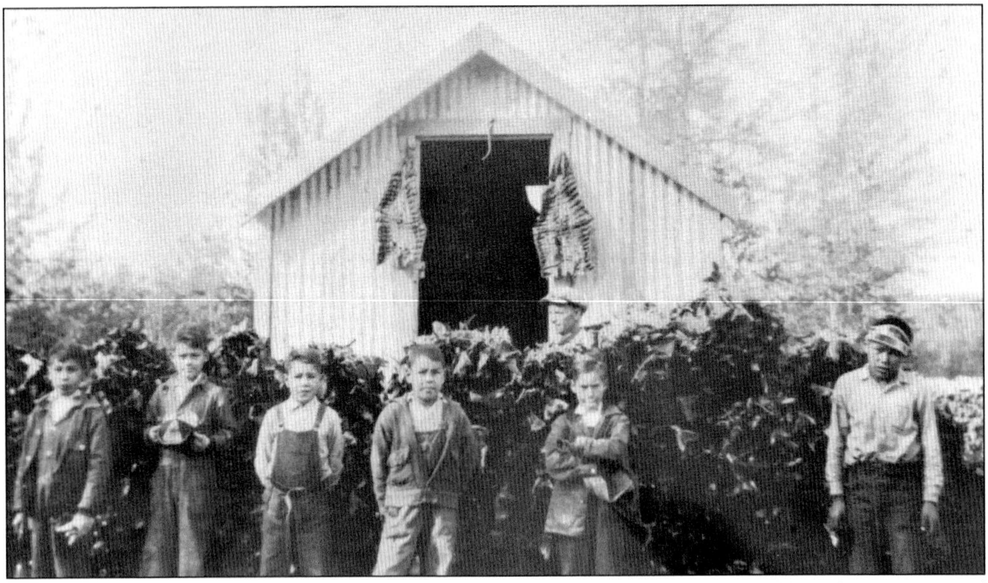

Not all youngsters had time to play. During the Great Depression, many children from farms and towns across the country were put to work. In this unidentified photograph taken around 1930, boys from the Wake Forest area pose in front of a local slaughterhouse, where it is safe to presume they were gainfully employed. (Courtesy of the Wake Forest Birthplace Museum.)

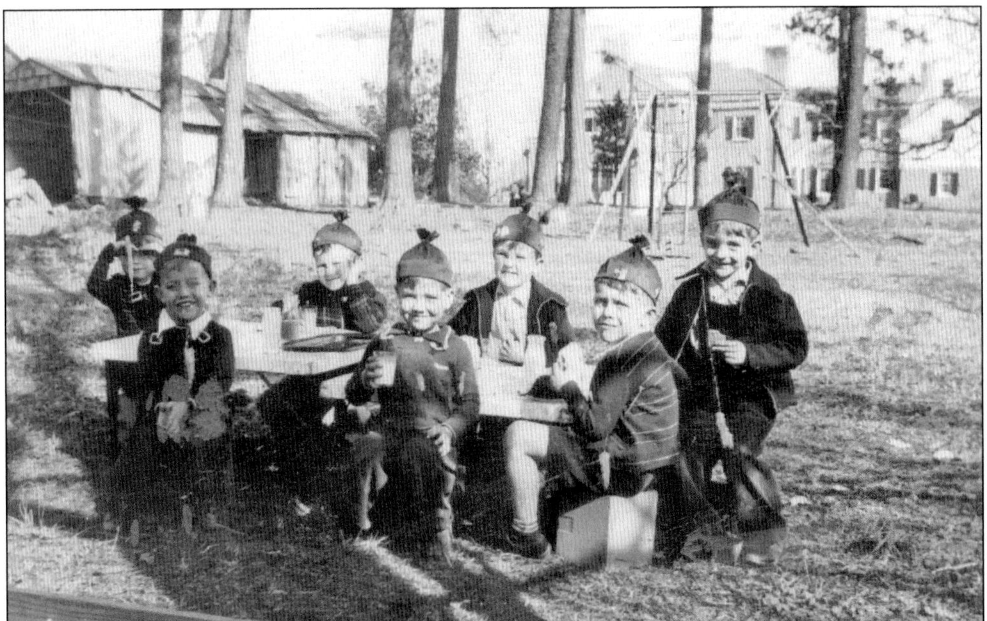

This children's party took place on Valentine's Day in 1938. The location was the former Faculty Avenue, now North Main Street, with the Mackie mansion visible in the background. The celebrants are, from left to right, unidentified, Coy Carpenter, Charles Sabiston Jr., John Mills, Roy Ray, Charles A. Wilkinson, and Frankie Fellows. (Courtesy of the Wake Forest Birthplace Museum.)

Grady Patterson Jr. and Jean Little are grandly costumed in this *c.* 1936 photograph for a theatrical production entitled *A Tom Thumb Wedding.* Patterson, born in Wake Forest in 1928, was the son of former Wake Forest College registrar Grady S. Patterson Sr. and grandson of Wake Forest College professor James L. Lake. (Courtesy of the Wake Forest Birthplace Museum.)

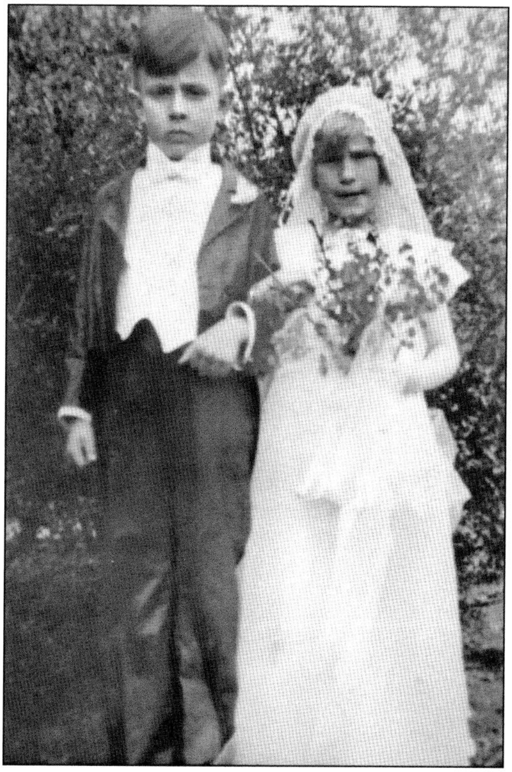

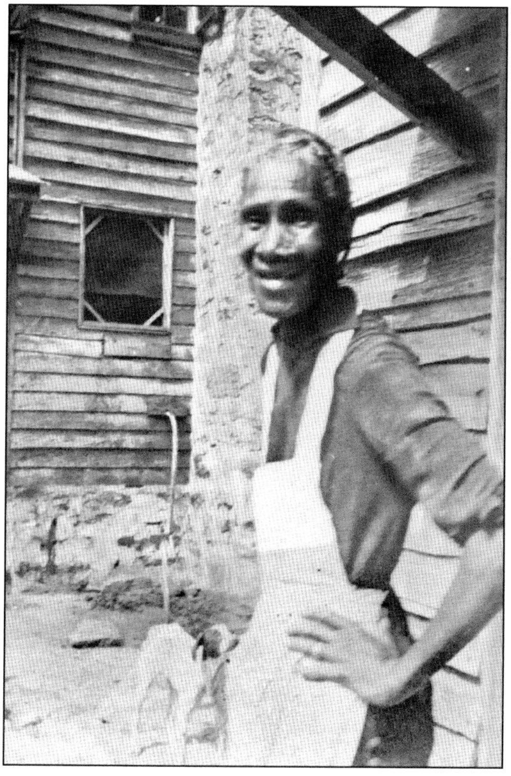

Recalled as "Clementine," this lady was a good friend and valued employee at Oakforest, where she worked as a cook during the 1930s and 1940s. Famous for baking sheets of buttery country biscuits, Clementine helped make the house a home for those who lived there during the Depression and war years. (Courtesy of Speed Massenburg and family.)

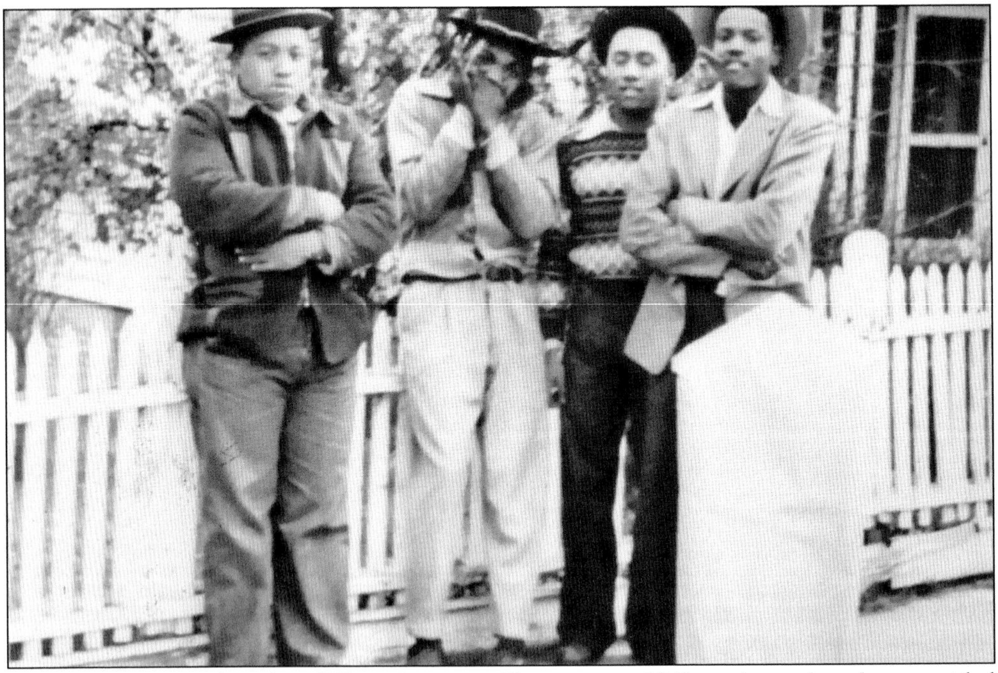

Four young men gathered on White Street at Christmas in 1942, and together they provided a musical interlude for passersby during the holiday season. This photograph appears in a wartime album collected by a soldier at the Army Finance School. (Courtesy of the Wake Forest Birthplace Museum.)

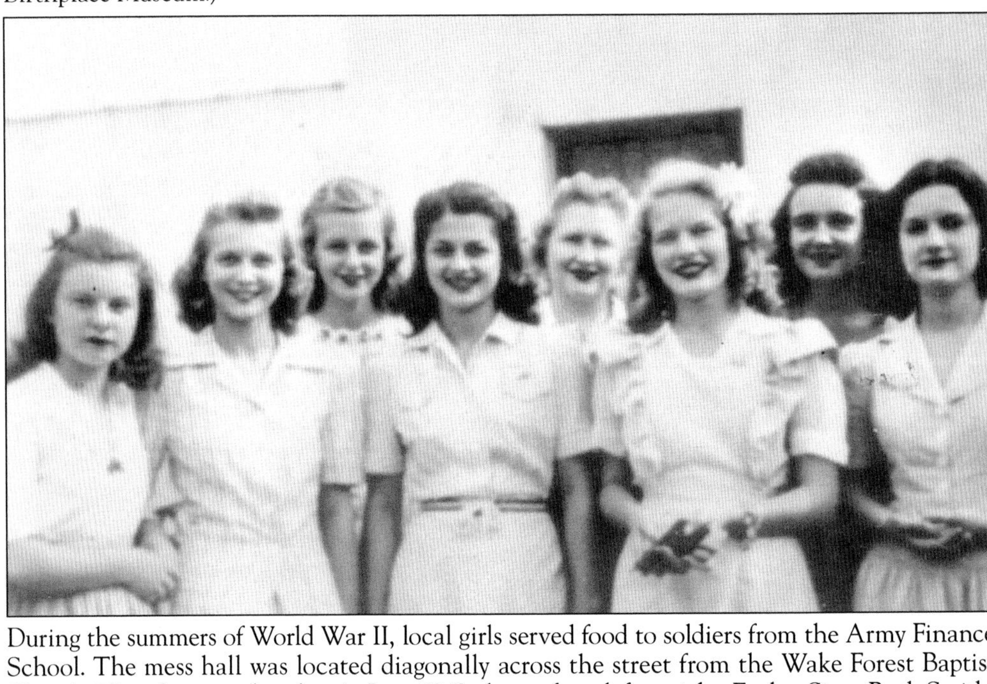

During the summers of World War II, local girls served food to soldiers from the Army Finance School. The mess hall was located diagonally across the street from the Wake Forest Baptist Church. This photograph, taken in June 1943, shows, from left to right, Evelyn Sims, Ruth Smith, Mary Gilmer Cocke, Virginia Wilkinson, Alice Holiday, Kitty Isbell, Betty Rose Holiday, and Emily Olive. (Courtesy of the Wake Forest Birthplace Museum.)

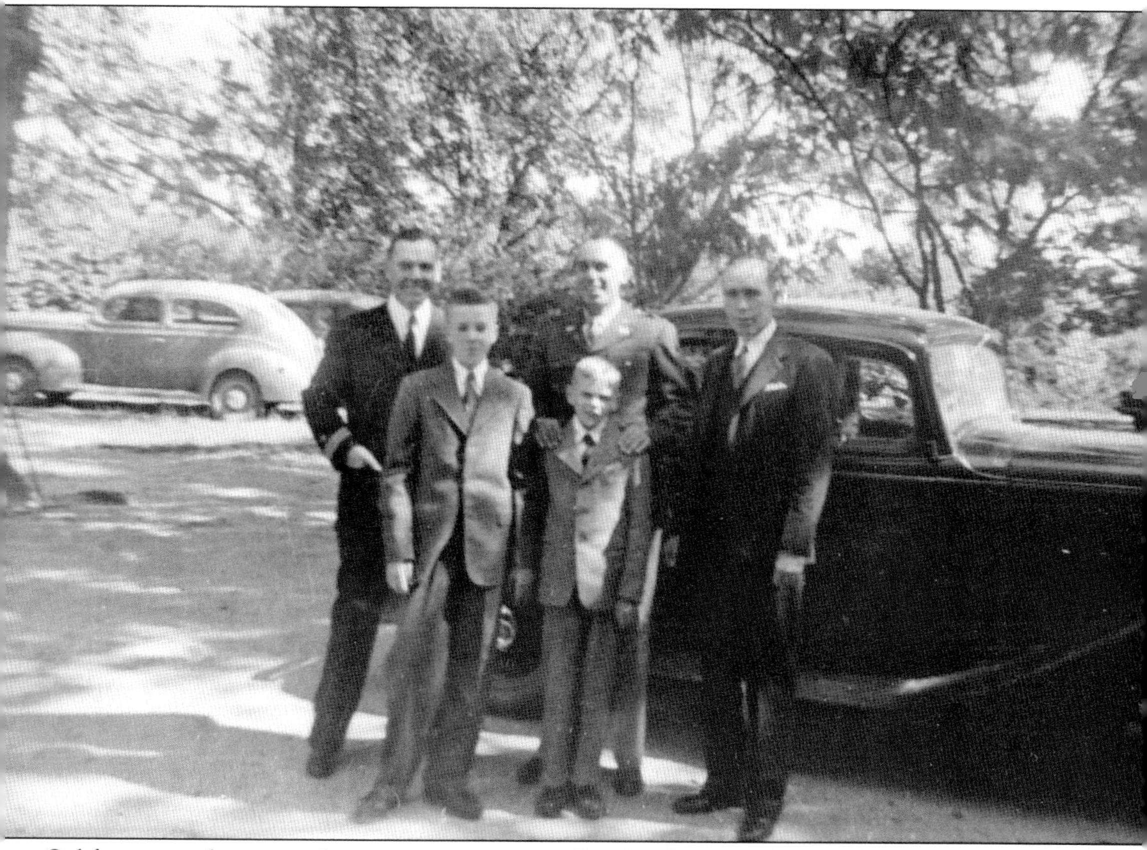

Oakforest was the scene of a wartime reunion on October 5, 1943, when brothers in arms (left to right) Henry, Kenan, and Richard Seawell (in back) came home to visit their nephews, Speed and Edward Massenburg (in front). Wake Forest responded to the war with paper drives, sewing bees for the ladies of the Red Cross, and USO functions held at the community house. The Shady Oaks Tourist Home on Faculty Avenue reportedly demolished the wrought iron fence decorating its front yard, donating the metal to the war effort. At least one contemporary newspaper article reported the wish of several Wake Forest families to rescue and house British children escaping the dangers of the German blitzkrieg. At the college, female students soon filled the seats vacated by men inducted into training camps or active duty, marking Wake Forest's first open admissions policy for women. And beginning in 1942, the college also housed the Army Finance School, with the mission of educating soldiers in the field of military financial management. (Courtesy of Speed Massenburg and family.)

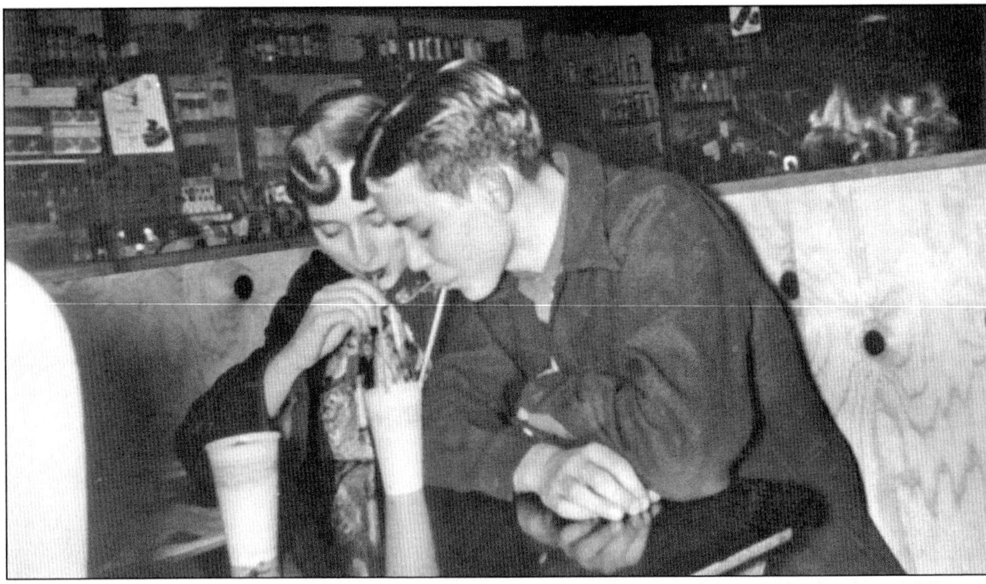

Bobbie Tribble, daughter of Wake Forest College president Harold Tribble (1950–1967), was photographed sharing a shake with Harvey Holding at Holding's Drug Store; the two later married. Kids from town loved stopping by the store for a milkshake after school. It was one of many downtown businesses that found prosperity catering to both the local and college crowds. (Courtesy of the Wake Forest Birthplace Museum.)

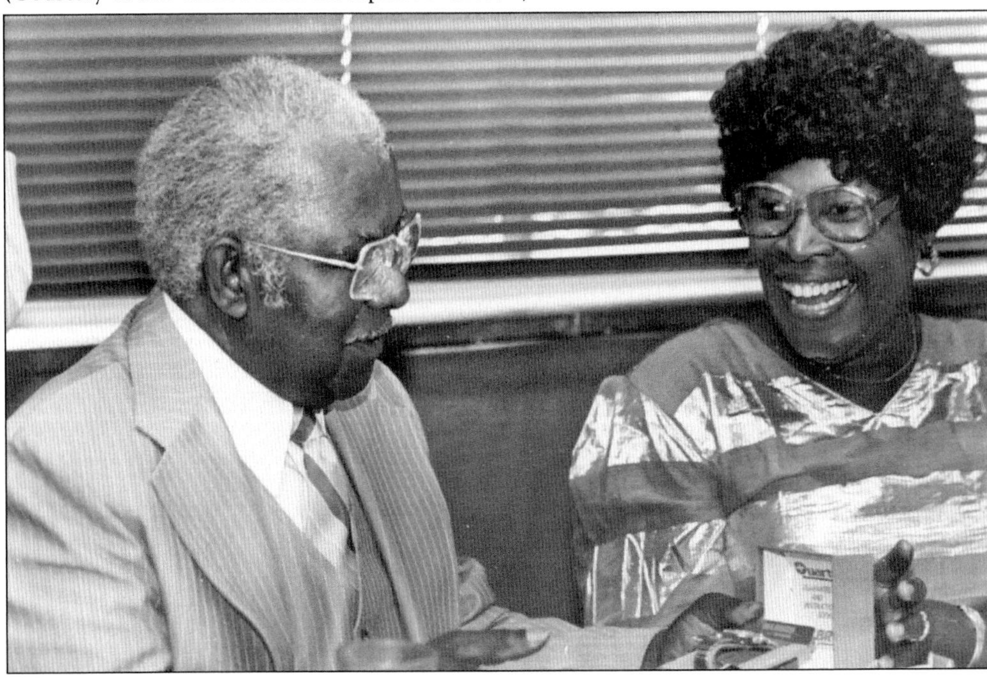

Fred Peppers, pictured with his wife, Pearl, was a valued employee of Southeastern Baptist Theological Seminary. In this c. 1985 photograph, Peppers appears to be receiving recognition for his many years of work as the custodian and friend of the seminary library and chapel. Peppers worked with Dr. H. Eugene McLeod, who built much of the library's collection. (Courtesy of Southeastern Baptist Theological Seminary.)

Three

BUSINESS AND INDUSTRY

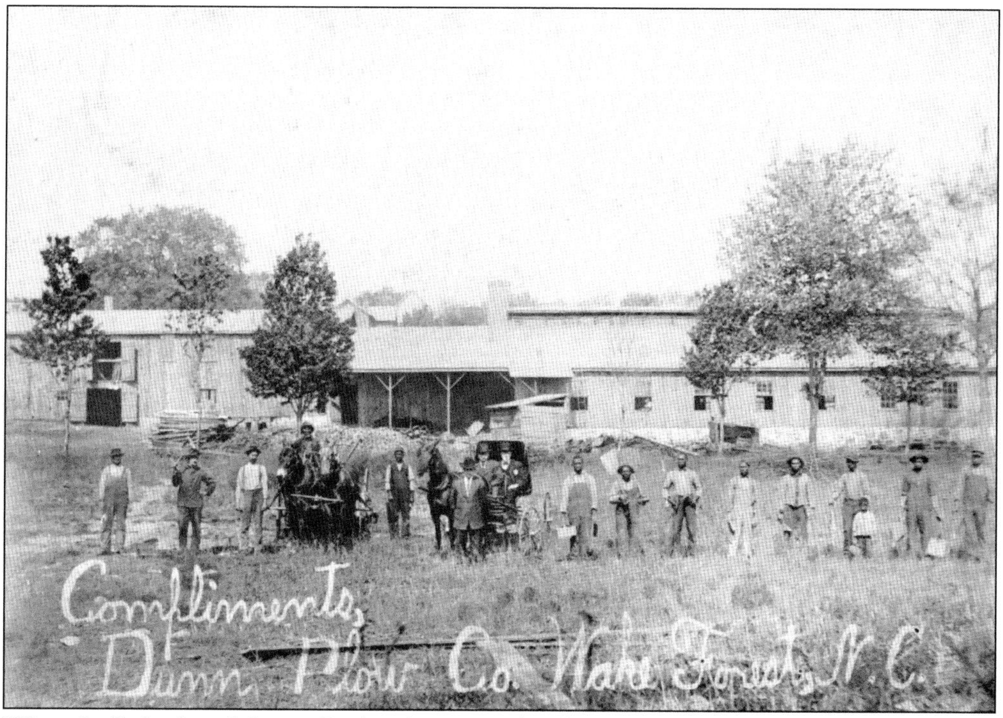

When the Raleigh and Gaston Railroad was completed in 1840, Forestville was the station. Wake Forest residents walked approximately one mile to catch the train for nearly 25 years. When Henry Clay made his historic visit to Raleigh in 1844, even he disembarked in Forestville. But things changed when the railroad at last moved the depot to Wake Forest. Being the center of transit allowed the town to grow, and it showed its respect for the college by naming streets after early college personalities. The W. D. Dunn and Company Plow Factory, *c.* 1890, was located on Brooks Street and was one of two foundries in Wake Forest that made plowshares in the late 19th through the early 20th centuries. This view shows the north side of the relatively large factory and a posed group of workers, managers, and investors. (Courtesy of the Wake Forest Birthplace Museum.)

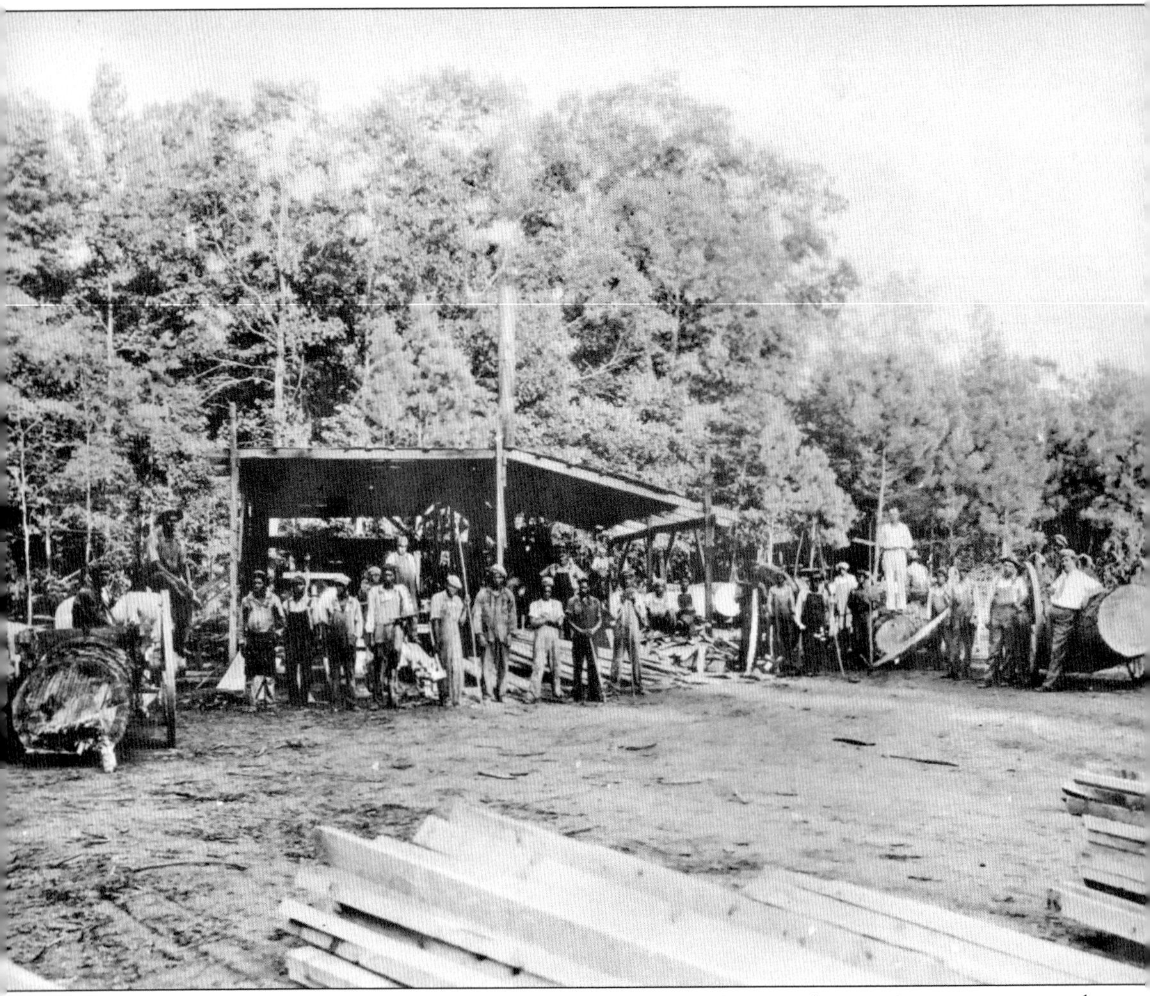

The George L. Mathis Lumber Company, *c.* 1940, was located on South Main Street approximately where Wake Forest–Rolesville Middle School stands today. It was a large operation that covered dozens of acres. An aerial view taken in the 1940s shows hundreds of stacks of drying wood that resemble small houses scattered across the landscape. The appearance and character of the town's business district changed significantly with the arrival of paved roads and streets in the 1920s. No longer solely dependent on the college, the town began developing its own commercial economy. The population was growing quickly as well with 1,443 residents in 1910 exploding to 3,898 by 1940. Soon the town was applying its newfound strength to the effort of attracting industrial jobs. The Wake Finishing Plant, a unit of Burlington Men's Wear Division of Burlington Industries, Inc., built a large plant south of town in 1948. Scovill Manufacturing followed in 1964 and Athey Products in 1965. Attracting large manufacturing plants kept the town afloat in the years following the college's departure. (Courtesy of the Wake Forest Birthplace Museum.)

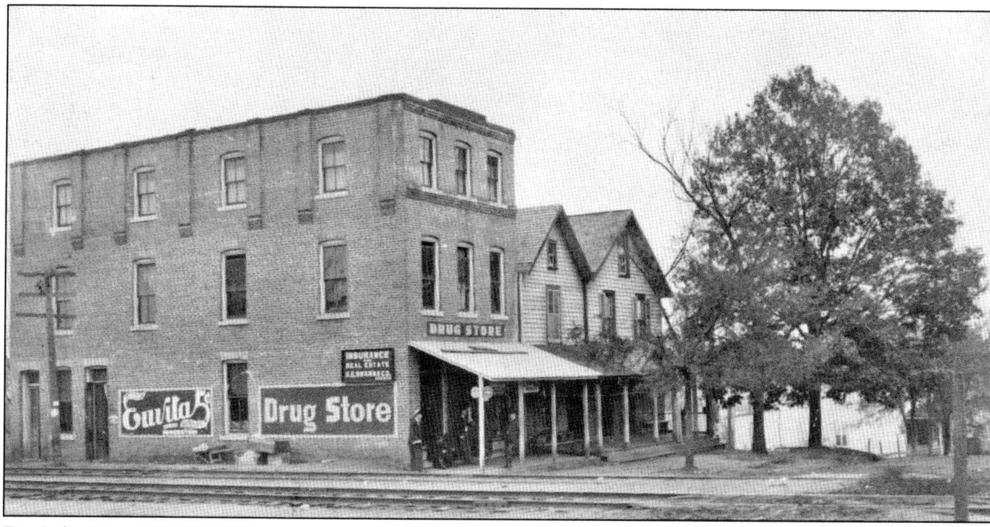

Dr. John Benjamin Powers, soon joined by pharmacist Thomas E. Holding, opened Powers Drug Store in this building alongside the railroad tracks around 1880. The drugstore, seen beside the Wake Forest Hotel and Dining Room, remained until the 1940s. Later identified as Hardwicke's Pharmacy, the business was twice damaged when trains jumped the tracks into the back of the building. (Courtesy of the Wake Forest Birthplace Museum.)

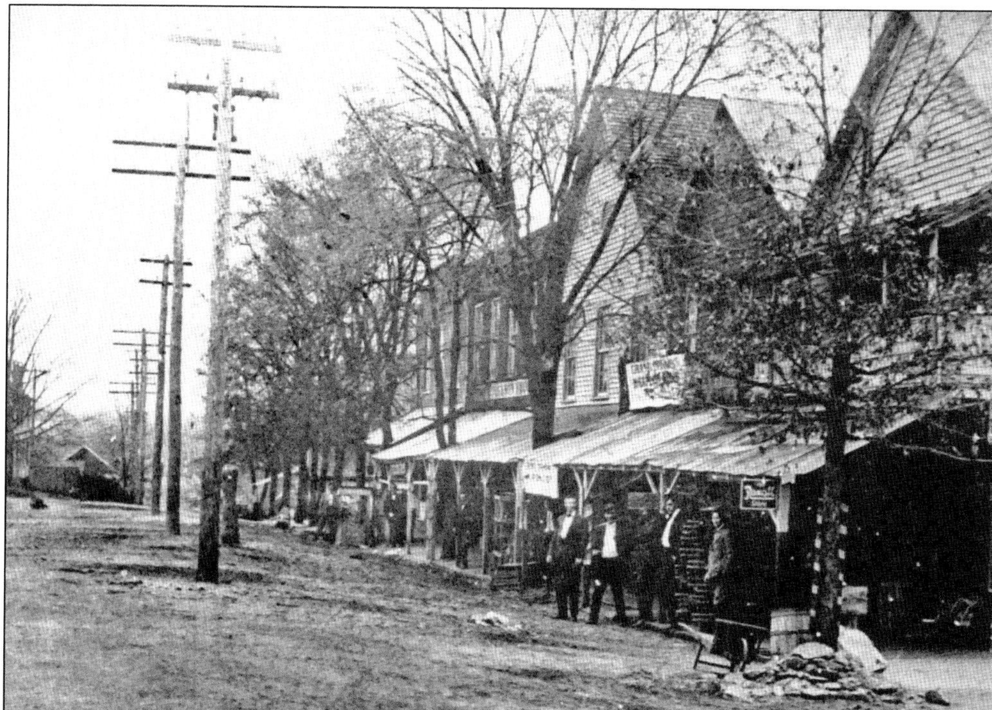

This photograph of the T. E. Holding Drug Store, *c.* 1900, shows the original establishment at the corner of Jones and White Streets. Thomas E. Holding began working as a pharmacist for Dr. John Benjamin Powers. After dissolving their partnership in 1888, Holding opened this business. He founded the Bank of Wake in the same building, before losing it during the Great Depression. (Courtesy of the North Carolina State Archives.)

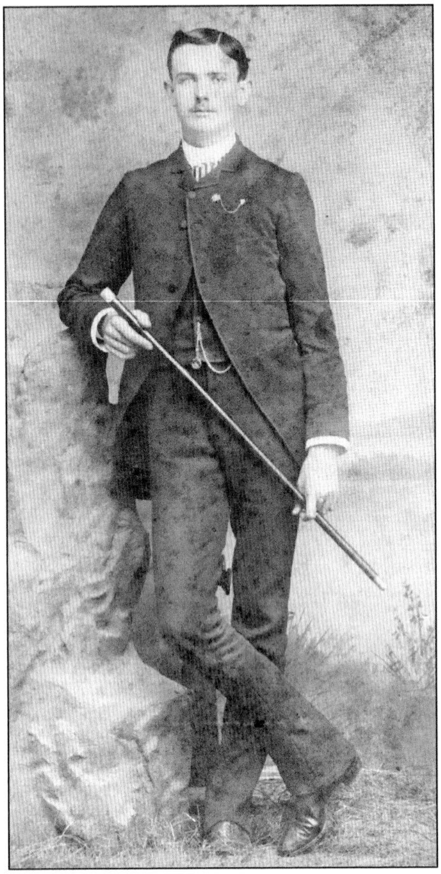

Finely dressed and sophisticated for his era, William Dickson, pictured c. 1900, was one of the proprietors of Dickson Brothers' Department Store. The family business operated for many years in Wake Forest. Residents recall department stores in those days selling dresses on approval. Ladies took the frocks home to try on and returned the selections they didn't like. (Courtesy of the Wake Forest Birthplace Museum.)

Primarily a dry goods establishment, Dickson Brothers' Department Store, seen here around 1900, survived through the mid-20th century. Its main competition, Bolus Department Store, was founded by Lebanese immigrant George Bolus, who started out in retail with goods sold from a horse-pulled wagon. (Courtesy of the Wake Forest Birthplace Museum.)

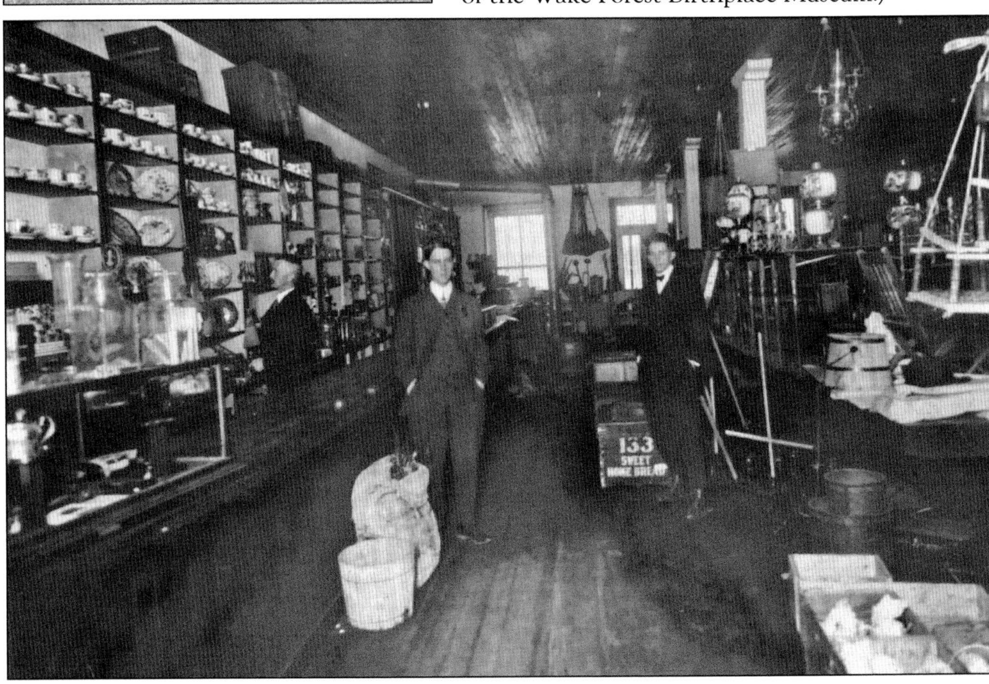

William Royall Powell was the son of Royall Cotton Mill founder William C. Powell. Also a town commissioner, he built a large, white, Classical Revival home on six acres near the north end of Faculty Avenue. His wife, Susie Powell, founded the Wake Forest Garden Club in 1924. (Courtesy of the Wake Forest Birthplace Museum.)

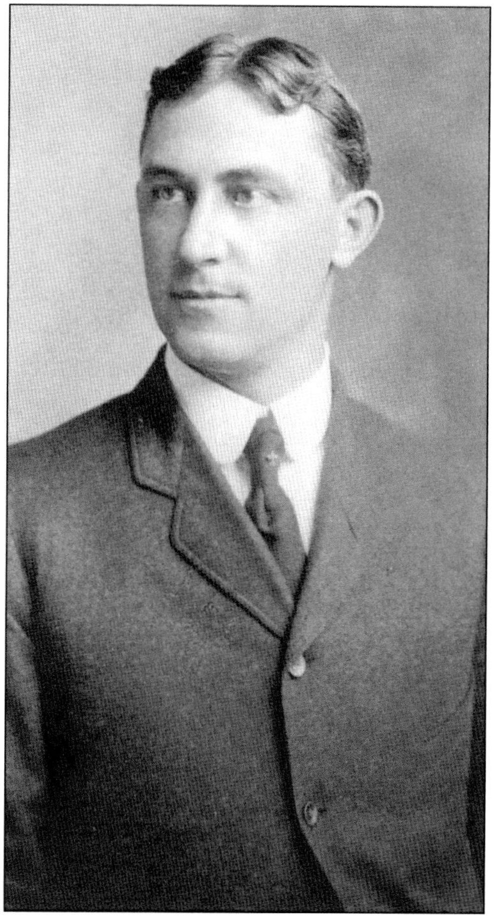

The Falls of the Neuse Manufacturing Company, built around 1855, used water's natural energy to power the production of everything from cotton to iron. For a time just before the Civil War, it was the only significant producer of paper in eastern North Carolina. The location operated primarily as a textile mill from the late 19th century until its closing in 1959. (Courtesy of the North Carolina State Archives.)

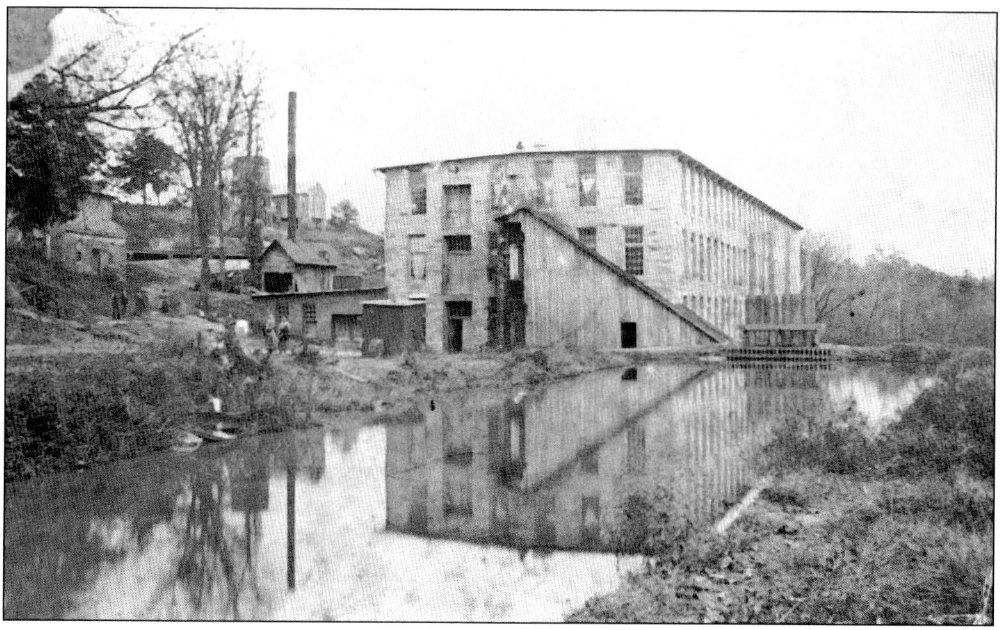

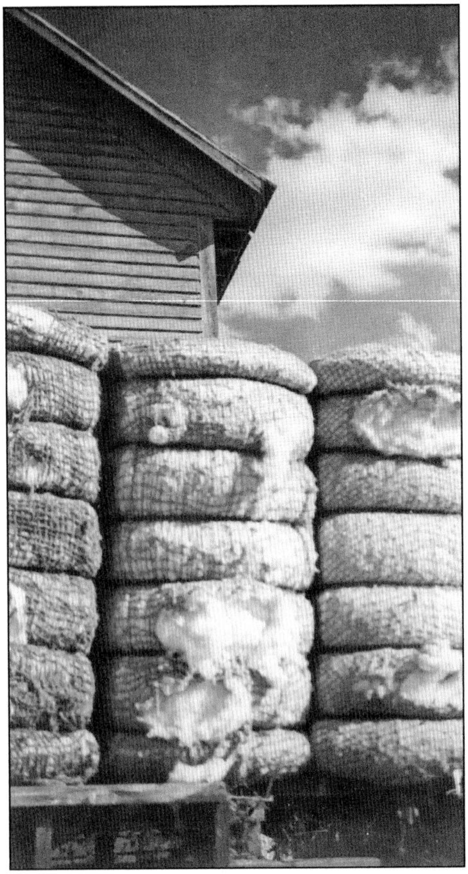

The second oldest business doing more than local trade was the W. W. Holding Company on South White Street. Started about 1890, the store first dealt in heavy groceries, cotton seed, fertilizer, and general merchandise, with a main interest in cotton. Cotton soon took over, as this 1940s-era image illustrates. The company became a major cotton supplier throughout the southeast. (Courtesy of the Wake Forest Birthplace Museum.)

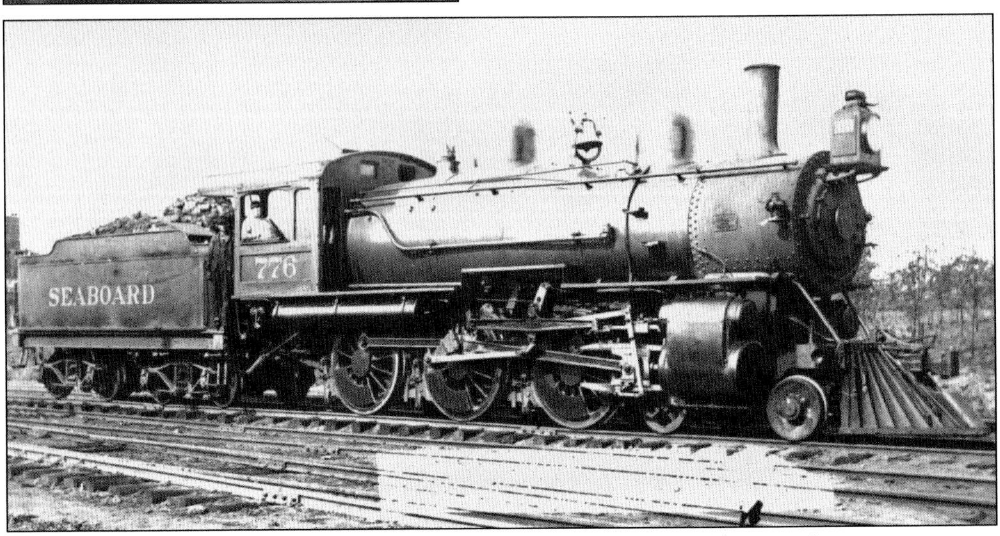

Soon after the railroad moved to Wake Forest, for the princely sum of $3,000, the town grew into a transportation center and place to trade. Forestville faded soon after, eventually becoming part of Wake Forest. The rails later switched to Seaboard Air Line and then Seaboard Coast Line, as pictured in this 1911 image of a new 10-wheel Seaboard freight engine. (Courtesy of the North Carolina State Archives N.95.9.47.)

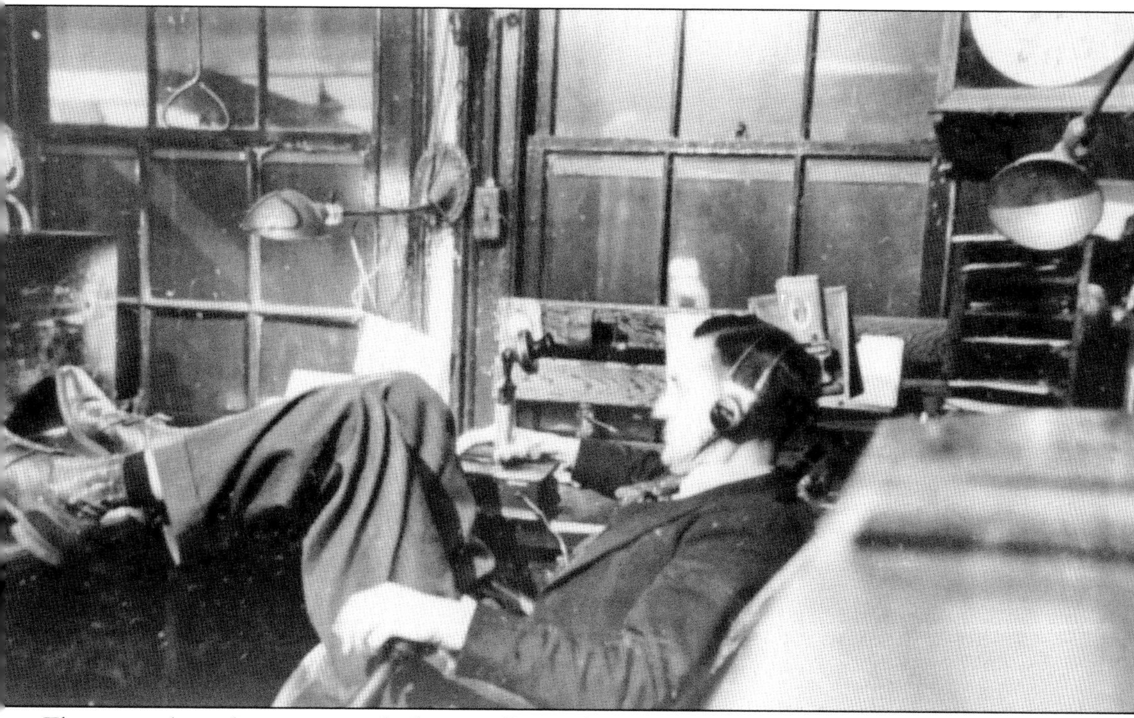

The town telegraph operator worked in an office at the train depot where he spent as much time socializing with visitors as operating machinery. This photograph, taken during World War II, shows operator James E. Anderson. In this era when telegraph and telephone were the main modes of communication, those in charge of running the systems were central figures in the social structure of a small town. Ruby Reid, later a notable Wake Forest businesswoman, started out as the community's telephone operator. One resident, writing to a friend from Atlanta in the 1920s, described the situation this way: "Miss Ruby Reid . . . listens to all the calls, and if the girls call and I'm not at home she tells them where I am. There are no secrets in Wake Forest." The letter was reprinted in a local history article appearing in the *Wake Forest Gazette*. (Courtesy of the Wake Forest Birthplace Museum.)

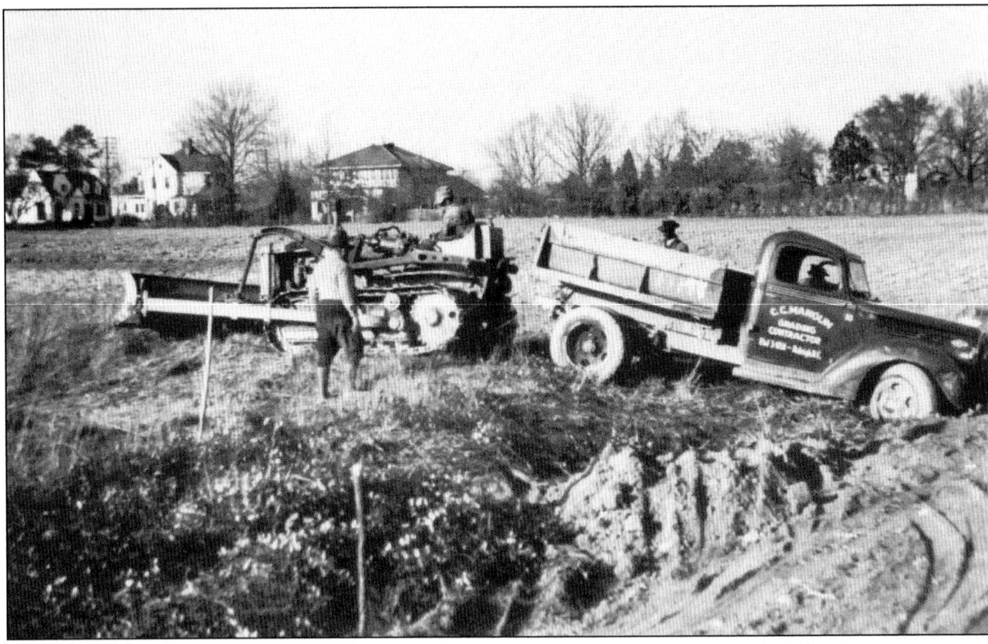

This Mangum grader was preparing land for a new wartime railroad track. The Mangums were a well-known local family. Priestly Hinton Mangum Jr. devoted his life to scientific agriculture and introduced the Mangum Terrace, an agricultural method that eliminates hillside ditches by terracing the slope and saving more land for cultivation. The practice has received worldwide attention. (Courtesy of the Wake Forest Birthplace Museum.)

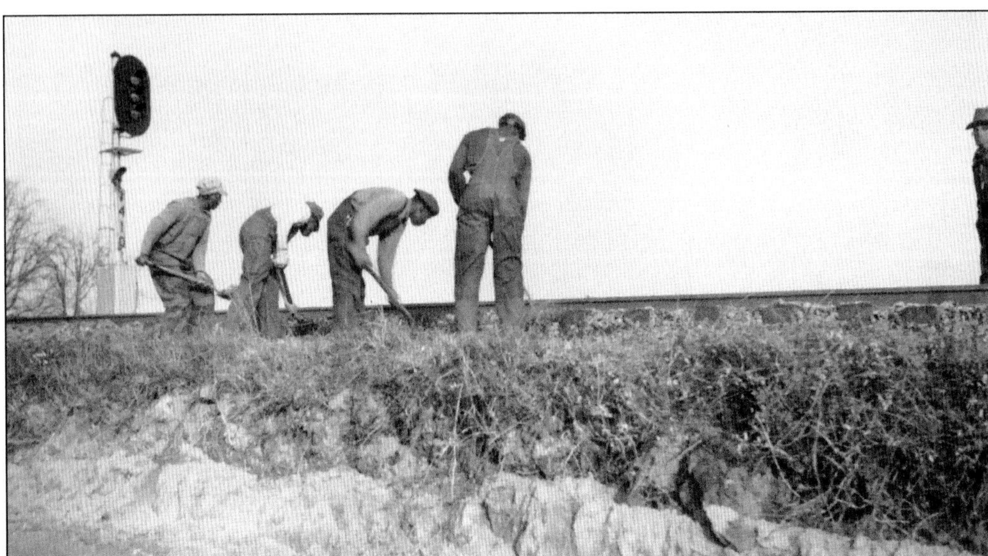

This photograph of railroad workers constructing new track for World War II shipments appears in an album compiled by a soldier who spent some of the war years at the Wake Forest Army Finance School. (Courtesy of the Wake Forest Birthplace Museum.)

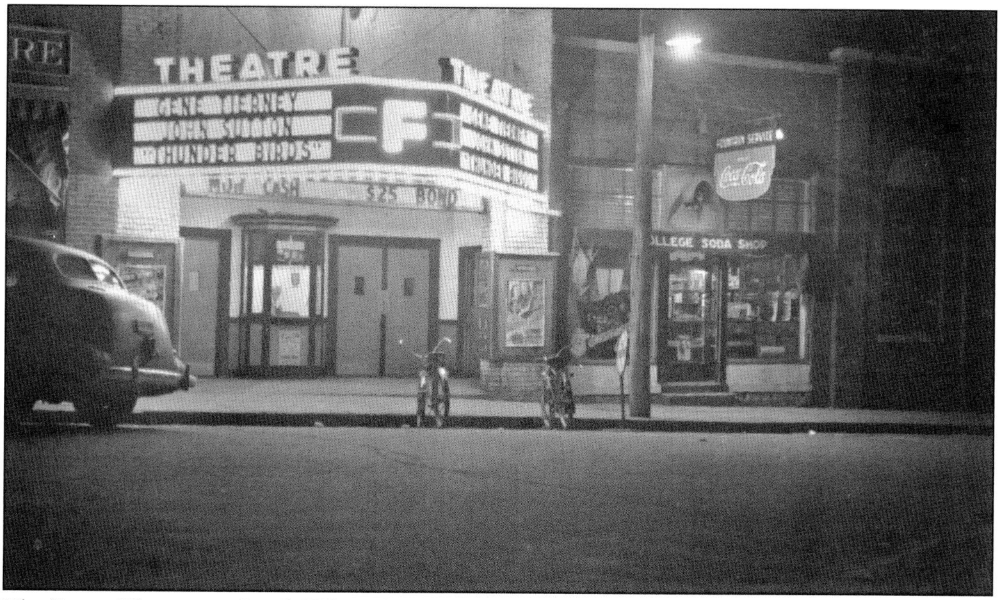

The Forest Theater on South White Street, *c.* 1942, was a popular destination for college students and town residents, particularly after it became the first local business to install air-conditioning. In the first part of the 20th century, the town had two movie theaters, and a ticket cost 12¢. The Collegiate and the Forest Theaters both closed after the college left town. (Courtesy of the Wake Forest Birthplace Museum.)

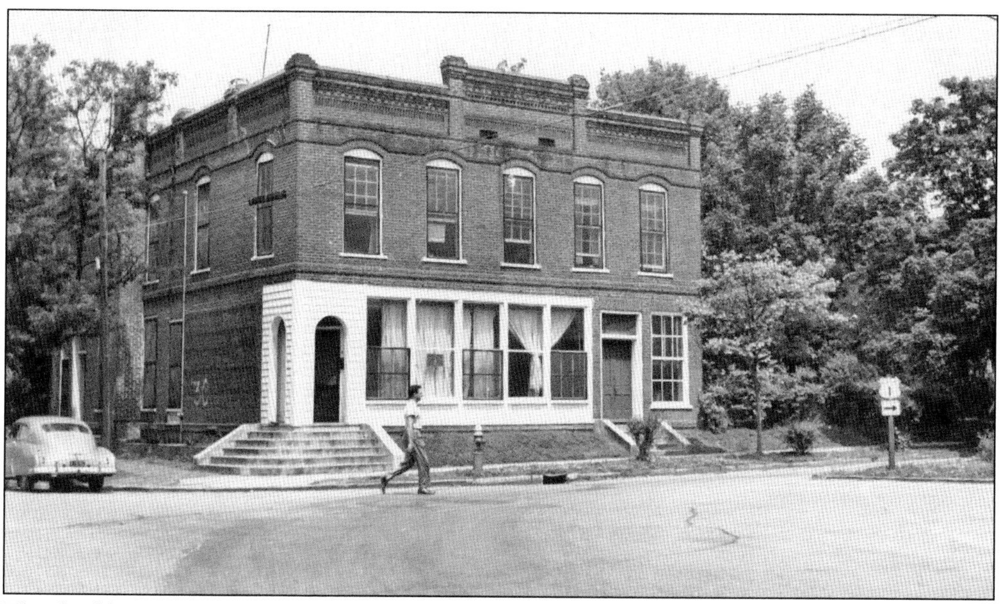

This building at the corner of North Main Street is commonly called the Corner. Once the site of Dickson Brothers' Department Store, it has also housed a campus law fraternity, Miss Jo Williams' Eatery, and the College Book Store. For many years, the location served as an ice cream and sandwich parlor, before costly new water treatment requirements forced it to shut down. (Courtesy of Southeastern Baptist Theological Seminary.)

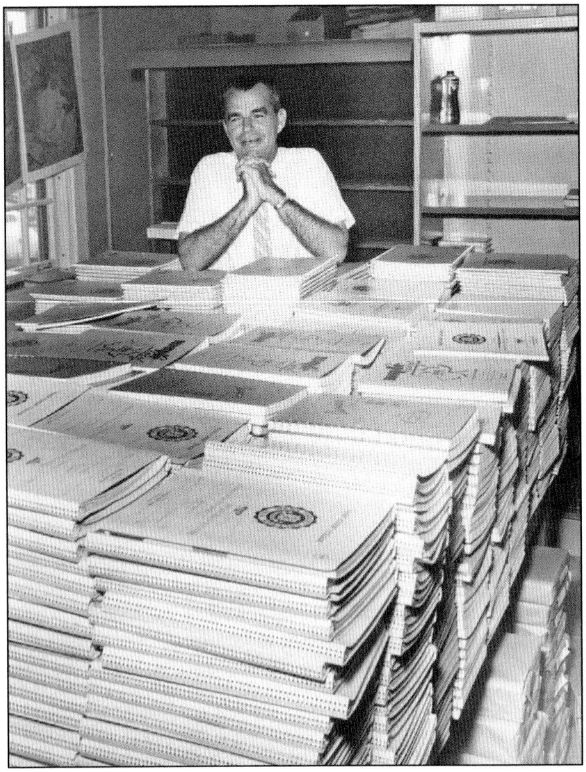

There was a time when everyone in town knew Everette Snyder, manager of the College Book Store from 1930 to 1960. And he, in turn, was famous for knowing the names of all 1,500 members of the student body and faculty. This photograph was taken by Grigg Studio on the Campus of Wake Forest College. (Courtesy of the Wake Forest Birthplace Museum.)

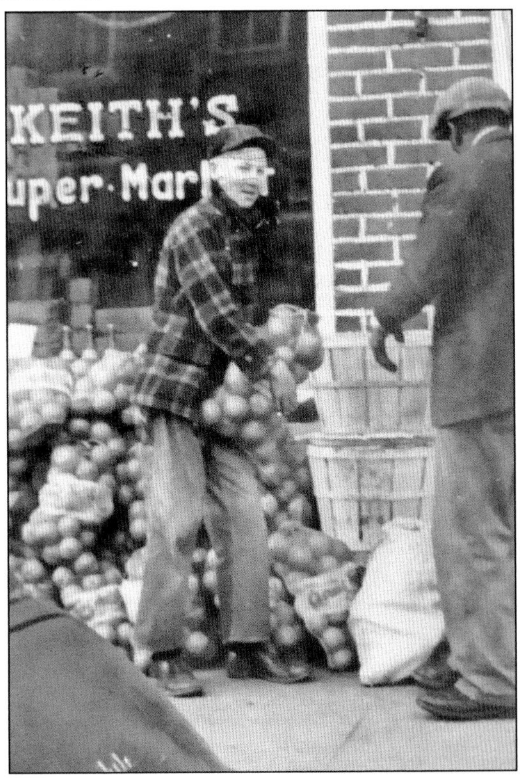

Keith's Grocery Store on South White Street was another popular local business. This photograph, taken in December 1942, shows a grocer stacking bags of Christmas oranges on the sidewalk outside the store. The store occupied various locations over a 60-year period. (Courtesy of the Wake Forest Birthplace Museum.)

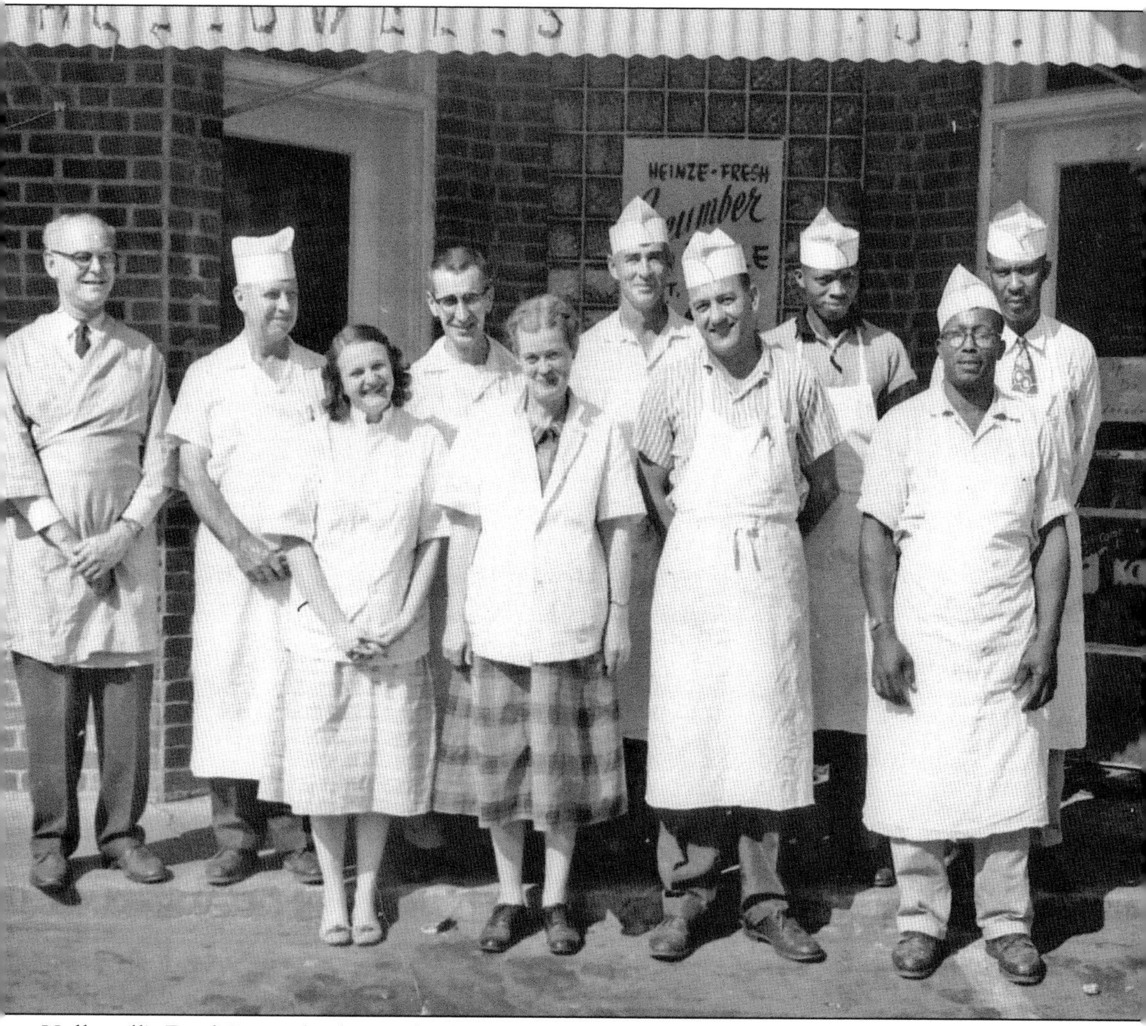

Hollowell's Food Store also boasted a large and happy clientele in the years before big chain grocery stores moved to town. Here owner Jesse Hollowell poses with employees. Pictured from left to right are (first row) Annie Mae Keith Lowery, May Kearney Ray, Gene Alford, and Isaac Harris; (second row) Jesse Hollowell, Lee Owen Pearce, Mickey Corchran, Ross Wiggins, Robert Jones, and Otis Stallings. The picture was taken in front of Hollowell's first new grocery store building, constructed some time between 1948 and 1950 and located on Roosevelt Avenue. The original store, opened in 1933, was located on South White Street. The local grocery, along with competitors Lyon's, Keith's, and Lowery's, catered to its customers with phone-in orders and at-home delivery. Regulars were allowed to pay their grocery bills at the end of the month. (Courtesy of the Wake Forest Birthplace Museum.)

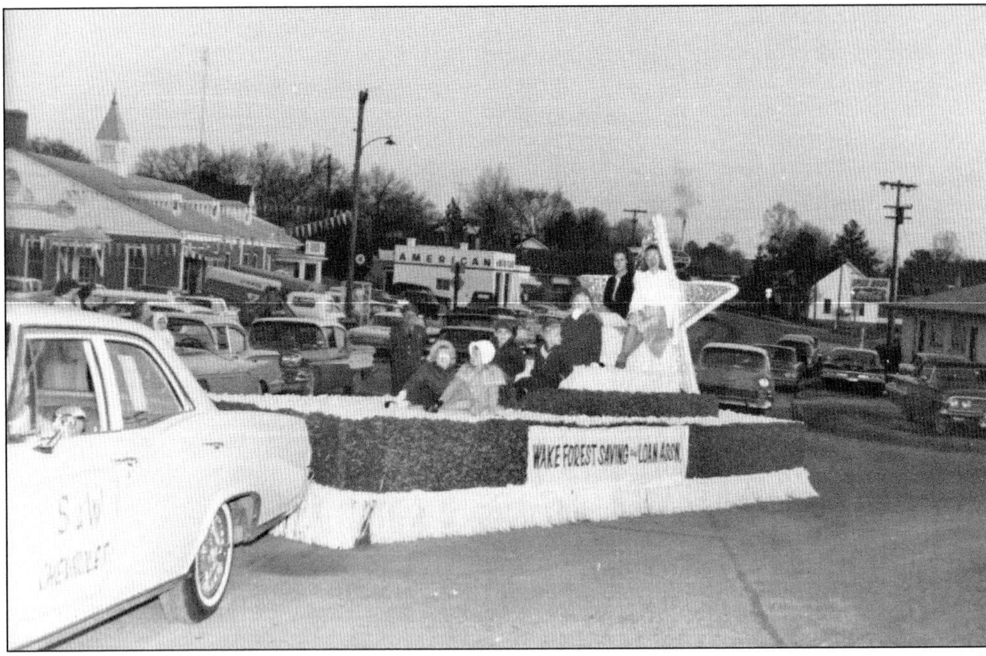

The Wake Forest Federal Savings and Loan, started by a group of local men in 1922, was the only local financial institution to survive the Great Depression, staying afloat as both local banks failed. This float was the savings and loan's entry in the 1964 Christmas parade. (Courtesy of Wake Forest Federal Savings and Loan.)

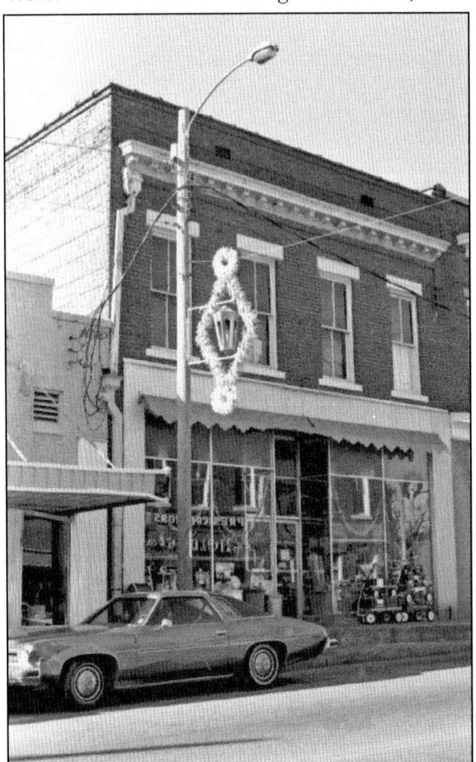

Ira Otis Jones founded the Wake Forest Supply Company in 1906, eventually passing the business on to his son, Leland, who renamed it Jones Hardware Company. The store on South White Street moved to the Durham Road in 1991. It closed just before its centennial in 2006, replaced by a Walgreen's. (Courtesy of the North Carolina State Archives N.79.9.867.)

Four

PROGRESS

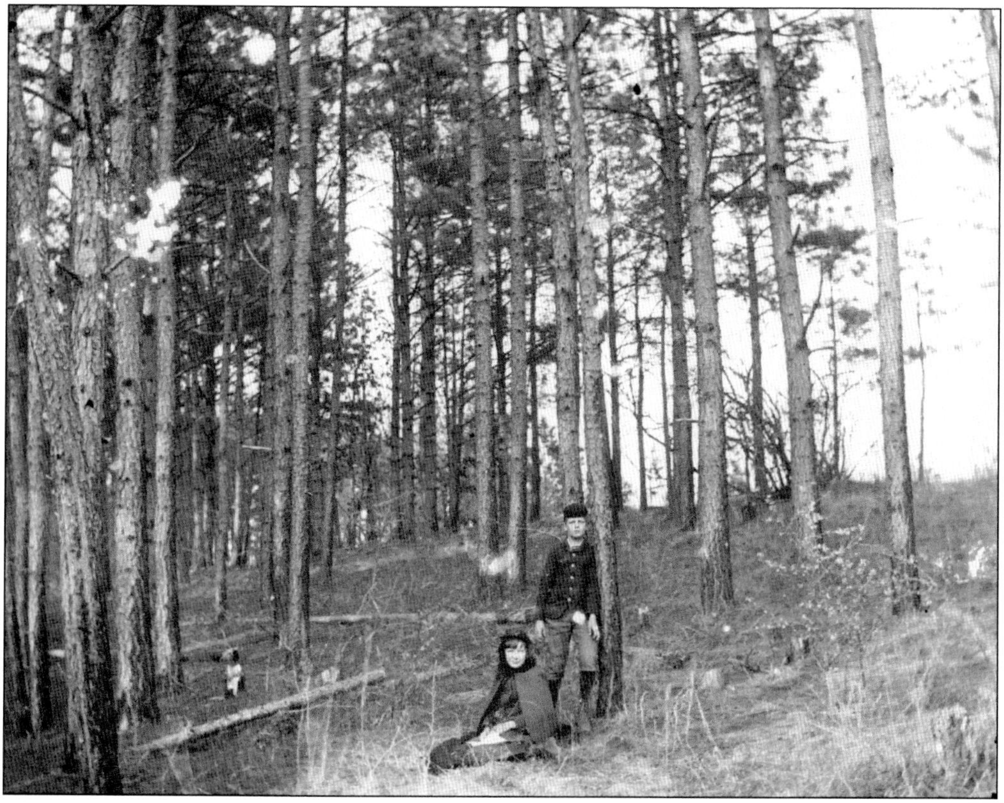

The Forest of Wake, named for its many trees, forms the backdrop of this photograph. The two children amid a patch of scrub pines are members of the Dr. Charles Taylor family, dating this photograph to the period between the Civil War and World War I. While the Industrial Revolution and railroad construction were improving the financial situation for many families, it was also chipping away at the township's forested landscape. In nearby Raleigh, rows of brick store buildings and offices rose into viable commercial centers aimed at a mixed clientele of town and farm families, both landowners and tenant farmers. Those farmers enjoyed a brief boom following World War I before stumbling again upon economic hardship and moving where the jobs were—to the cities and towns wired for electricity and modern conveniences. Wake Forest followed the trend, moving quickly into the 20th century with growth as a center of transportation, construction, education, and industry. (Courtesy of the Wake Forest Birthplace Museum.)

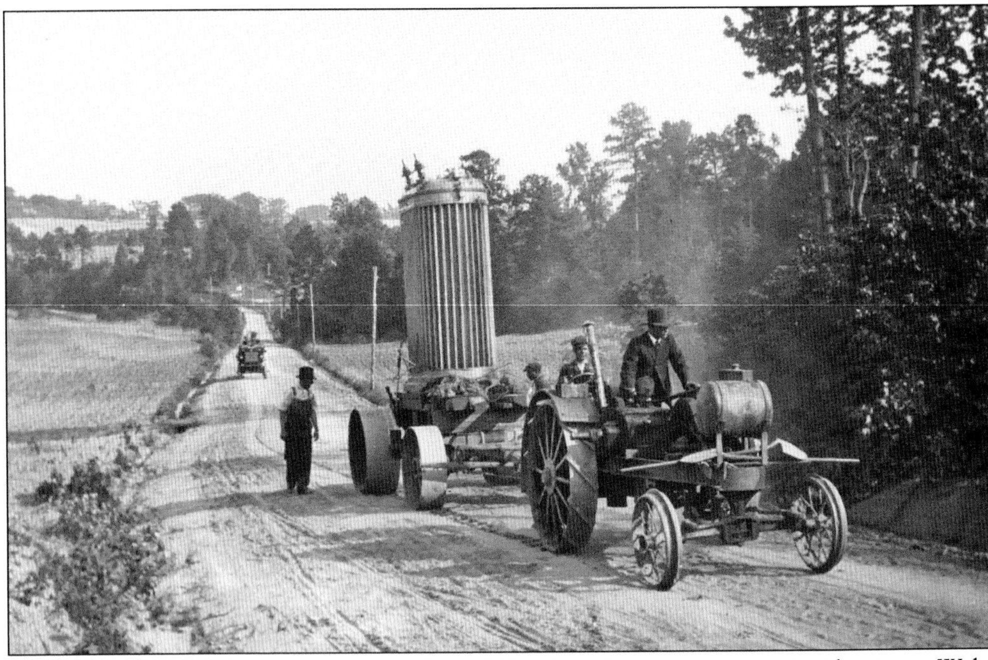

Wake Forest's electrification was sparked in 1909, when the town gave up its identity as Wake Forest College to become, more simply, the Town of Wake Forest. It also gained the authority to issue bonds for an electric light plant. This utility crew from the Carolina Power and Light Company is transporting transformers from Raleigh to Wake Forest around 1912. (Courtesy of the North Carolina State Archives phC68.1.268A and B.)

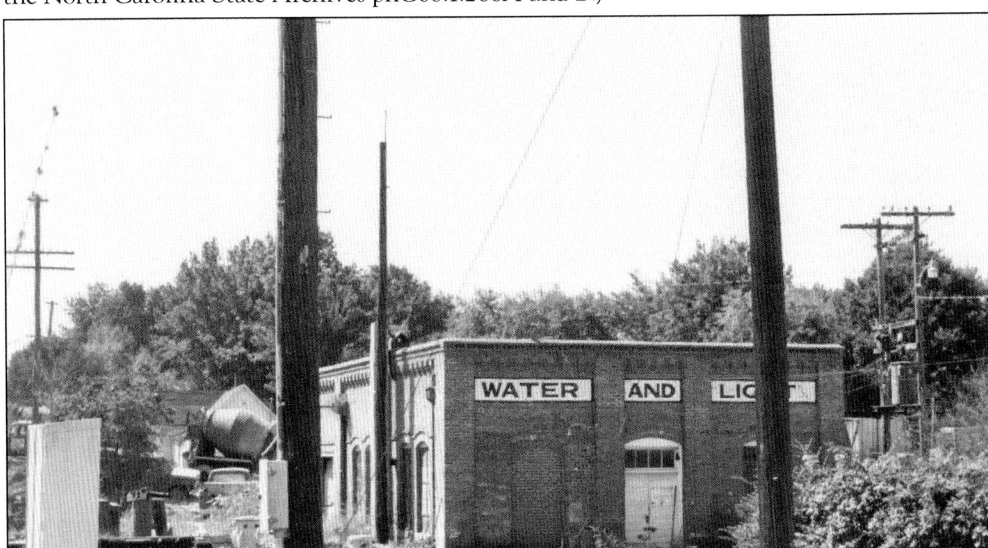

The Water and Light Plant came as a result of the 1909 legislative act giving the Town of Wake Forest its charter and a corporate identity. Next came a $15,000 bond election to build this electric light plant. The building in this photograph now serves as the funeral home crematorium along the railroad tracks on South White Street. (Courtesy of the Wake Forest Birthplace Museum.)

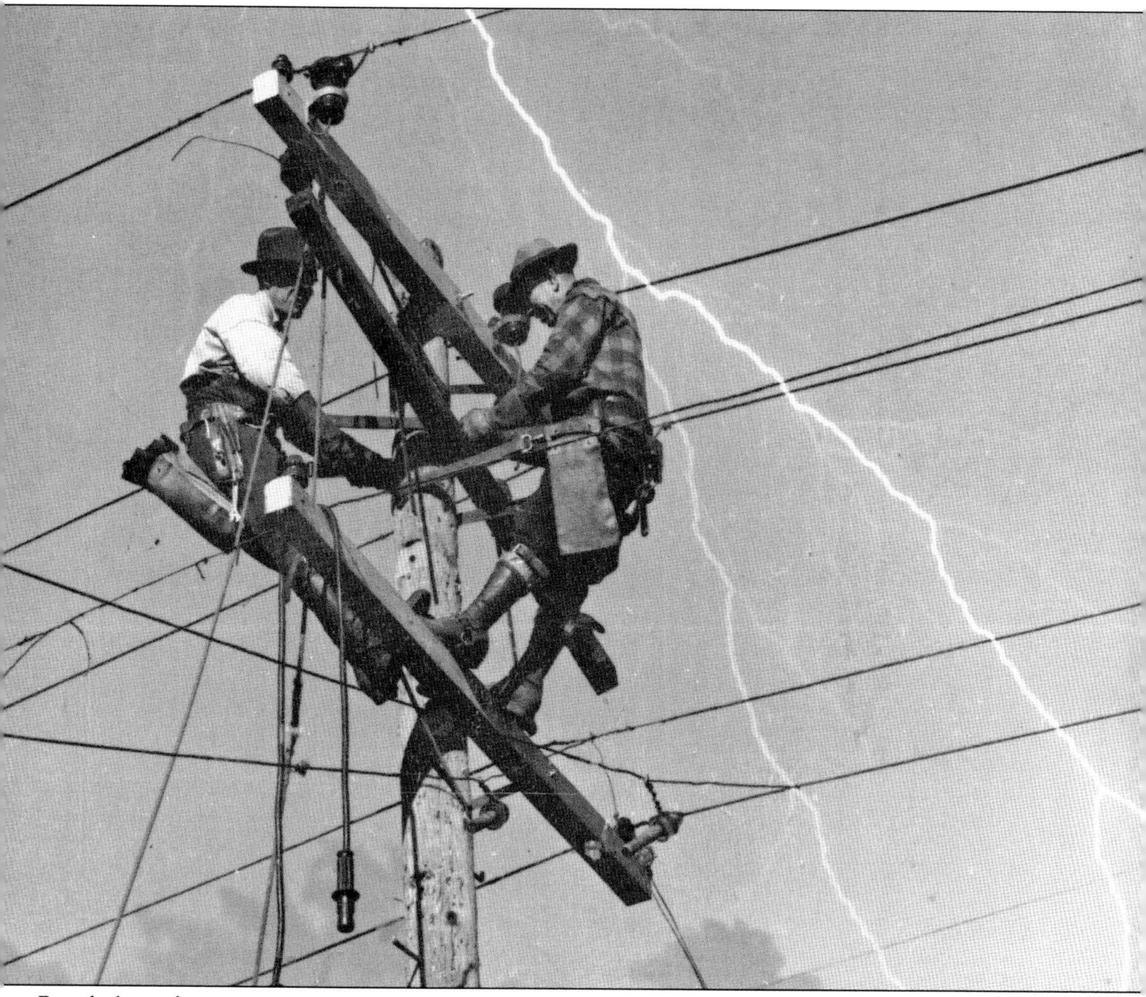

Rural electrification came along in the 1930s as part of an effort to save the family farm. The government hoped affordable electricity would improve rural conditions, make farming more profitable, and staunch the exodus of families from the country to the cities. Indeed, in those days, only 10 percent of farm families had electricity, compared to nearly 90 percent of town and city dwellers. When private utility companies opposed the effort, claiming it was too difficult and expensive, Pres. Franklin Delano Roosevelt created the Rural Electric Administration. Carolina Power and Light (CP&L) still hadn't run lines along the dirt roads to reach the region's many farmhouses. This dramatic photograph of CP&L linemen furiously working on a pole in a thunderstorm was taken in 1935, the year the national Rural Electrification Administration was established. It was 1940 before the first meeting was held in Wake Forest to form the Wake Electric Membership Cooperative. (Courtesy of the North Carolina State Archives PhC68.1.249.)

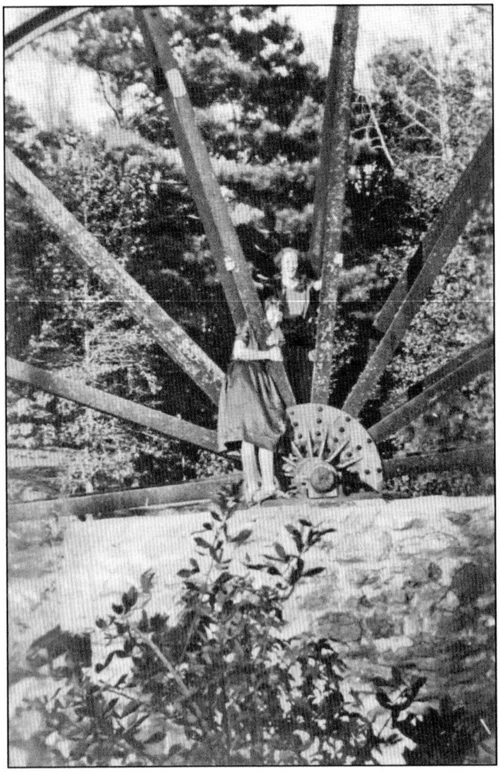

This large mill wheel still stands at the site of Deacon's Ridge, near the end of South White Street. It was a popular picnic site in the early part of the 20th century, arrived at by car and, as recalled by older Wake Forest residents, much fun to climb. (Courtesy of the Wake Forest Birthplace Museum.)

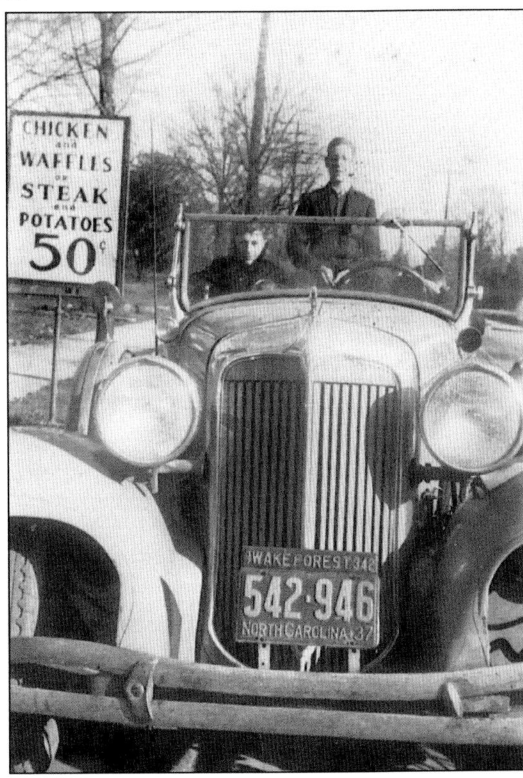

This photograph of Johnny Newsome and his new car was taken on New Year's Eve 1937. Automobiles were becoming very popular, and in 1924, town voters approved $175,000 in bonds to start paving streets. Soon folks heard tell of the new north-south interstate coming to town and a paved road linking Wake Forest to Durham. (Courtesy of the Wake Forest Birthplace Museum.)

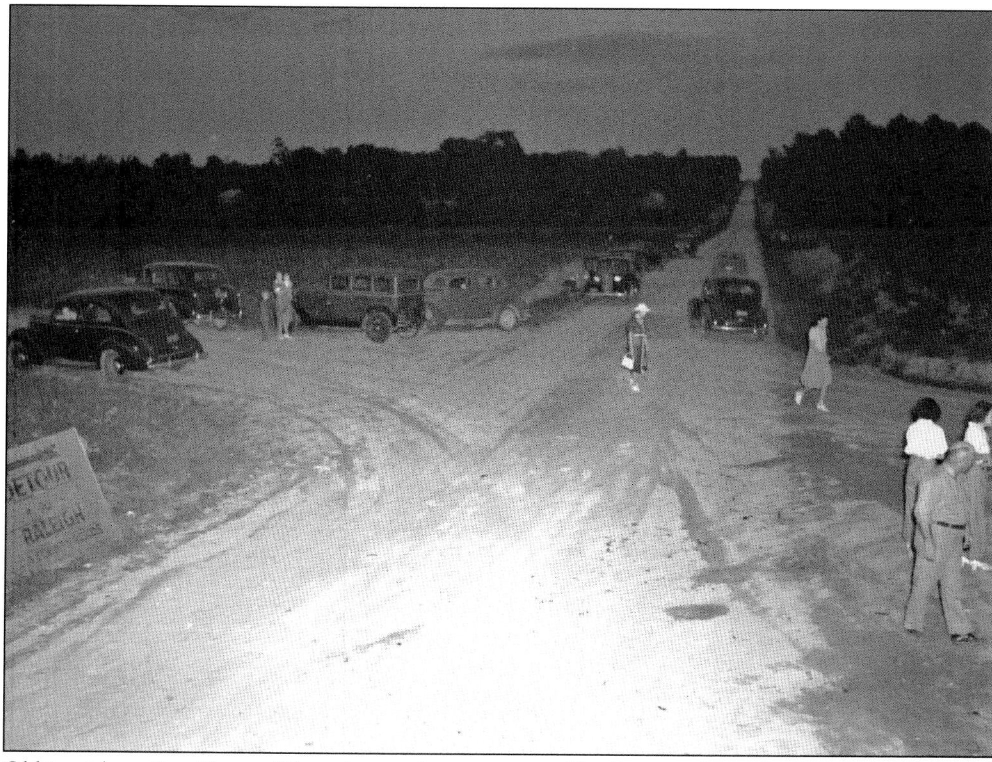

Old Louisburg Road began life as the northern stage road leading northeast from Raleigh. Residents around William Roles's store and post office, where the town of Rolesville grew up, were busy in the 19th century establishing well-respected schools of their own. (Courtesy of the *News and Observer* and North Carolina State Archives NO.39.13.402-408.)

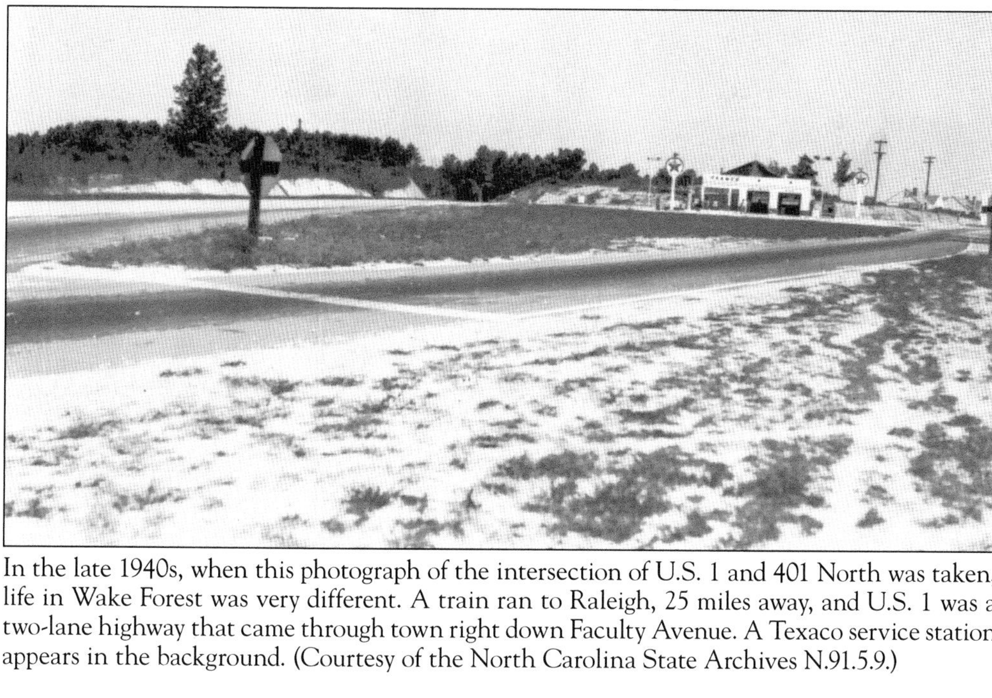

In the late 1940s, when this photograph of the intersection of U.S. 1 and 401 North was taken, life in Wake Forest was very different. A train ran to Raleigh, 25 miles away, and U.S. 1 was a two-lane highway that came through town right down Faculty Avenue. A Texaco service station appears in the background. (Courtesy of the North Carolina State Archives N.91.5.9.)

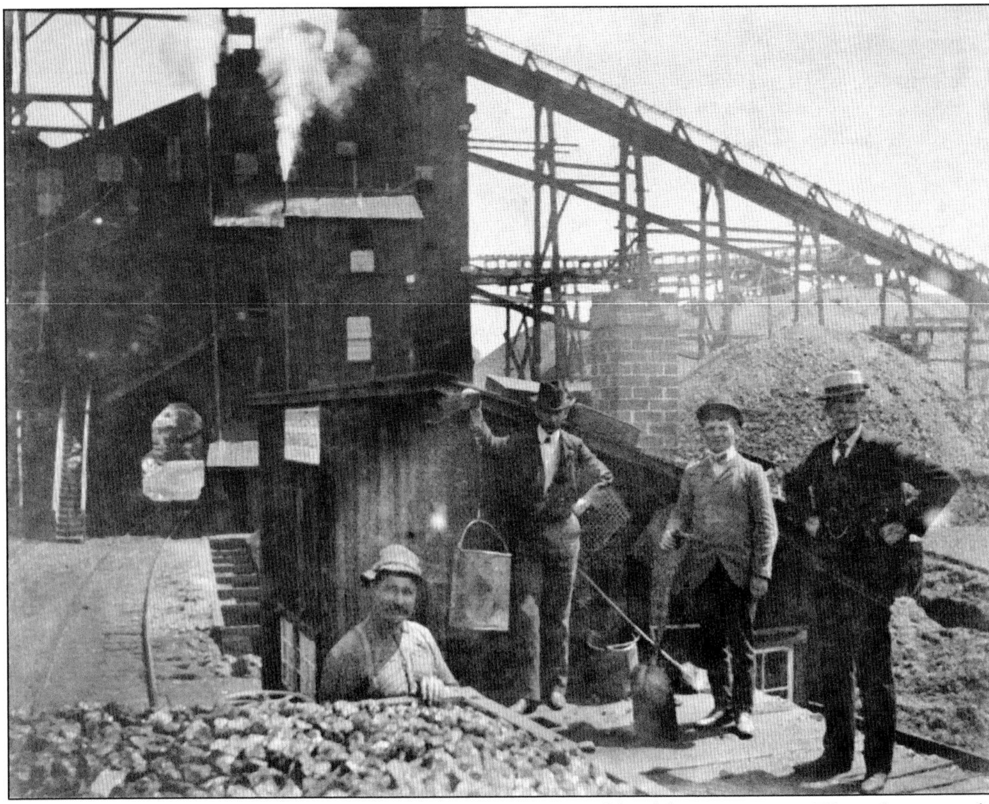

Local rock was often quarried for road construction and building projects. This photograph, from a collection at the Wake Forest Birthplace Museum, appears to show workers at the rock quarry on U.S. 1 in the early part of the 20th century. (Courtesy of the Wake Forest Birthplace Museum.)

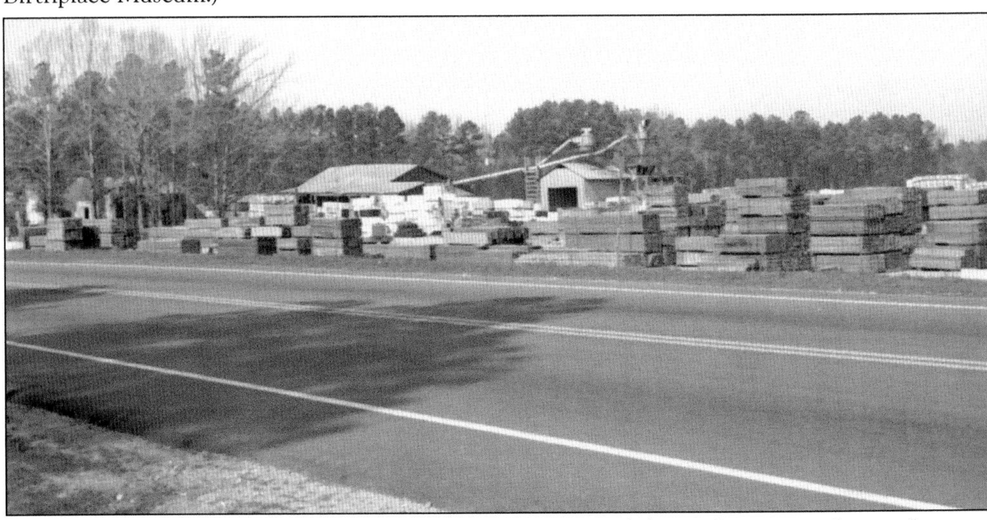

Goldston's Lumber Company operated throughout most of the 20th century. Located several miles west of town on Highway 98, it nonetheless has maintained a Wake Forest address and identity. Goldston's materials were used for many Wake Forest construction projects. (Courtesy of the North Carolina State Archives N.93.7.1085-1086, 1094.)

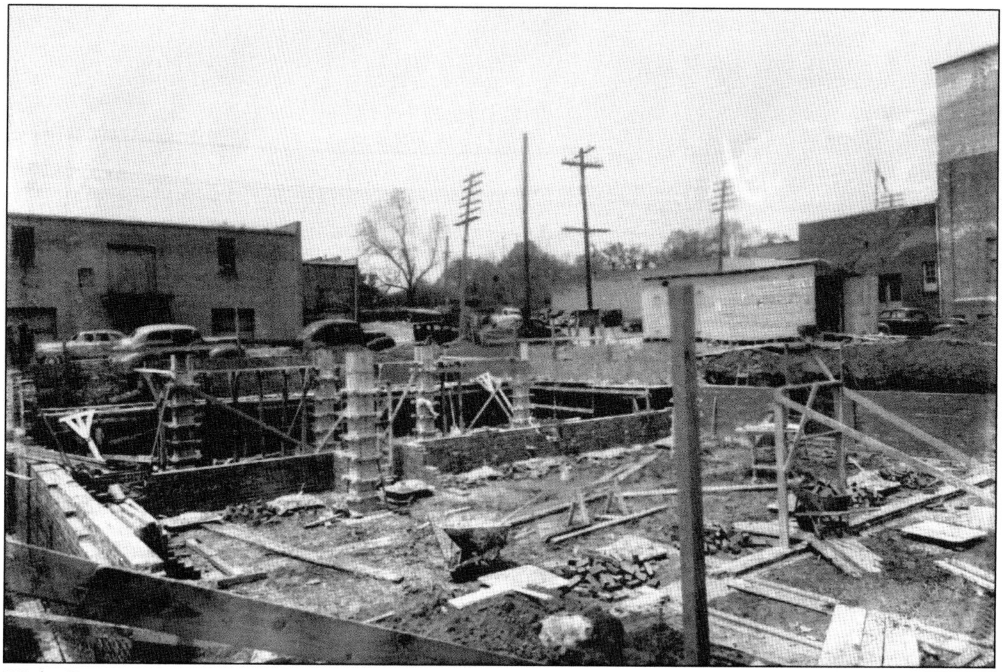

Wake Forest's new post office was constructed on South White Street in 1940. Funded by a grant from the Works Project Administration, the $43,000 building would become the town's first government-owned post office building in its 117-year history. Previously postmasters operated out of their homes or rental space. (Courtesy of the North Carolina State Archives N.53.15.4425.)

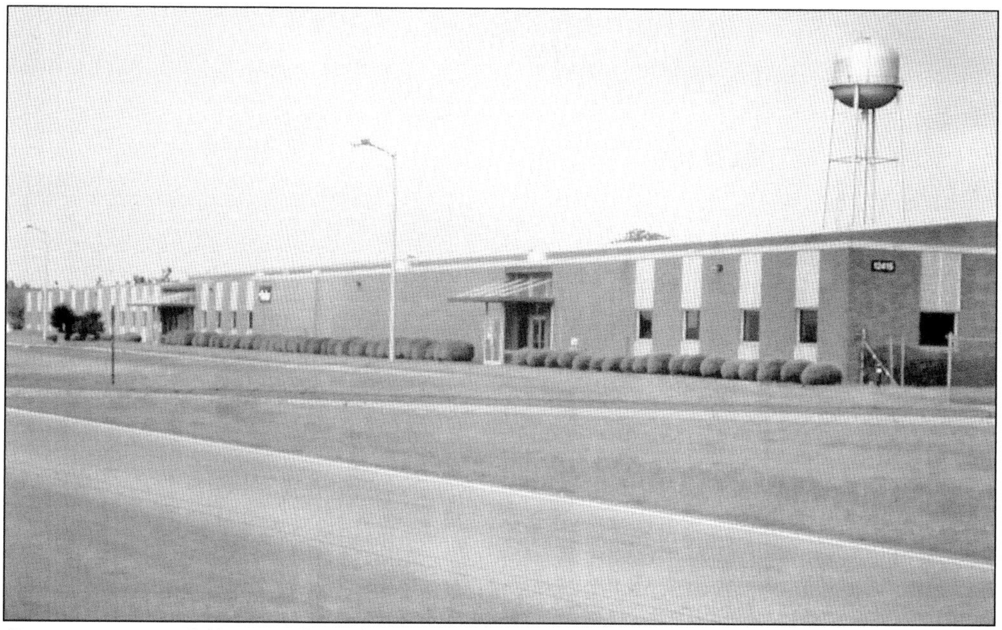

Cows once peacefully grazed on the 33-acre tract of land that, in 1964, became the Schrader Plant along U.S. 1. The metalworking factory, which made more than 10,000 varieties of machine parts, employed more than 200 people, and made regular shipments to distributors throughout the United States and overseas. (Courtesy of Millridge Companies.)

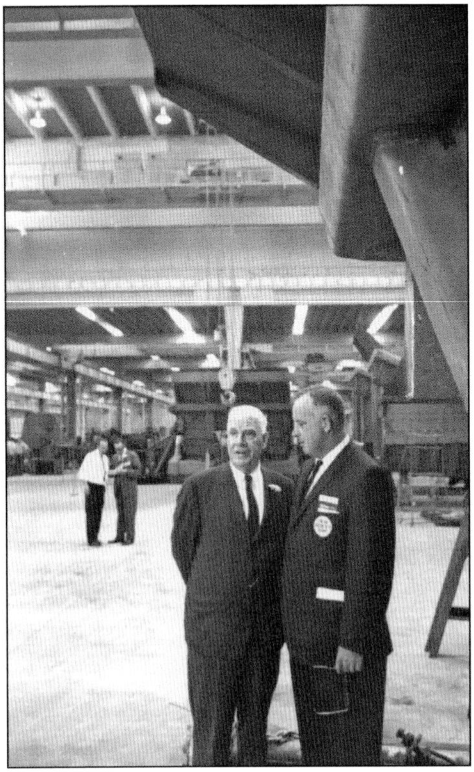

In June 1965, former governor Luther Hodges (left) was the principal speaker at ceremonies dedicating the 147,000-square-foot Athey Plant, a factory for the manufacture of heavy material moving equipment for mining, quarrying, and highway construction. (Courtesy of the *News and Observer* and North Carolina State Archives NO.6-28-1965Fr17 and Fr24.)

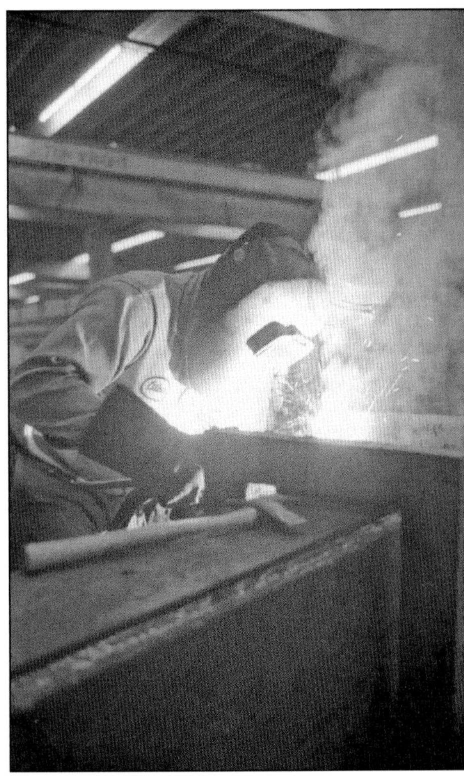

In the 1960s, Athey employed approximately 250 skilled workers in the Wake Forest area, manufacturing equipment shipped internationally to developing nations. It was Wake Forest's largest employer when layoffs hit just before Christmas 2000. A few months later, the plant was closed. (Courtesy of the *News and Observer* and North Carolina State Archives NO.6-28-1965Fr17 and Fr24.)

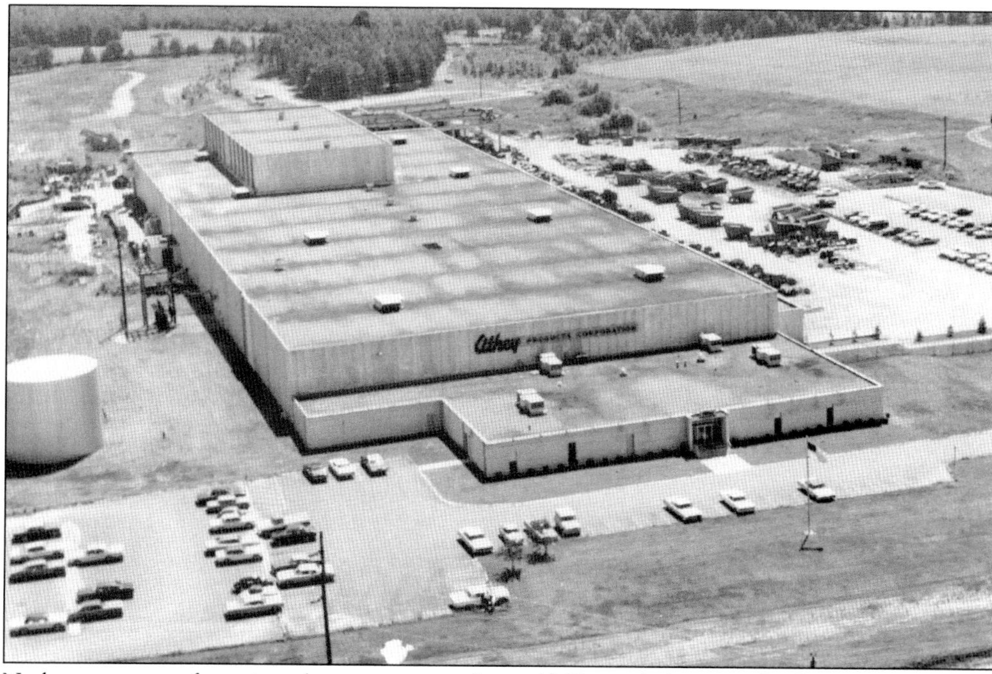

No longer a manufacturing plant, as seen in this *c.* 1965 aerial photograph, the Athey Plant has now become the Factory, the family activity and sports and entertainment center developed by the Ammons Group. (Courtesy of Southeastern Baptist Theological Seminary.)

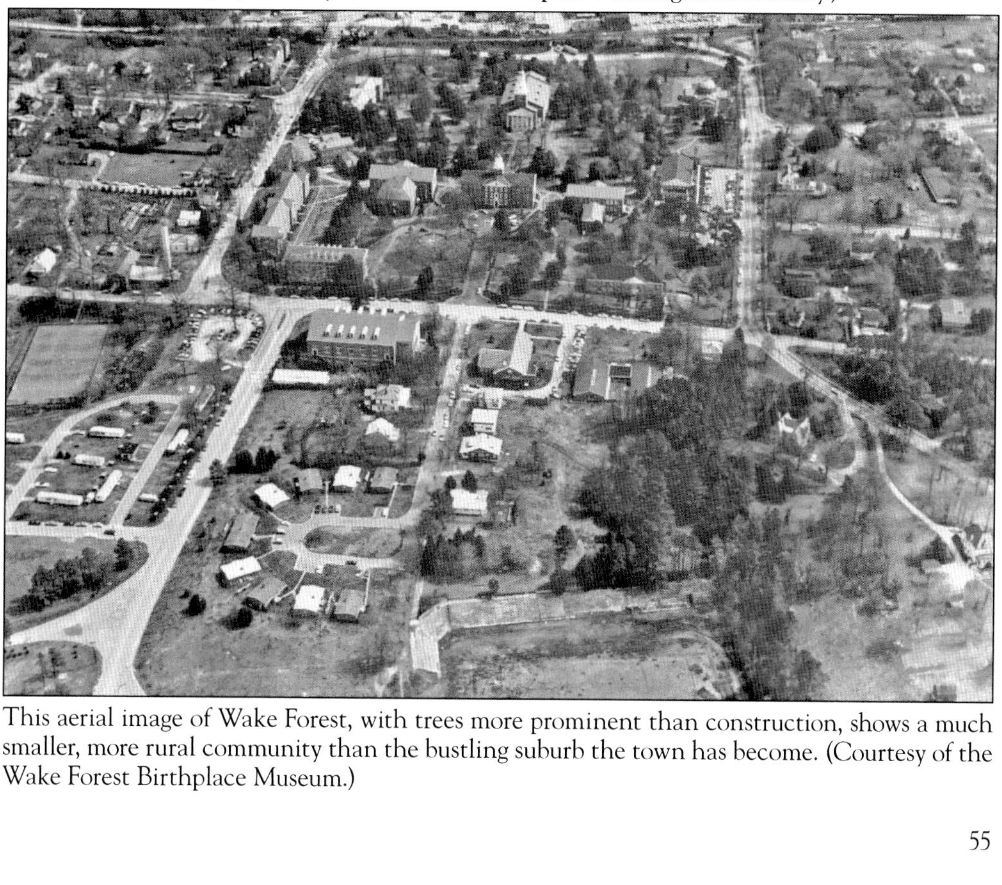

This aerial image of Wake Forest, with trees more prominent than construction, shows a much smaller, more rural community than the bustling suburb the town has become. (Courtesy of the Wake Forest Birthplace Museum.)

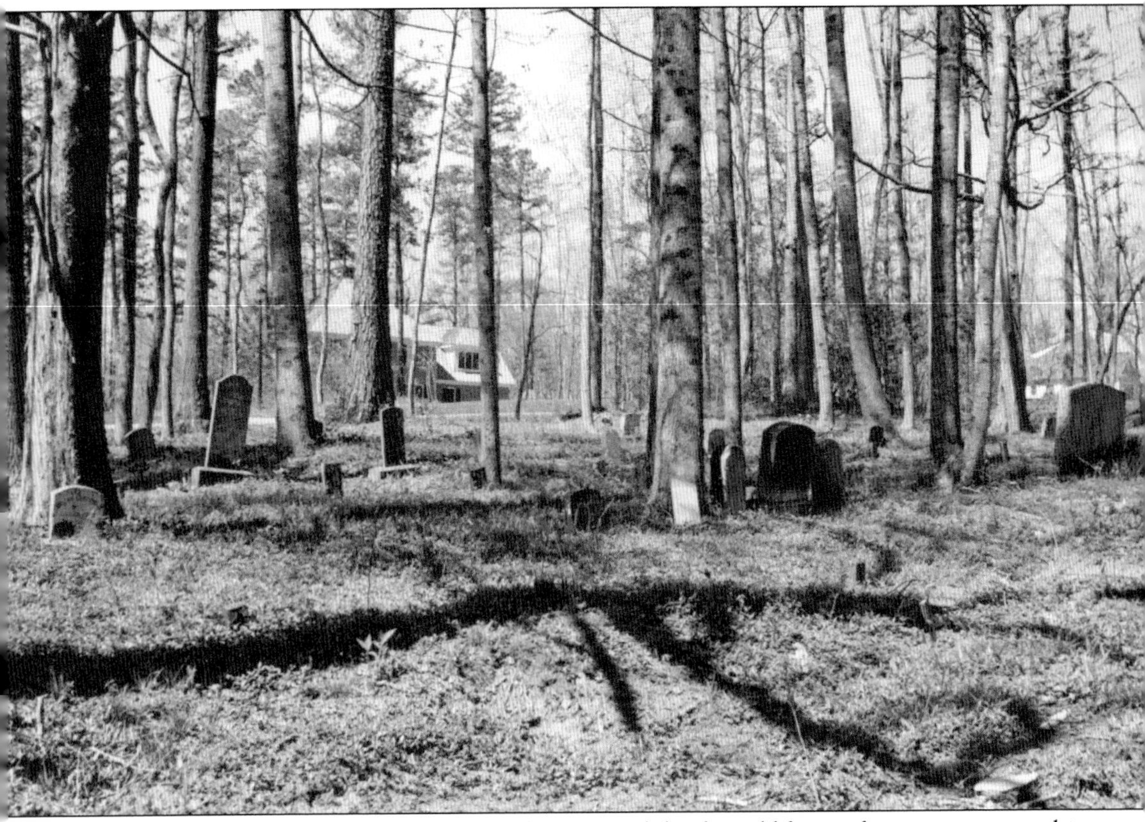

Family cemeteries pose a problem for developers, as subdividing old farms often means encroaching on past burial grounds. The Thompson cemetery, located on what once was farmland along Horse Creek, was overgrown and untended when discovered by builder Jim Adams of Millridge Companies, who chose to leave the historic site intact while constructing new homes on all sides. Buried in the quarter-acre plot are John Martin Crenshaw, the first student to enroll in Wake Forest College (then Institute) in 1832 at the age of 12, and his father, George Thompson, one of the school's original trustees. The graves face east, traditionally positioned to more readily greet the rising sun on the morning of Christ's return. The cemetery also contains a number of slave graves marked with fieldstone and located in the back left corner of the property. No original house remains. But a plantation called Waterfall, said to resemble the Mordecai house in Raleigh, once stood across the road near the banks of Horse Creek. It burned in the 1970s. (Courtesy of the Smart family.)

Five

SCHOOLS AND EDUCATION

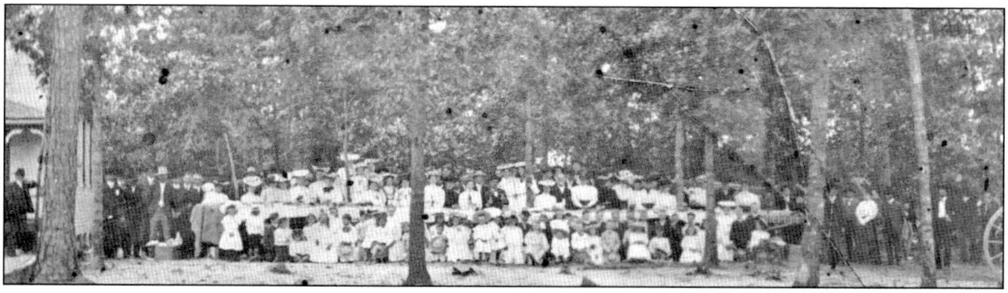

Wake Forest has a long association with learning, making an early mark as home to three private academies that educated children from all over the county. Clements Academy, a country school built in Wake Forest Township in the area north of Rolesville, was county funded and named for the Wake County superintendent of schools, W. G. Clements. Placed at a dirt-road intersection, the school had three teachers, each instructing students in three grades. Children graduated at the eighth- or ninth-grade level. This photograph, taken around 1905, shows the school soon after it opened. Although it closed in 1928, the building was made into a home in later years, allowing it to remain one of the county's only early-20th-century school buildings still in existence. (Courtesy of the Wake Forest Birthplace Museum.)

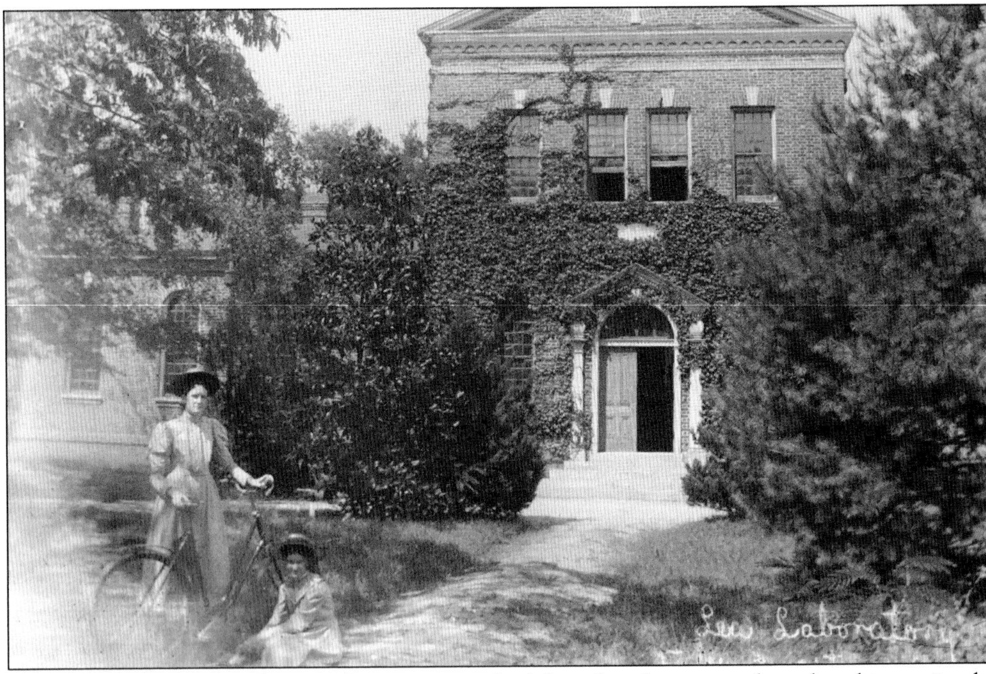

Opened in 1888, Lea Laboratory's vine-covered edifice already appeared aged and imposing by the time this *c.* 1900 photograph was taken. Named for Sydney Lea in recognition of a generous donation, the building was considered the most contemporary college science building of its time. It is now listed on the National Register of Historic Places. (Courtesy of the Wake Forest Birthplace Museum.)

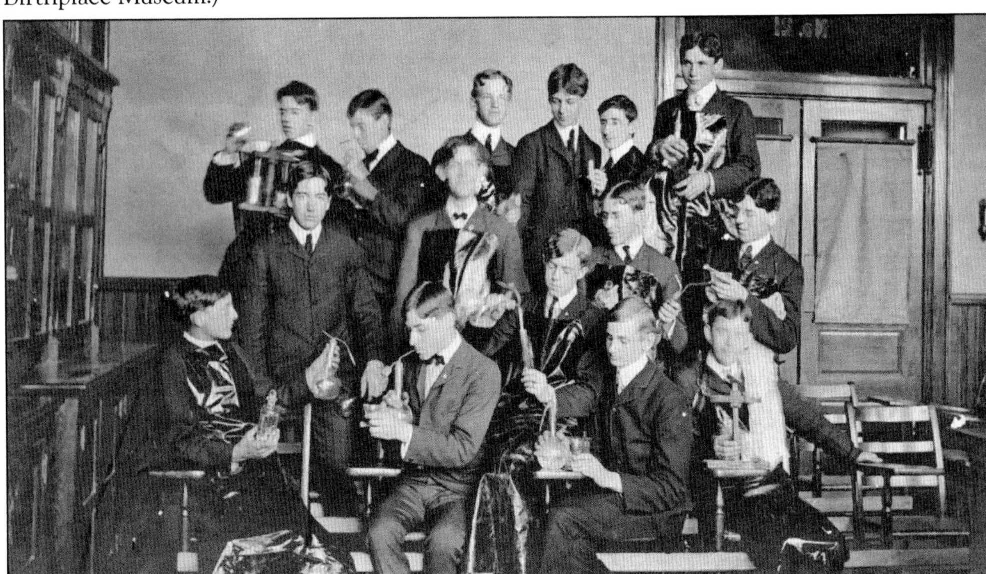

The chemistry classes held in Lea Laboratory were perhaps the most advanced in the nation for their era, with students performing hands-on experiments at a time when most colleges and universities provided science instruction only through lectures. The students in this 1903 chemistry class, many wearing laboratory aprons, pose with their test tubes and vials. (Courtesy of the Wake Forest Birthplace Museum.)

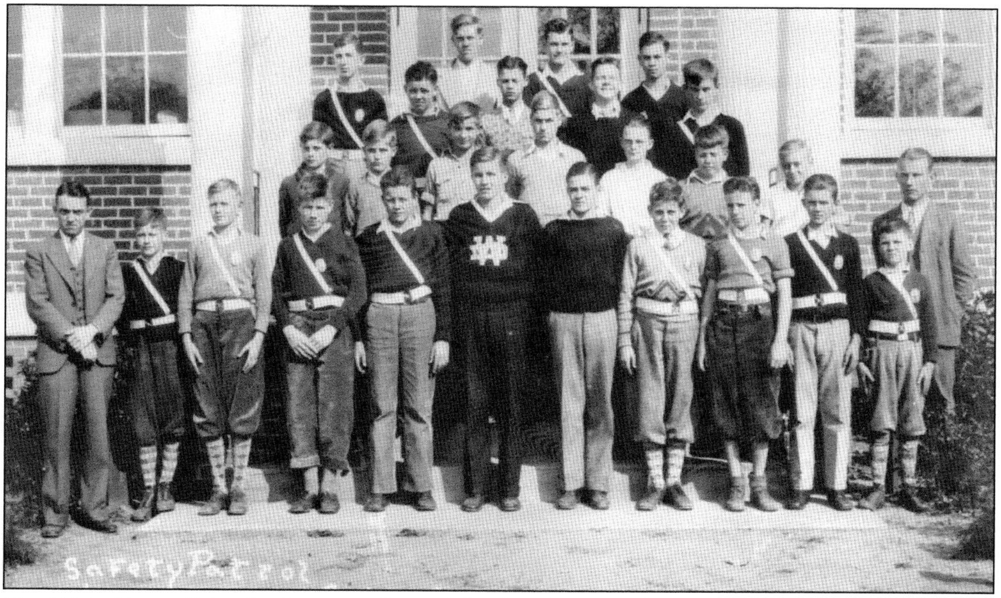

The Wake Forest School safety patrol posed for this photograph in 1931, when the school housed students in kindergarten through 12th grade. The school building burned three years later, a victim of the town's unsolved arsons in the mid-1930s, and elementary classes that year were held in the basement of Wake Forest Baptist Church. Upon its completion, students moved into the school on Sycamore Street, which is still used today. (Courtesy of the North Carolina State Archives N.53.15.5528.)

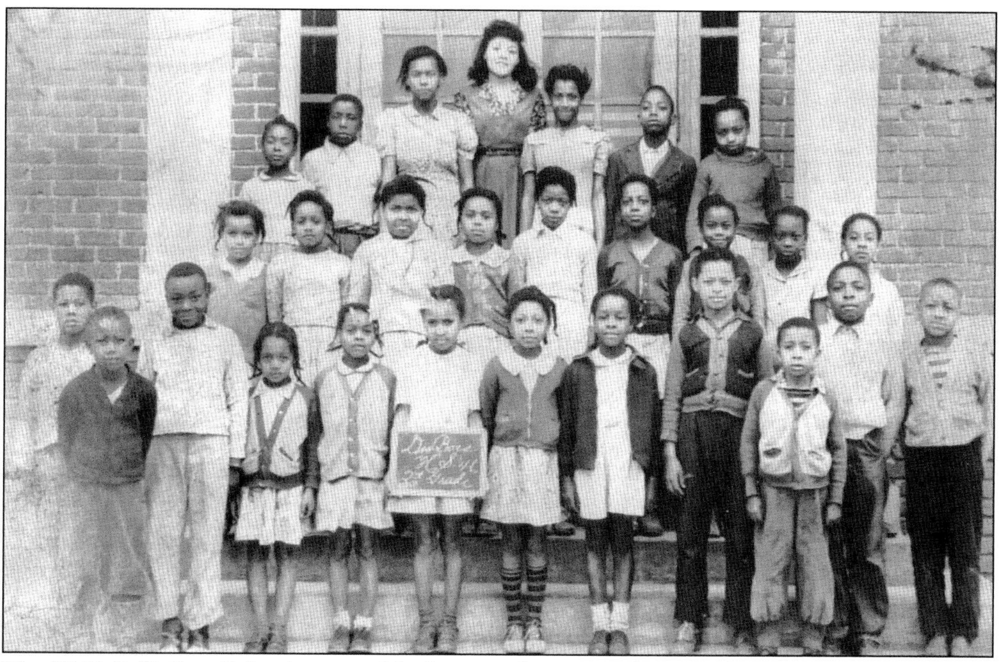

The W. E. B. DuBois School was paid for by a combination of private donations and money from the Rosenwald Fund. The first building consisted of eight classrooms, for grades one through seven, and a 366-seat auditorium. In 1946, the third-grade class posed in front of the school building. (Courtesy of the Wake Forest Birthplace Museum.)

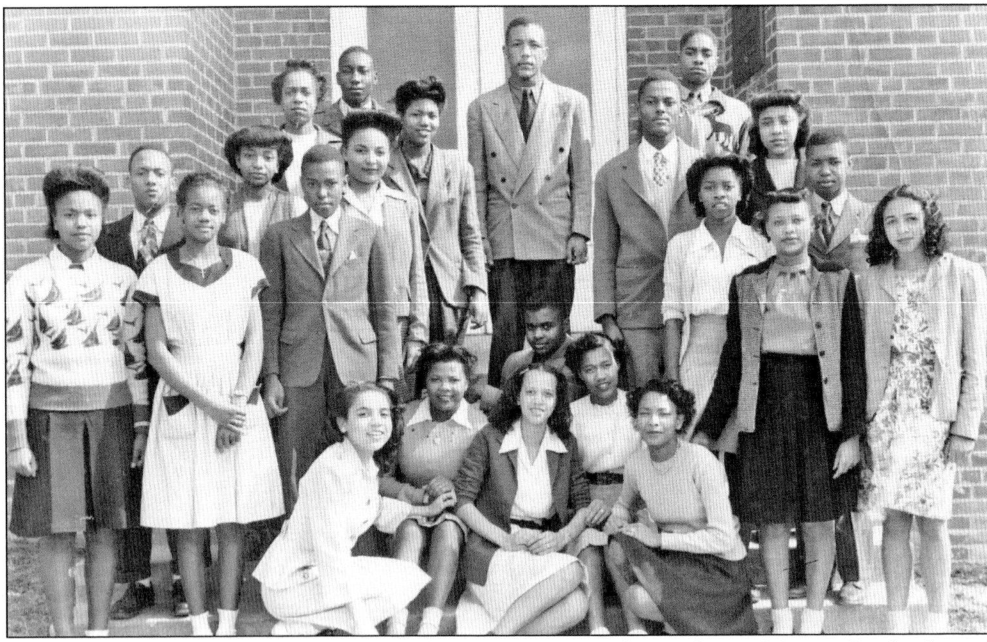

American businessman Julius Rosenwald, part owner and president of Sears, Roebuck, and Company, founded the Rosenwald Fund to improve educational opportunities for African American students. As public funding and private donations were also required, activists across the rural South raised millions of dollars to provide education for all. More than 5,000 schools, shops, and teachers' homes eventually received funding, and the Wake Forest Graded Colored School, founded in 1926, was among them. With the 1939 addition of a high school, the school's name changed to DuBois in honor of prominent philosopher and activist Dr. W. E. B. DuBois. These members of two DuBois High School classes were service club members and scholars around 1940. (Courtesy of the National Alumni Association DuBois School.)

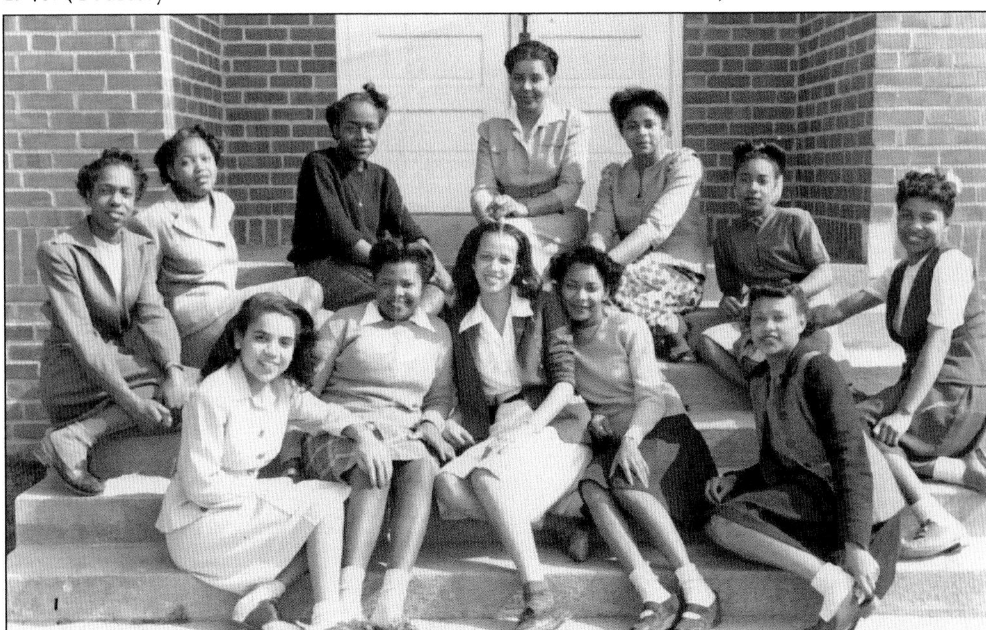

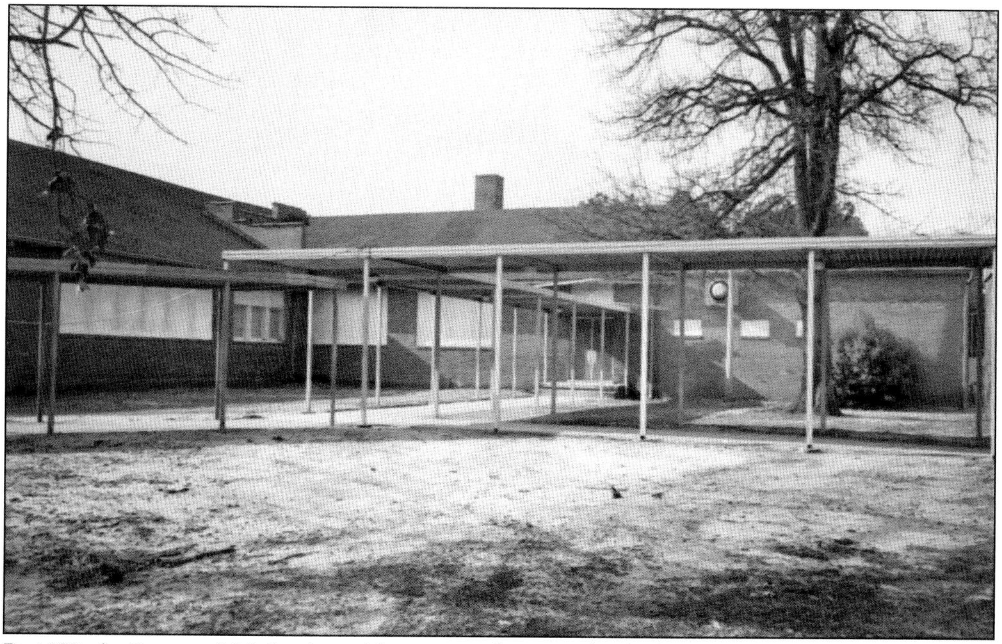

By 1932, the Rosenwald Schools could accommodate one-third of all African American children in the South. The surviving buildings, significant historically and as symbols of educational strength in the African American community, are endangered and in need of preservation. This image shows an architectural view of the DuBois School at Franklin and Cedar Streets. (Courtesy of the North Carolina State Archives N.93.3.350.)

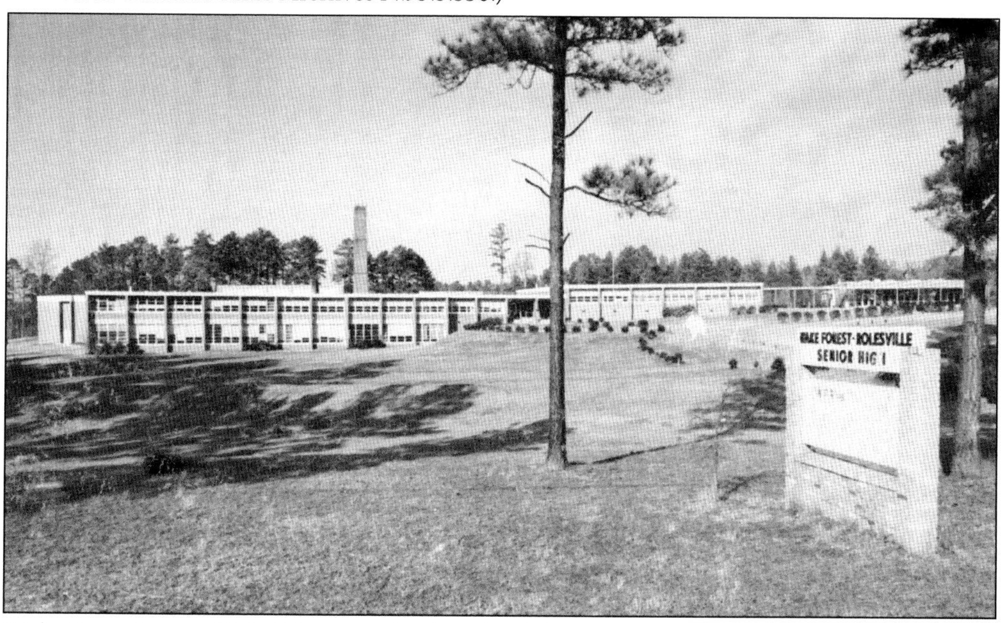

Wake Forest Senior High School was built on land the seminary sold to the town for $20,000 in 1955. The school building was finished in time to start the 1958–1959 school year. When Rolesville High School closed in the 1960s, its students were reassigned to the school in Wake Forest. The facility was also integrated, and the school was renamed Wake Forest–Rolesville High School. (Courtesy of the Wake Forest Birthplace Museum.)

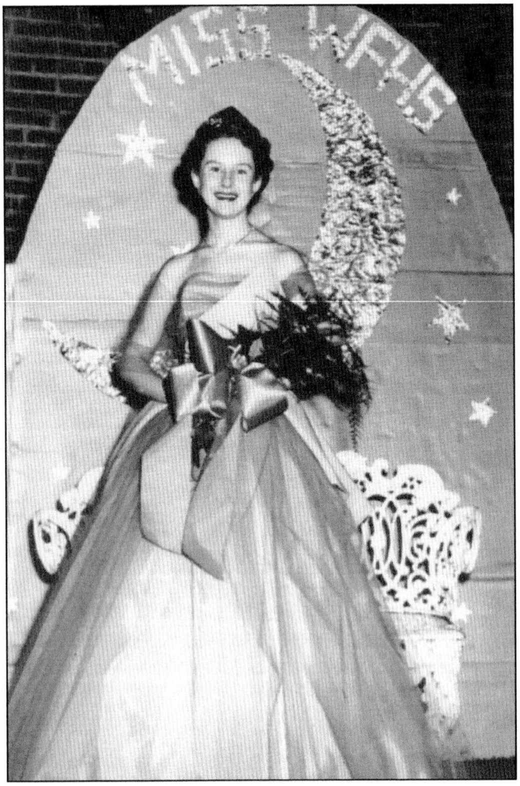

Sally Patterson, pictured as Miss Wake Forest High School, was the daughter of Wake Forest College registrar Grady S. Patterson Sr. and the granddaughter of Wake Forest College professor James L. Lake. (Courtesy of the Wake Forest Birthplace Museum.)

This fashion show, presented by Wake Forest's Senior Girl Scout Troop around 1961, provided a glimpse of contemporary teen styles. From left to right are (first row) Suzanne Whellus, Anne Tull, Suzanne Mills, and Stella Forrest; (second row) Bunny Barnes, Ginger Maupin, Marveen Addleton, Mrs. John Wayland, Lynn Lovelace, Mrs. Elmo Scoggin, Libby Briggs, Scarlet Scoggin, and Sally Osborne. (Courtesy of the Wake Forest Birthplace Museum.)

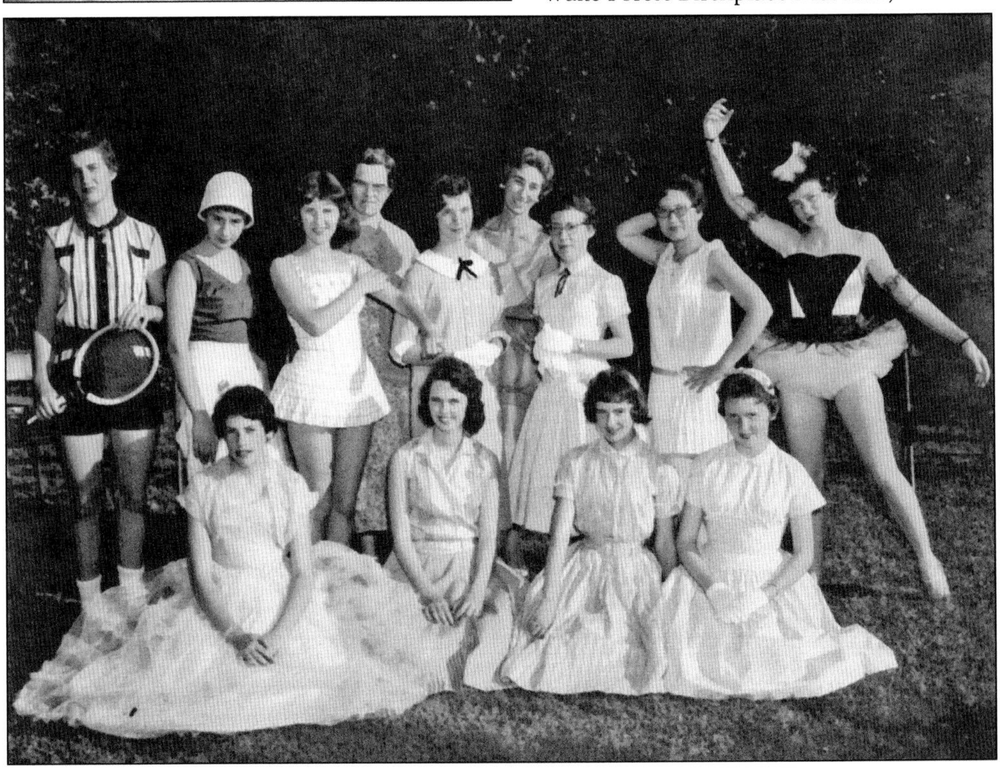

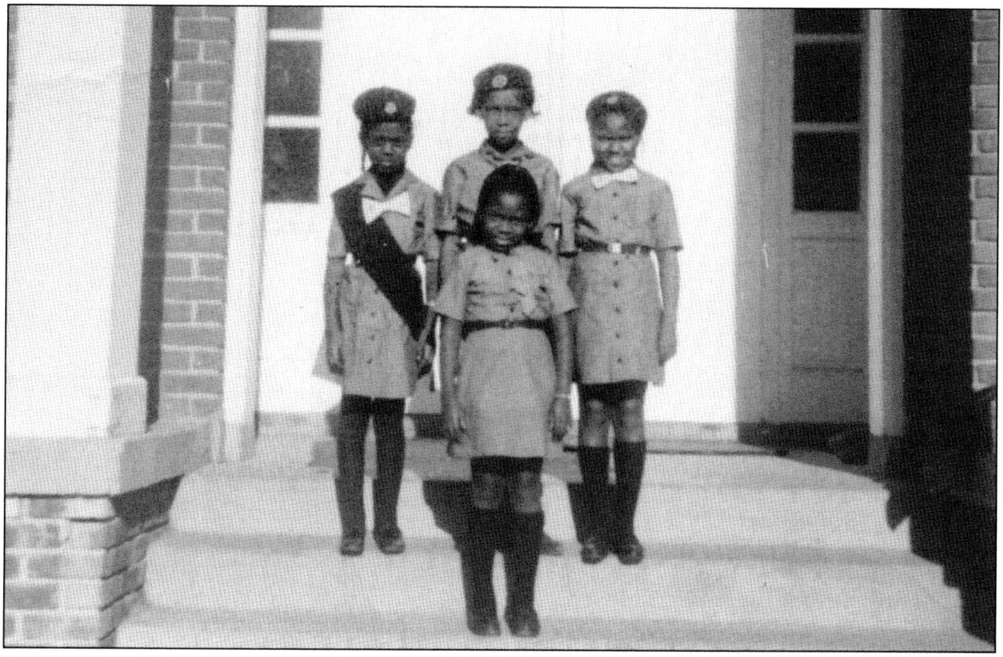

A group of Girl Scouts poses on the steps of the DuBois School, *c.* 1955. (Courtesy of the National Alumni Association DuBois School.)

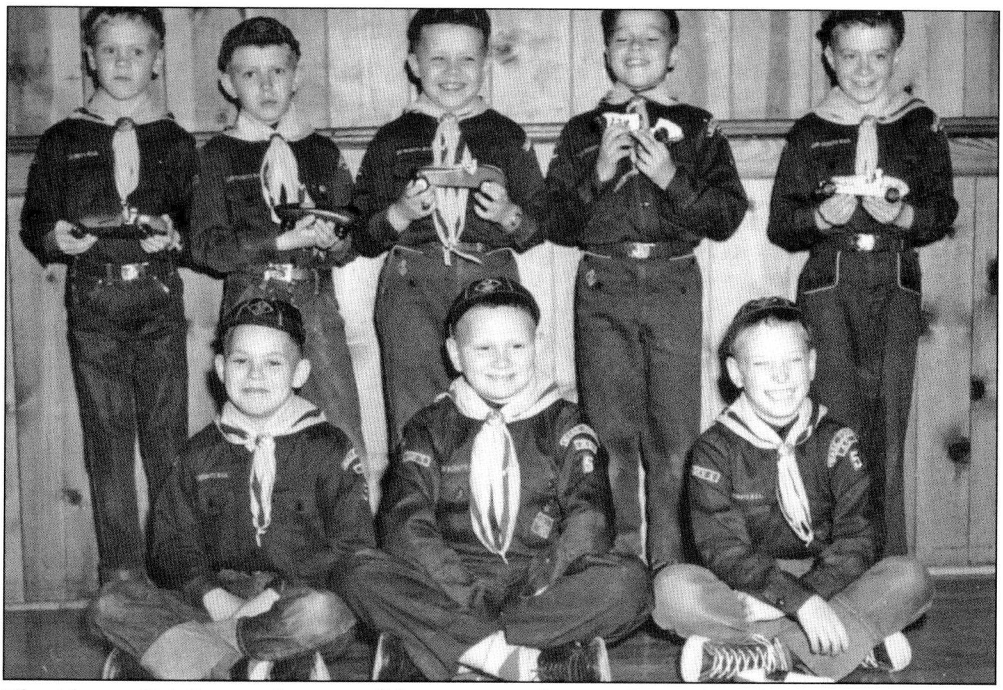

These happy Cub Scouts, showing off their pinewood racers that took top honors at the local Cub Scout Derby, were headed to district competition at the April 1958 Scout Exposition at Reynolds Coliseum in Raleigh. Pictured from left to right are (first row) Freddy Daniel, Sherril Daniel, and Mike Hobgood; (second row) Paul T. Harrell Jr., James Warren, Butch Joyner, Maynard Harding, and Johnny Wooten III. (Courtesy of the Wake Forest Birthplace Museum.)

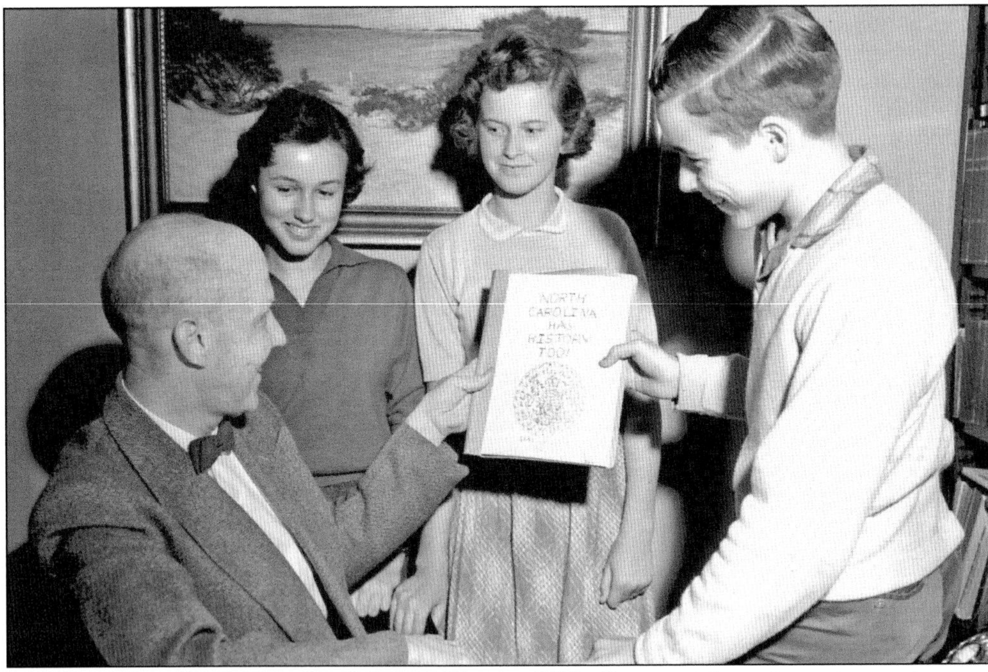

Charles Christopher Crittenden (1902–1969) was a Wake Forest professor, historian, author, and state agency visionary. He was executive head of the North Carolina Historical Commission, which was the forerunner to the Department of Archives and History. He was also a Wake Forest native. In this 1957 photograph, Dr. Crittenden is receiving a book from schoolchildren. (Courtesy of the North Carolina State Archives N.57.12.16.)

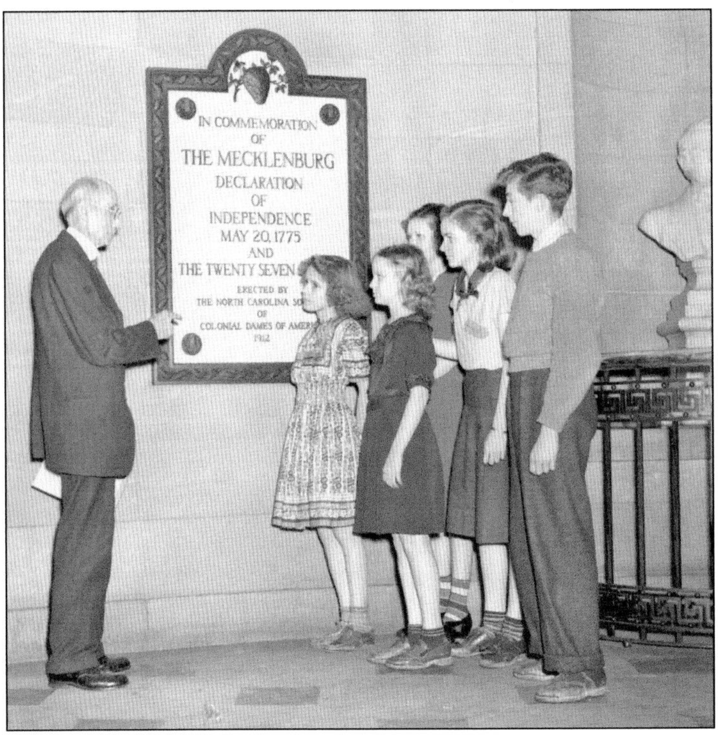

In this February 1939 photograph, a group of Wake Forest schoolchildren are taking a tour of the state capitol in Raleigh. Legislative information clerk George Snell is discussing a plaque commemorating the Mecklenburg Declaration of Independence. The seventh graders listening intently are, from left to right, Rebecca Ballentine, Nancy Easley, Audrey Poole, Nola May Ray, and Frankie Mansfield. (Courtesy of the *News and Observer* and North Carolina State Archives NO 39.2.56.)

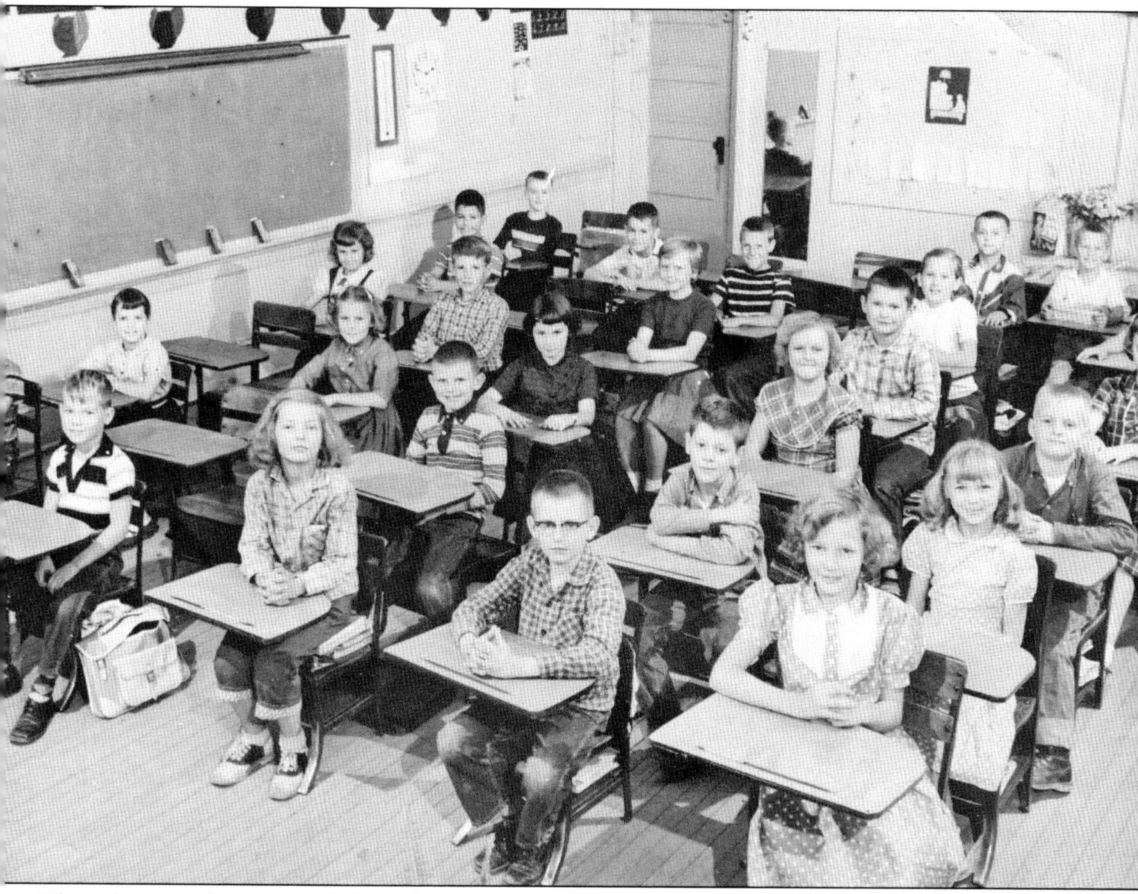

These busy students paused for a class photograph commemorating their third-grade year at Wake Forest Elementary School in 1958–1959. Wake Forest's graded public school system began in 1913 with a legislative act providing a bond vote for $25,000 for a graded school. Schools in Forestville and Wake Forest were established in 1919. Wake Forest Elementary School's original building went up in the mid-1920s and initially served as the town's high school. A two-story brick structure with Colonial Revival details, it was much like others in the county. In 1935, an addition brought more classroom space. Although that structure still stands, the first building was razed in 1991, and with an ever-increasing student population, the school has undergone a number of renovations since. (Courtesy of the Wake Forest Birthplace Museum.)

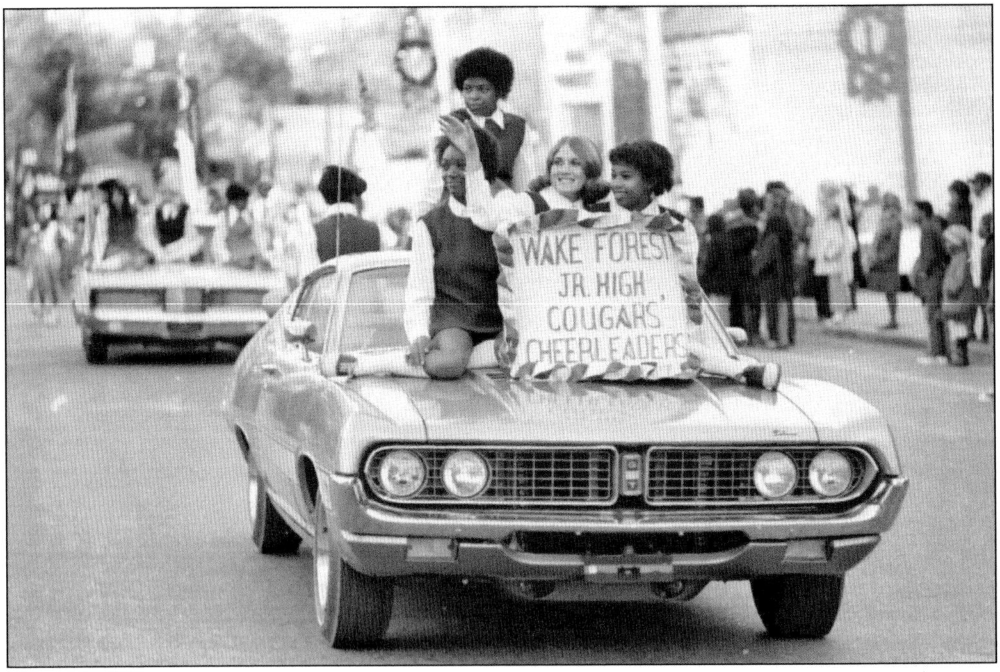

Cougar cheerleaders rode in the December 8, 1970, town Christmas parade. This was the year Wake County integrated DuBois High School, renaming it Wake Forest Junior High. Older DuBois students moved to Wake Forest High School, which expanded to also include students from Rolesville. (Courtesy of the *News and Observer* and North Carolina State Archives NO.12-8-1970.Fr31.)

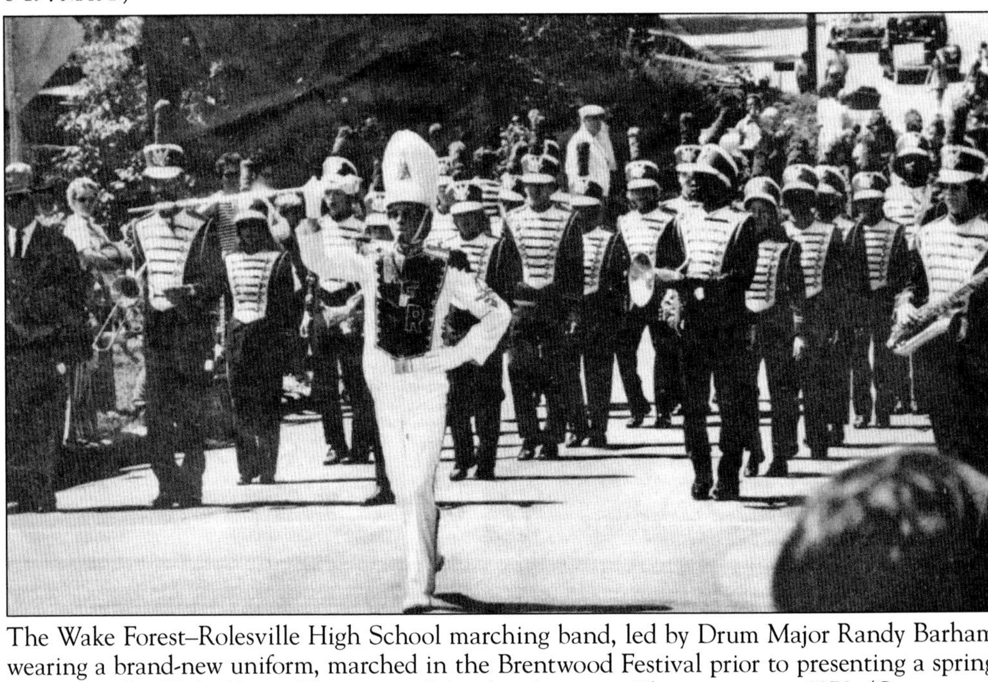

The Wake Forest–Rolesville High School marching band, led by Drum Major Randy Barham wearing a brand-new uniform, marched in the Brentwood Festival prior to presenting a spring concert at the Wake Forest Elementary School auditorium. The year was c. 1970. (Courtesy of the National Alumni Association DuBois School.)

Six

The Seminary and Religious Life

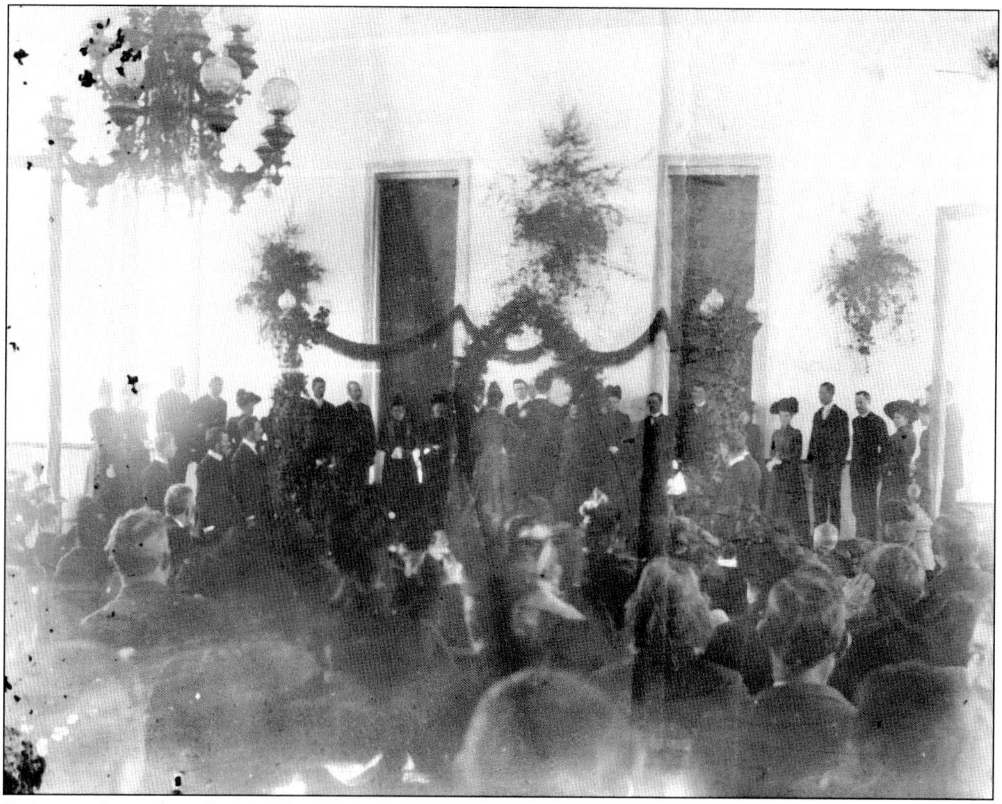

Religion has played a vital role in Wake Forest's history. The North Carolina Baptist State Convention created the college. The college, in turn, created the town. The late 19th century was a time of religious expansion, with emancipated slaves, revival meetings, and population growth accounting for at least 55 new Wake County churches in the years following the Civil War. Most were Baptist, and many flourished around railroad towns and newly established textile mills. Baptist pastors typically stayed only a few years, and many were ministerial students from the college who left after graduation. This religious scene is classic Victorian. Fannie Taylor, daughter of Wake Forest College president Dr. Charles Taylor, married Dr. Joseph Gorrell in what is believed to be the Small Chapel on campus. The guests are dressed in dark clothing; branches of cedar and ivy decorate the wall and wedding arch. (Courtesy of the Wake Forest Birthplace Museum.)

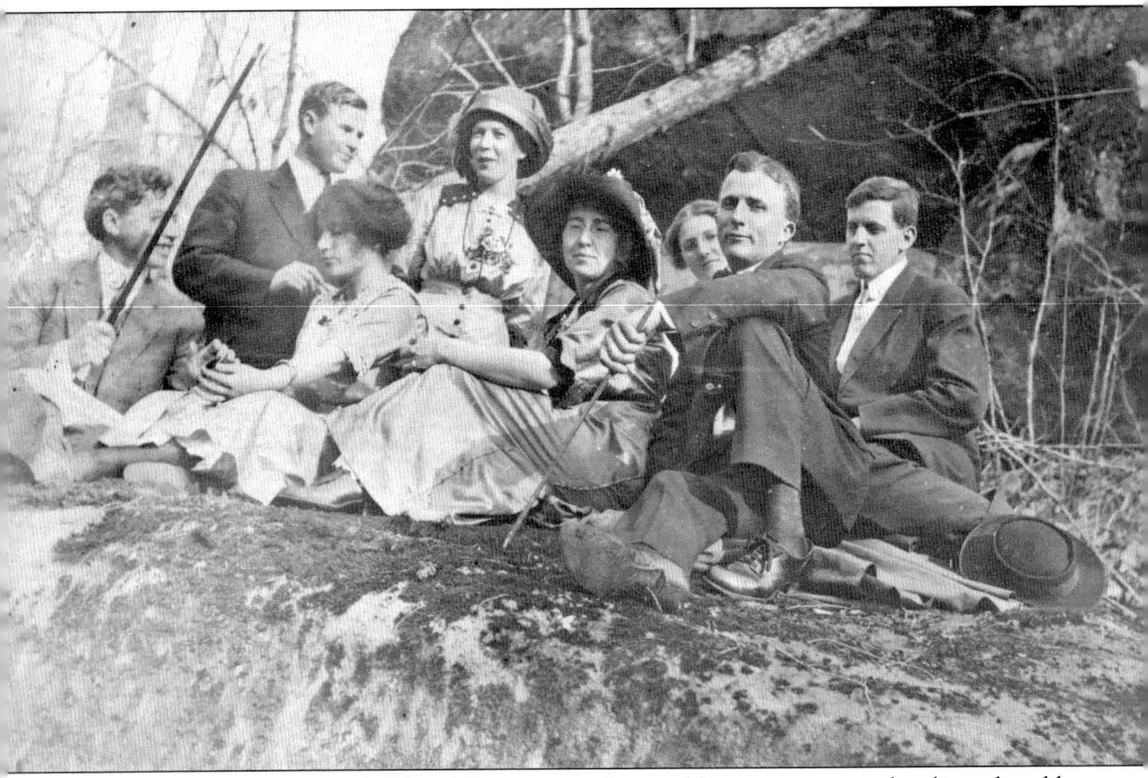

The Cat Den, a series of odd rock formations where wildcats were rumored to live, played host to an annual Easter egg hunt in the first part of the 20th century. Although the exact location remains unclear, the Cat Den's rocks at one place met together to create a room that visitors to the site called "the church." Another rock formation made a high cliff looking down straight to the creek below. This was called Lover's Leap. "The leap to the bottom would probably have been the last leap anyone would have taken," recalled Wake Forest resident Annie Laurie Hunt Pearce. The annual Easter egg hunt never used candy eggs—just "good old country eggs that we colored all colors of the rainbow. We used crayons to make our own patterns and designs." (Courtesy of the Wake Forest Birthplace Museum.)

Wake Union Church has an interesting history. Founded around 1779 on land deeded to the Sutherland family by Lord Granville of England, it was once home to all Protestant denominations, becoming Wake Union Baptist in 1803 after the other congregations built their own houses of worship. The original structure dates to about 1792 and has been repeatedly remodeled. (Courtesy of the North Carolina State Archives N.94.8.1132-1139.)

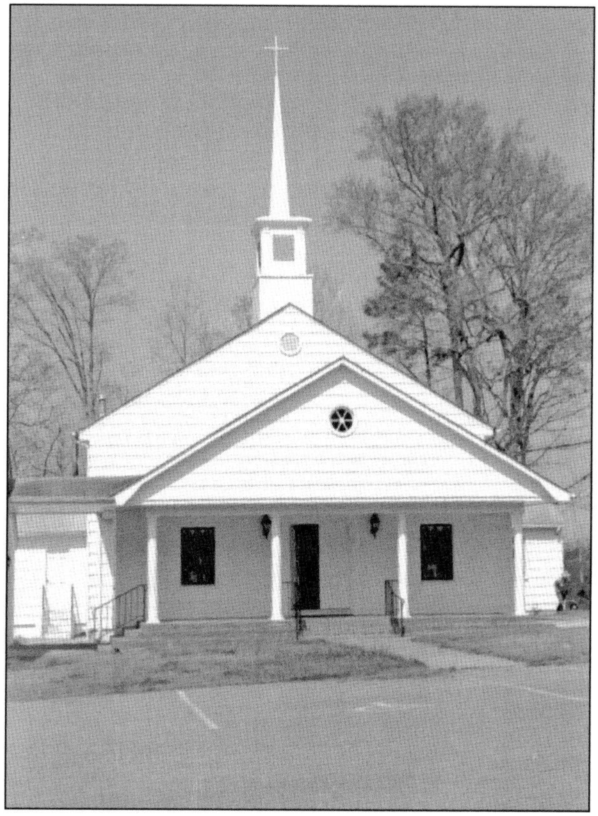

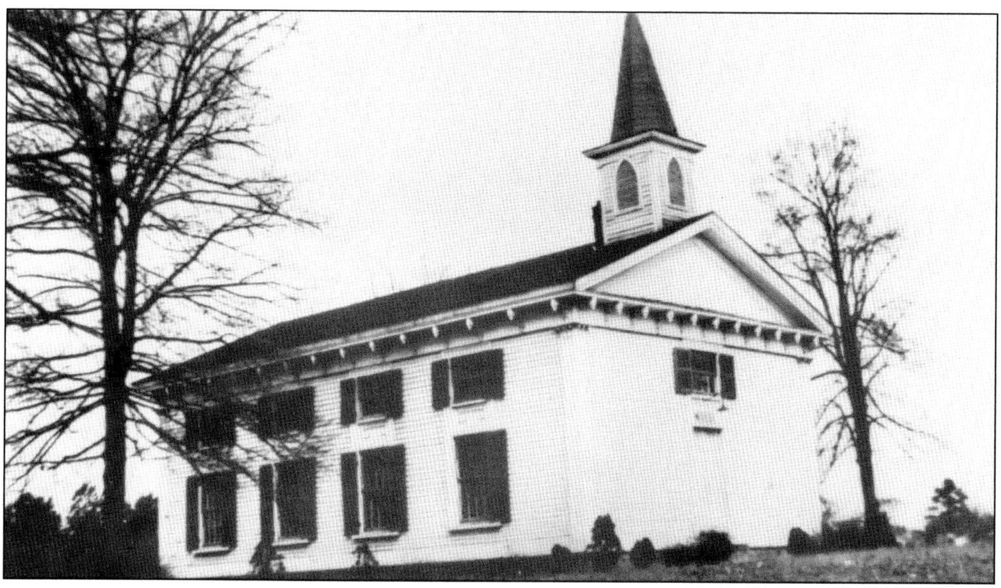

A picturesque and elegant architectural achievement, Forestville Baptist Church is easily the former town's most recognizable remaining structure. Organized in 1859 and built in 1860, it was church home to many Wake Forest College professors. The controversial moving of Forestville's train station to Wake Forest angered some worshippers and eventually split the congregation. (Courtesy of the Wake Forest Birthplace Museum.)

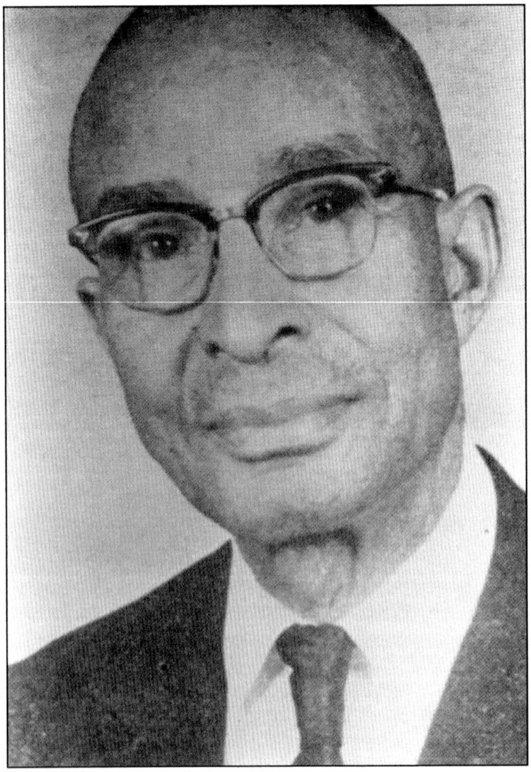

The Reverend George Stokes led Friendship Chapel Baptist Church from 1931 to 1972, through the Great Depression, construction of the new sanctuary, and the civil rights movement. Although he ministered four churches on a rural circuit, Friendship Chapel was his church home. Formally established in 1866, Friendship Chapel still has a large and devoted congregation. (Courtesy of Friendship Chapel Baptist Church.)

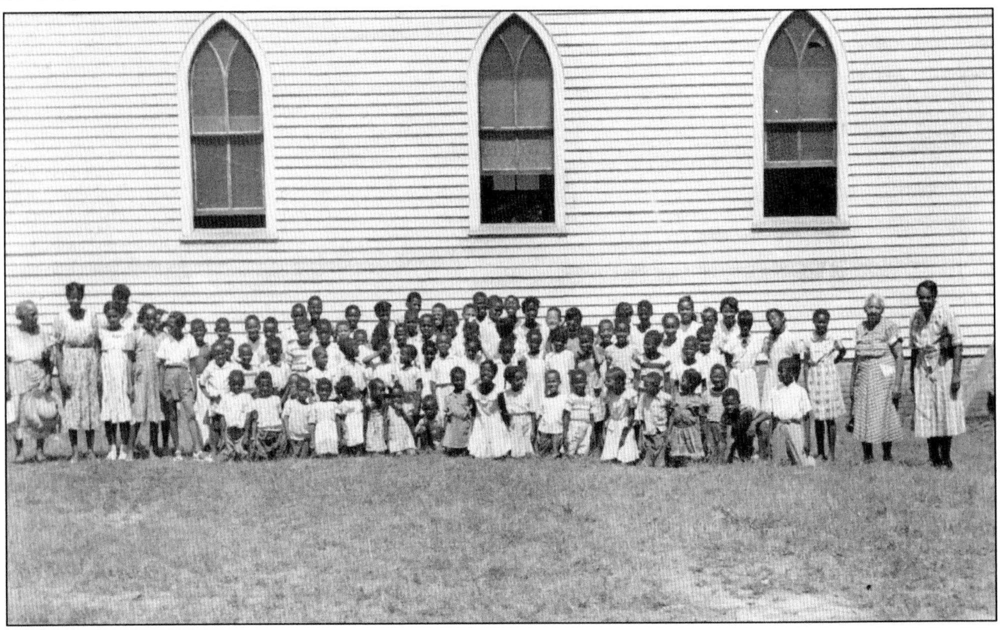

During the Civil War, slaves worshipping at Wake Forest Baptist Church broke away to create their own congregation. First located on the college grounds, Olive Branch Baptist Church eventually moved to a town location. In this *c.* 1945 photograph, Sunday school children pose with teachers, including Ellen Powell (right) and Lucy Harris (left). The building burned in 1956 and was replaced with a brick structure. (Courtesy of Geraldine Hall-Taylor.)

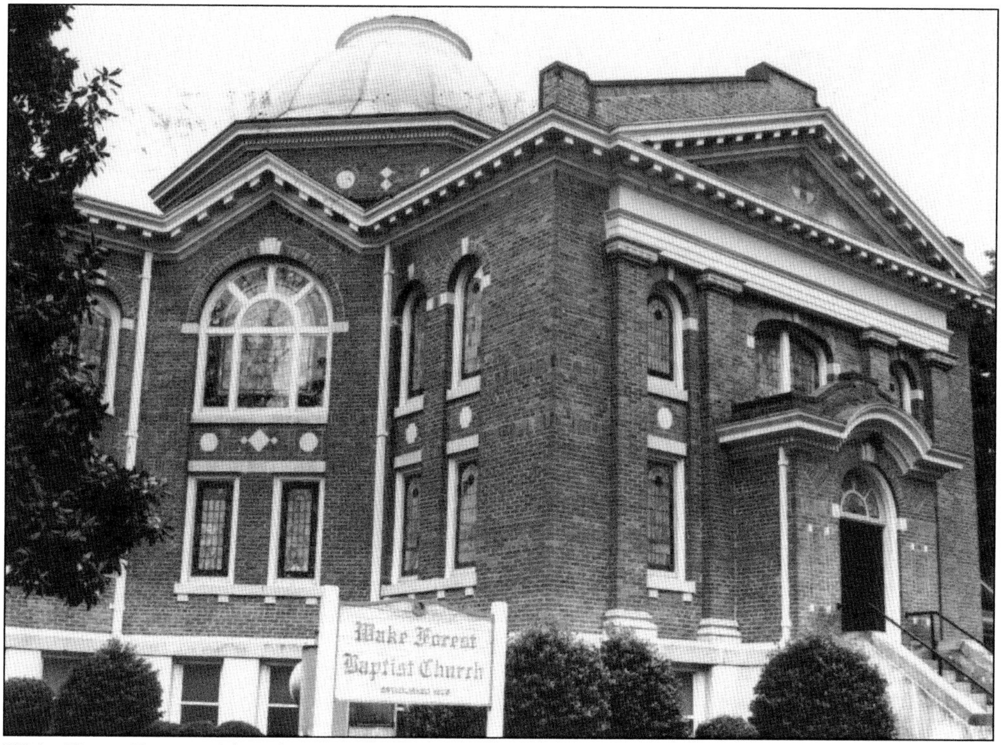

Wake Forest Baptist Church marked a departure from common church architecture of the period. A fancier, more sophisticated structure than most of its contemporaries, the domed, cruciform brick building is the work of Charlotte architect James J. McMichael, who created similar plans for congregations in Elizabeth City, Lincolnton, and other towns. (Courtesy of the Wake Forest Birthplace Museum.)

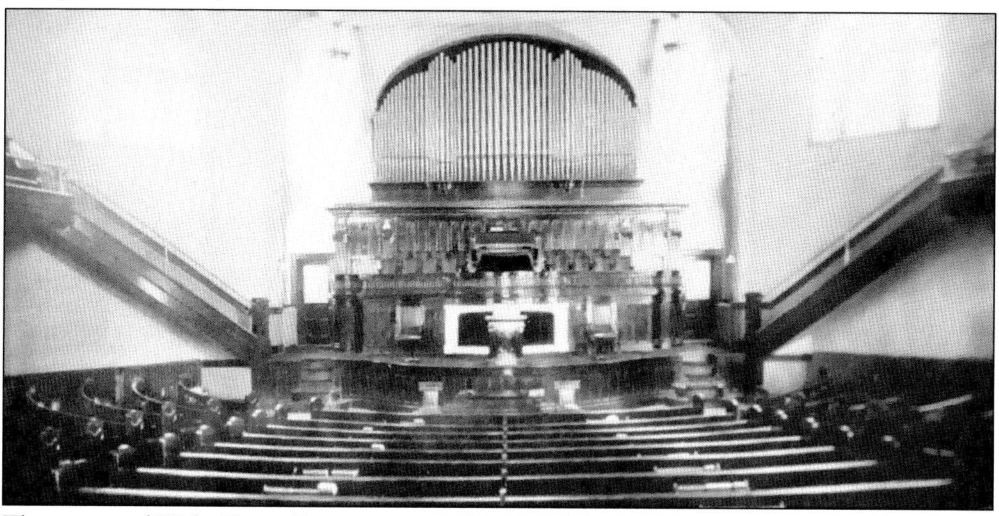

This image of Wake Forest Baptist gives a glimpse of the church's classically inspired interior. Constructed in 1913–1914, the building features prominent porticoes and large stained-glass windows surrounding the traditional church pews. Also visible, near the choir balcony, is the extravagant pipe organ selected by former college president Dr. William Poteat in 1927. (Courtesy of the Wake Forest Birthplace Museum.)

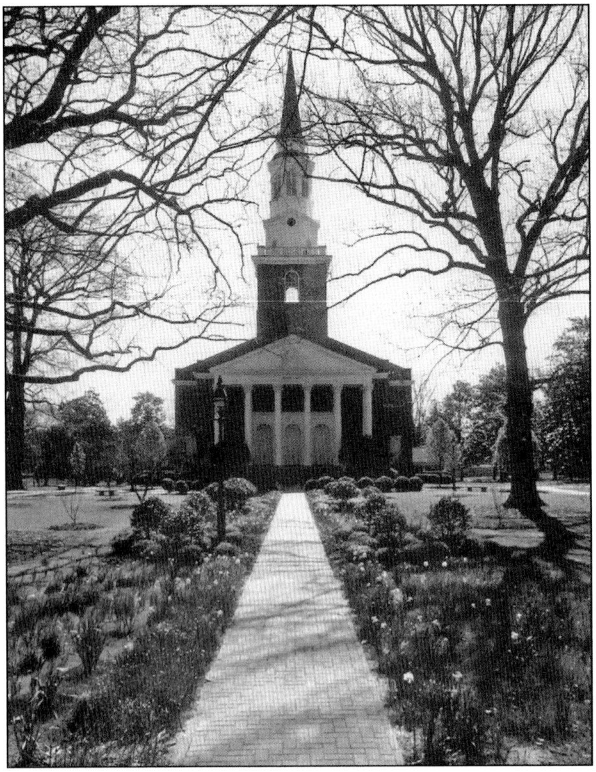

Binkley Chapel, built in 1943, is used as a student chapel three days a week. The chapel also plays host to lecture series and choral performances by the seminary's music department. (Courtesy of Southeastern Baptist Theological Seminary.)

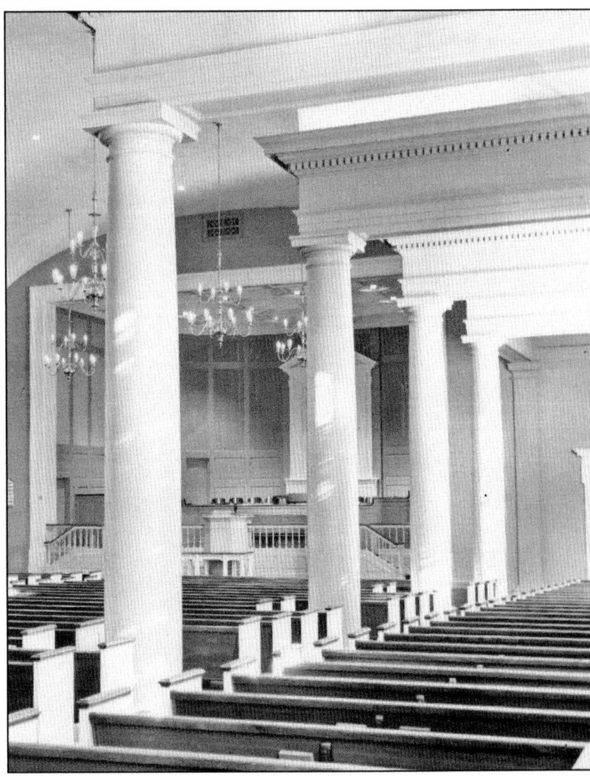

The chapel interior seems far removed from the towering spire that's come to characterize the campus skyline. It is named for Dr. Olin T. Binkley, who served as president of Southeastern Baptist Theological Seminary from 1963 to 1974. During his tenure, the campus changed significantly. Four outdated buildings were removed, and 13 new buildings were constructed. (Courtesy of Southeastern Baptist Theological Seminary.)

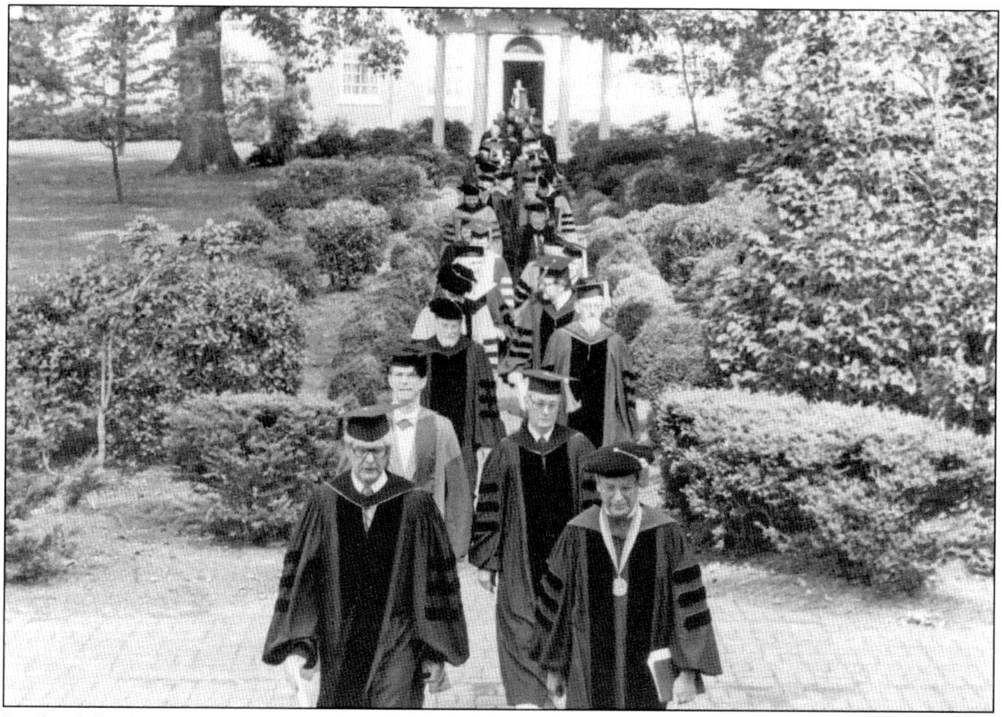

In the fall of 1951, seminary classes began with 85 students and three faculty members. The seminary and school shared campus space until Wake Forest College moved to Winston-Salem in 1956. The date of this academic procession is approximately 30 years later, with Dr. Morris Ashcraft (left), dean of faculty, and Dr. Randall Lolley (right), seminary president, leading the marchers. (Courtesy of Southeastern Baptist Theological Seminary.)

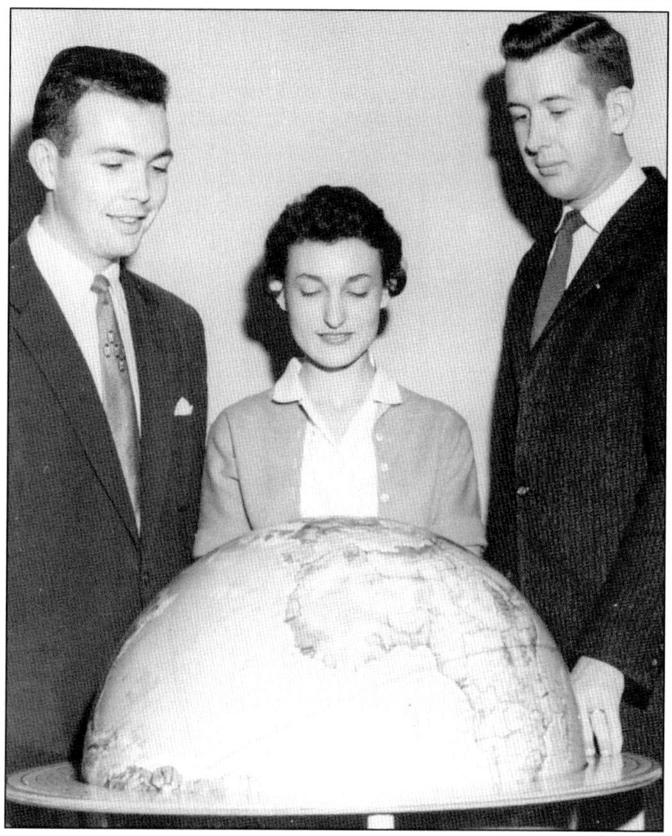

Those studying at the seminary have always been involved in global mission work. These students were photographed while taking part in the Missions Conference for Student Missions in 1959. (Courtesy of Southeastern Baptist Theological Seminary.)

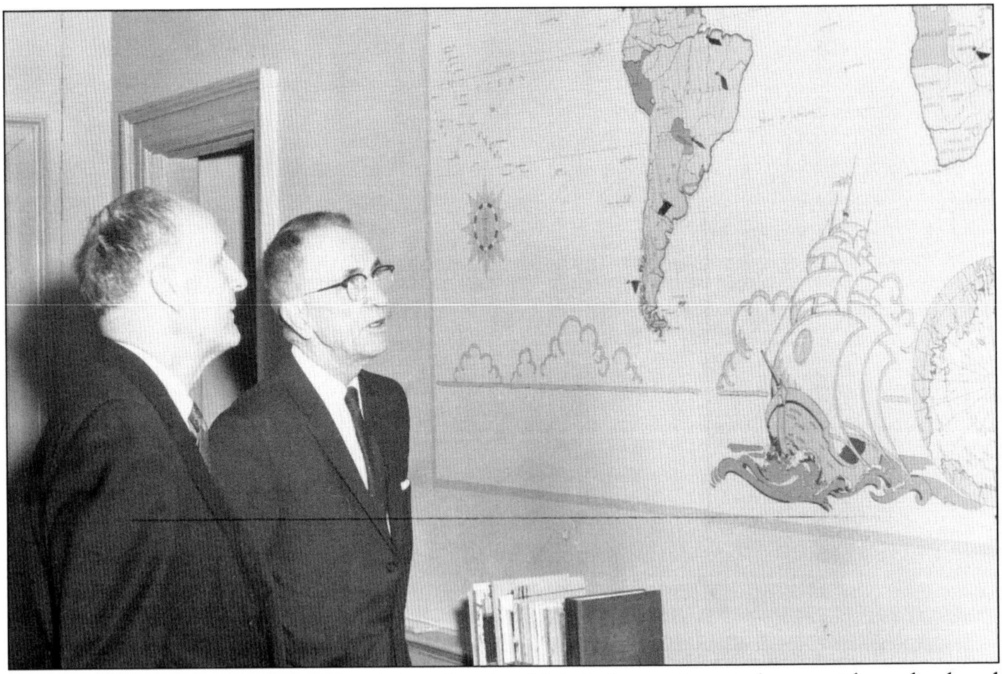

Dr. Theodore Adams (left) and Dr. Sydnor Stealey (right), the seminary's first president, displayed dedication to their evangelical cause with involvement in the Baptist World Alliance Committee. Dr. Stealey served as seminary leader from 1950 to 1963, when he retired and Dr. Olin T. Binkley became president. Seminary enrollment in that era stood at 575 students. The school had 28 faculty members. (Courtesy of Southeastern Baptist Theological Seminary.)

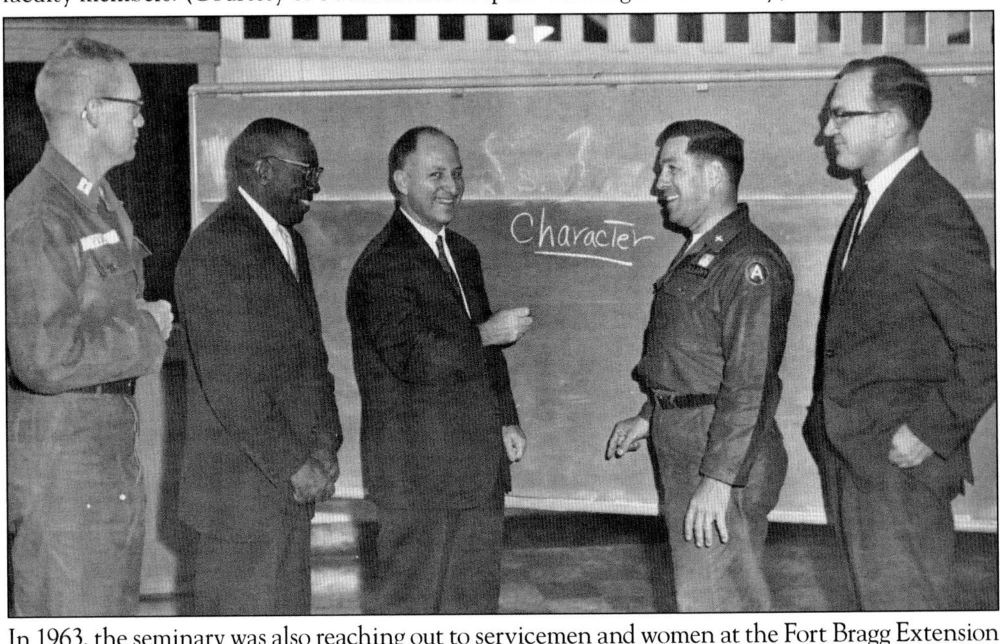

In 1963, the seminary was also reaching out to servicemen and women at the Fort Bragg Extension Center in Cumberland County. The participants are, from left to right, Chaplain Robert Floyd, the Reverend A. C. Jones, Dr. Denton Coker, Chaplain Donald E. Bloor, and the Reverend Robert L. Tilley. (Courtesy of Southeastern Baptist Theological Seminary.)

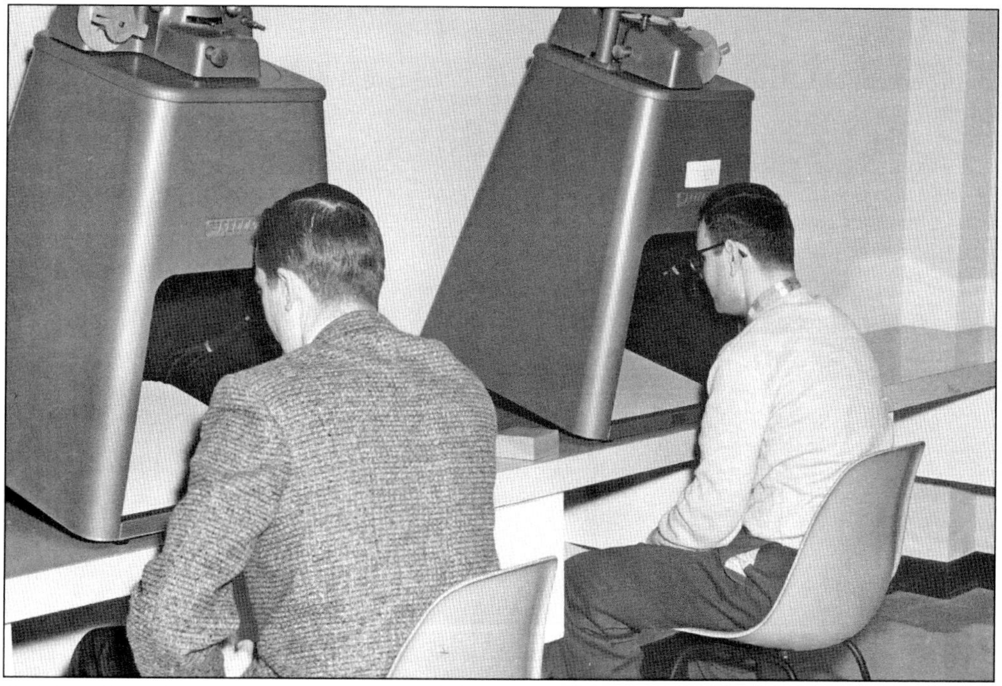

Binkley Chapel housed a library in the 1970s where students were able to conduct scholarly research via the seminary's early micro-readers. The chapel's ground floor was eventually turned into classrooms to accommodate the growing student population. (Courtesy of Southeastern Baptist Theological Seminary.)

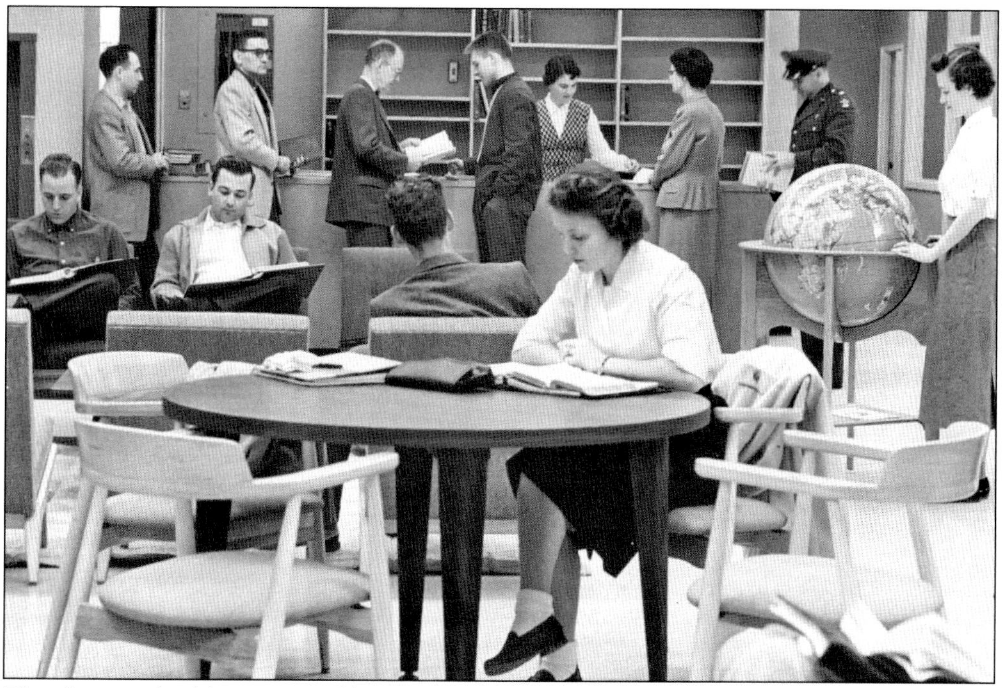

This photograph of the seminary library's main floor reading room was taken in 1958. The charging desk is in the background. (Courtesy of Southeastern Baptist Theological Seminary.)

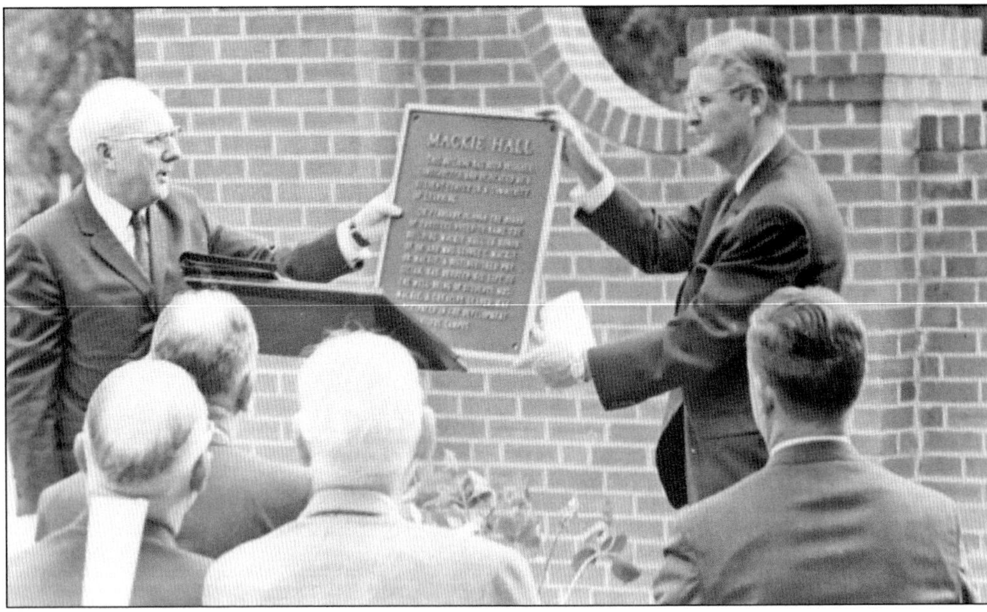

Dr. George Mackie, a physician associated with Wake Forest College as both an alumnus and professor, practiced medicine in the town of Wake Forest and also provided strong backing for the seminary. Dedicated in 1968, Mackie Hall was named in honor of George and his wife, Kathleen. Later renamed Stephens-Mackie Hall, the building was renovated and reopened as a professorial complex in 1999. (Courtesy of Southeastern Baptist Theological Seminary.)

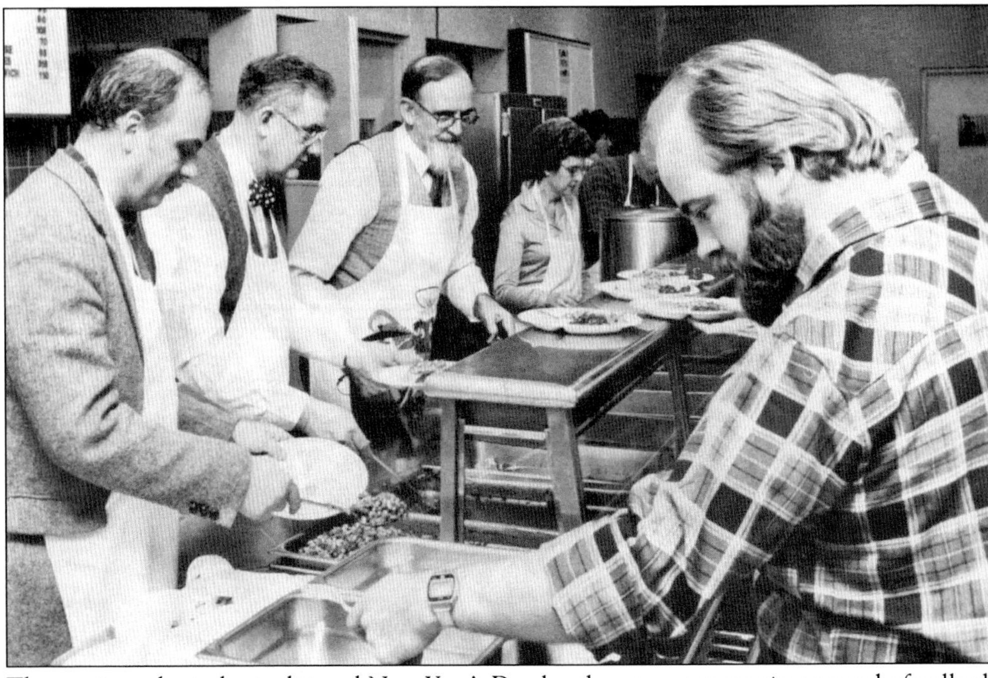

The seminary hosted a traditional New Year's Day lunch every year, serving a meal of collards and black-eyed peas to enthusiastic visitors. The event was the school's annual gift to the town. In this photograph, Nancy Byard (far right), Dr. James Mosely (center), and Dr. John Steeley (second from left) are serving. (Courtesy of Southeastern Baptist Theological Seminary.)

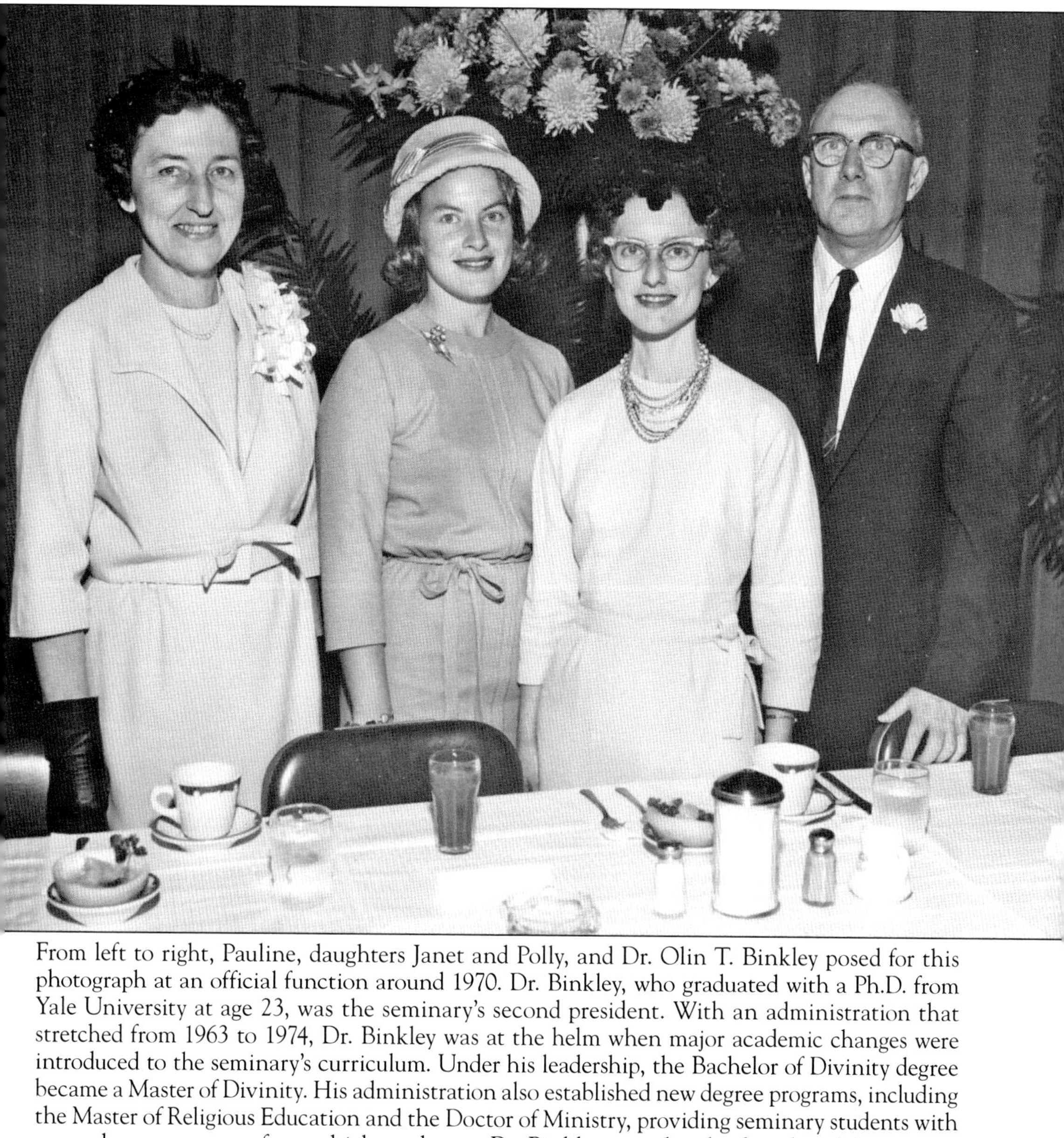

From left to right, Pauline, daughters Janet and Polly, and Dr. Olin T. Binkley posed for this photograph at an official function around 1970. Dr. Binkley, who graduated with a Ph.D. from Yale University at age 23, was the seminary's second president. With an administration that stretched from 1963 to 1974, Dr. Binkley was at the helm when major academic changes were introduced to the seminary's curriculum. Under his leadership, the Bachelor of Divinity degree became a Master of Divinity. His administration also established new degree programs, including the Master of Religious Education and the Doctor of Ministry, providing seminary students with seven degree programs from which to choose. Dr. Binkley was also the founder of the school's Alumni Giving Program. (Courtesy of Southeastern Baptist Theological Seminary.)

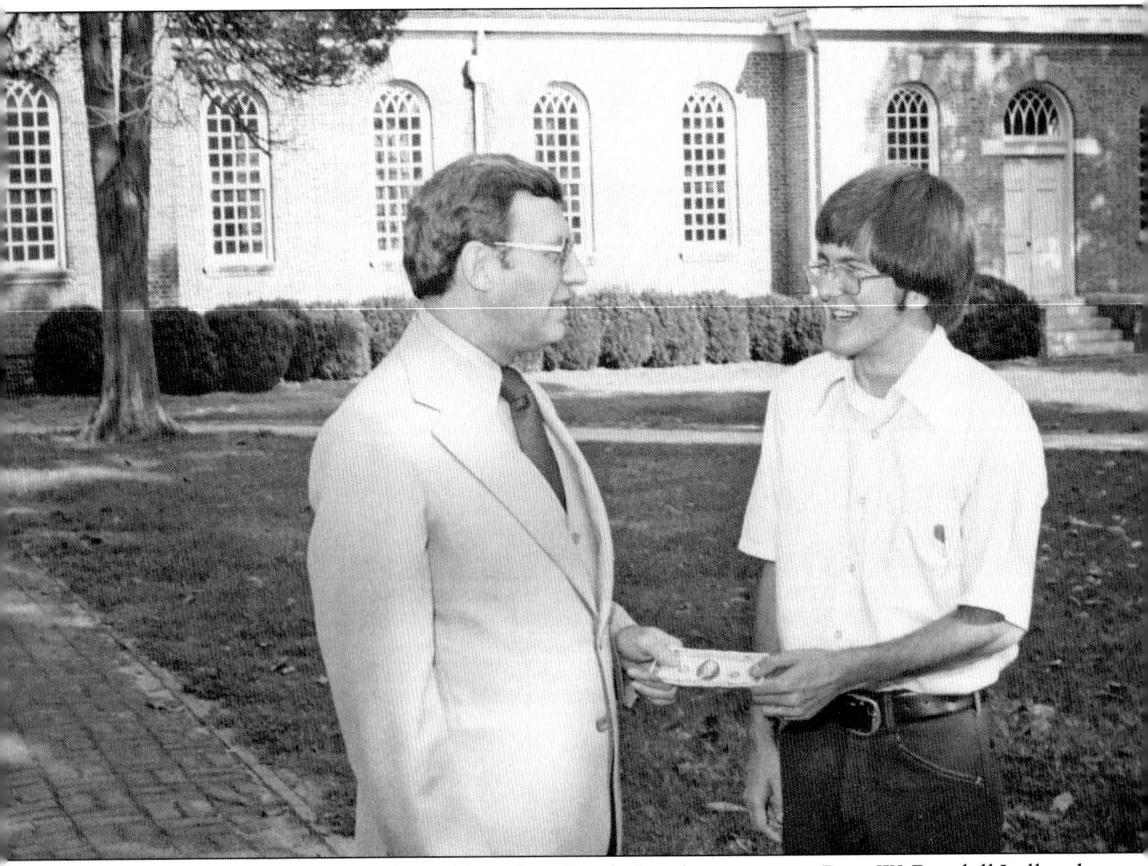

Seminary student Mike Barker, of Camden, South Carolina, presents Pres. W. Randall Lolley the first gift to help the seminary get started on its 15-year, $28-million program to renovate the 145-year-old campus. This initial donation, c. 1978, helped fund an overhaul that eventually included renovation and relocation of existing buildings, expansion of student housing, and modification of the campus heating/air system, parking, and lighting. As the seminary's third president, Dr. Lolley initially led a campus of 663 students and 24 faculty members, kicking off a period of sustained prosperity and growth. (Courtesy of Southeastern Baptist Theological Seminary.)

Seven

HEADLINES

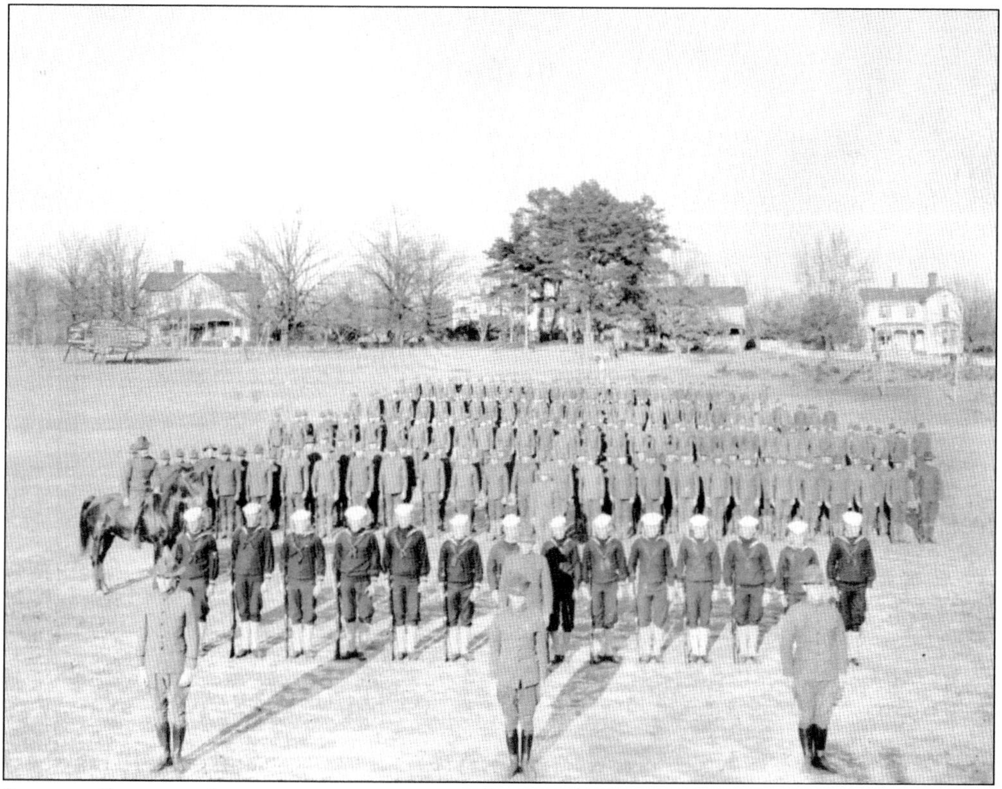

For a small town with easy access to a strong religious education as the foundation for its original claim to fame, Wake Forest has nabbed a good number of news headlines over the years. Oddly, the town and its campus have repeatedly touched on stories with broad political or cultural impact, brushstrokes reaching far beyond the expected limits of a quiet, rural community. Swings in fundamentalist religious beliefs have always deeply resonated here. But so, too, have other current events. From 11th-hour rescue operations to rare books lost at sea, Wake Forest has earned more than a moderate amount of newsprint over the years. One reliable story that brought reporters to the campus twice in the first half of the 20th century was war. Wake Forest College was used by the military during both world wars, most notably becoming the Army Finance School during World War II. This group was photographed during Army-Navy Student Training in World War I. Marching soldiers made an exciting addition to small town life. (Courtesy of the Wake Forest Birthplace Museum.)

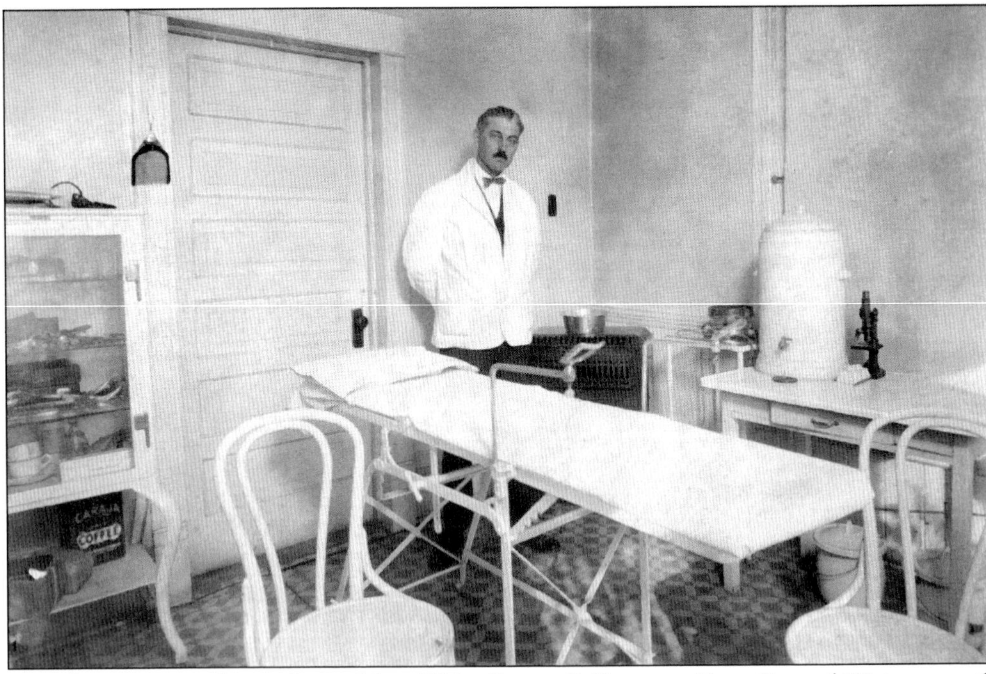

Dr. John Powers, a descendant of first Wake Forest College president Samuel Wait, was still practicing medicine when the Spanish flu epidemic hit town on September 14, 1918. All available beds in the college hospital were filled by nightfall. Sixty percent of the students fell ill, and one died. (Courtesy of the Wake Forest Birthplace Museum.)

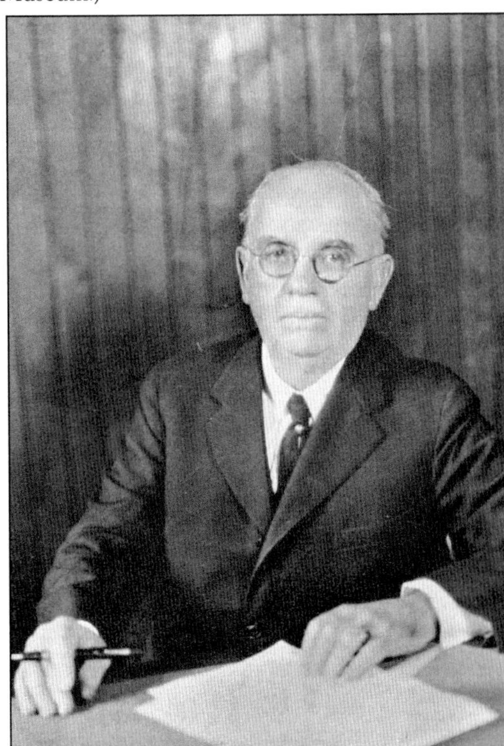

Dr. William Louis Poteat, president of the college from 1905 until 1927, was ahead of his time in teaching both evolution and modern laboratory techniques. In 1923, he made news with an unexpected broadside aimed directly at the Ku Klux Klan. "We don't want . . . the assistance of an organization of irresponsibles. The general tone and spirit of North Carolina is against any such organization." (Courtesy of the Wake Forest Birthplace Museum.)

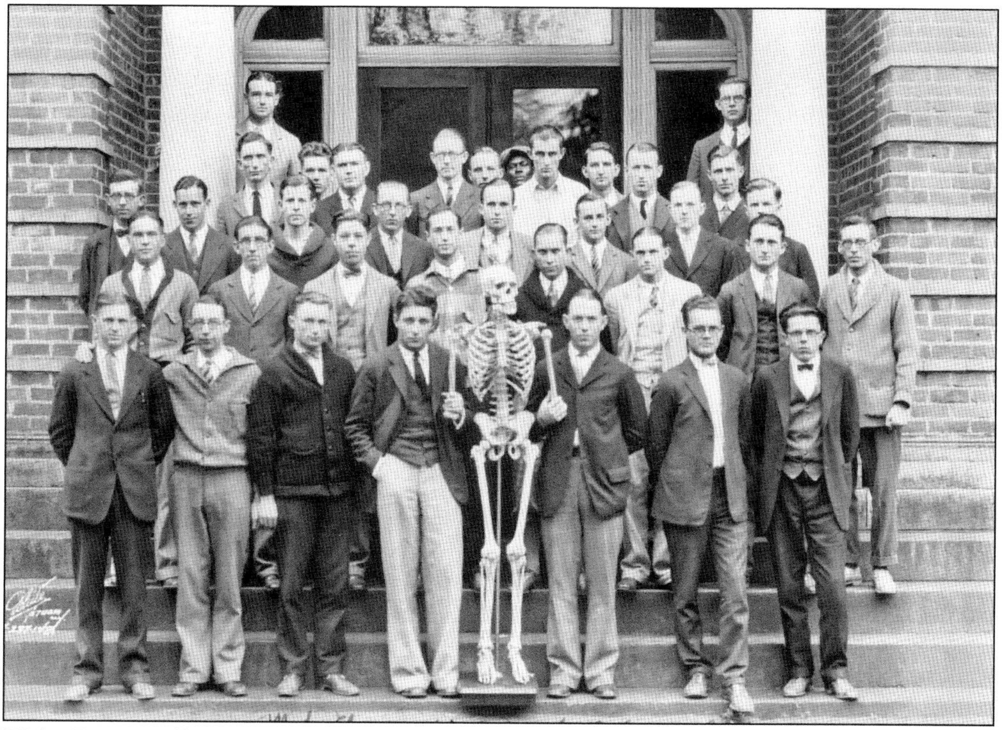

Wake Forest College established a leading medical school in 1902. Its students, *c.* 1920, made news decades after graduation when a large collection of human bones, minus their skulls, were unearthed in an old trash pit. A construction worker uncovered the skeletons while working at a site behind the campus, and general consensus held they were the remains of cadavers, dissected and discarded by early medical students. As for the missing parts, Dr. George Mackie supplied a possible answer with his reply, "I understand medical students used to make ashtrays out of the skulls." (Courtesy of the Wake Forest Birthplace Museum.)

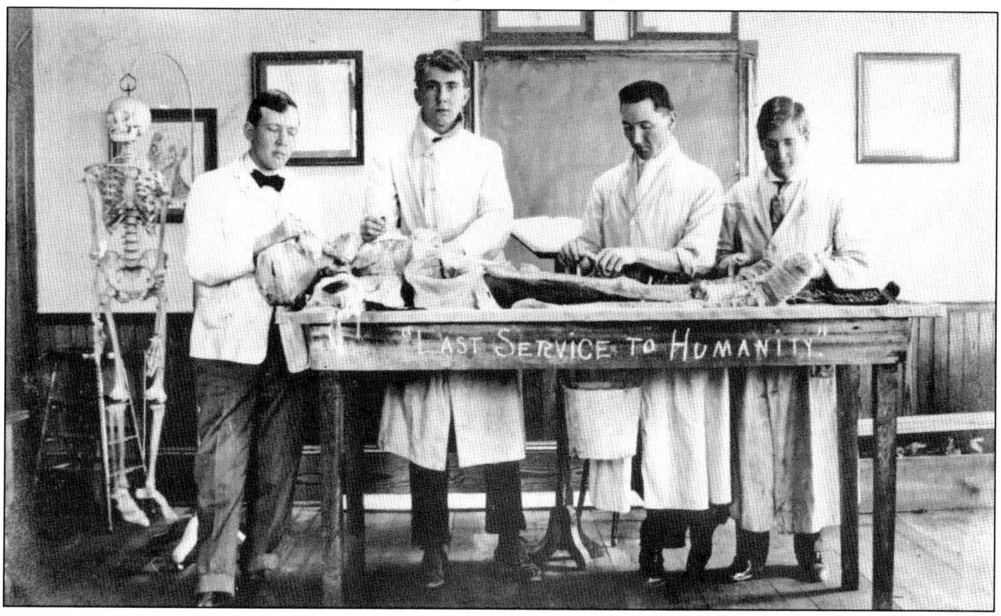

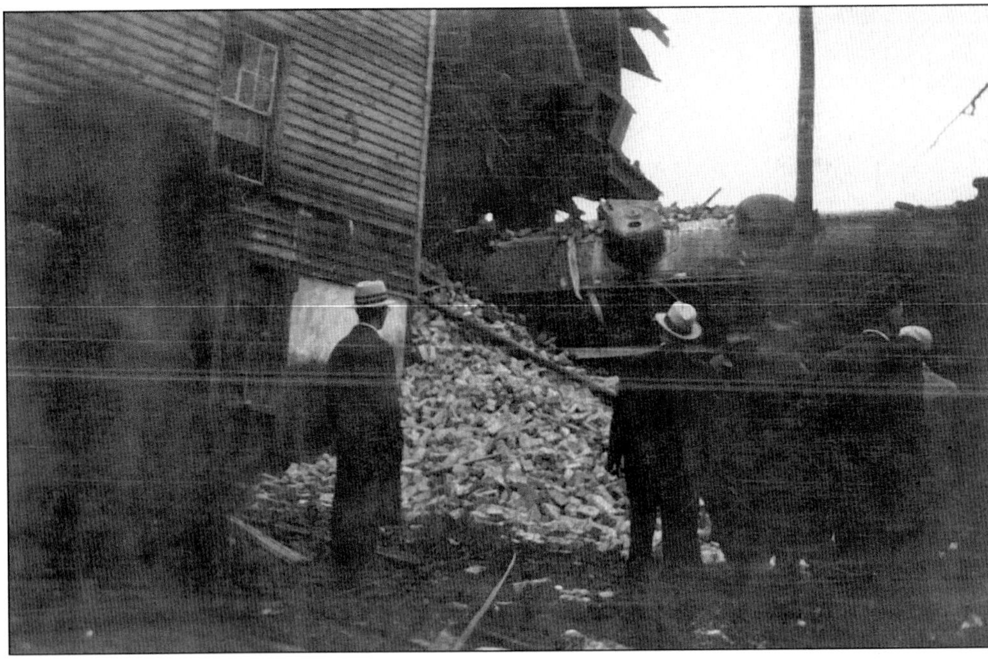

This appears to be the 1928 train wreck in which the Powers Drug Store was smashed and one man was killed. Early Wake Forest grade crossings had a grim history. At least four other accidents claimed five lives by 1963. (Courtesy of the Wake Forest Birthplace Museum.)

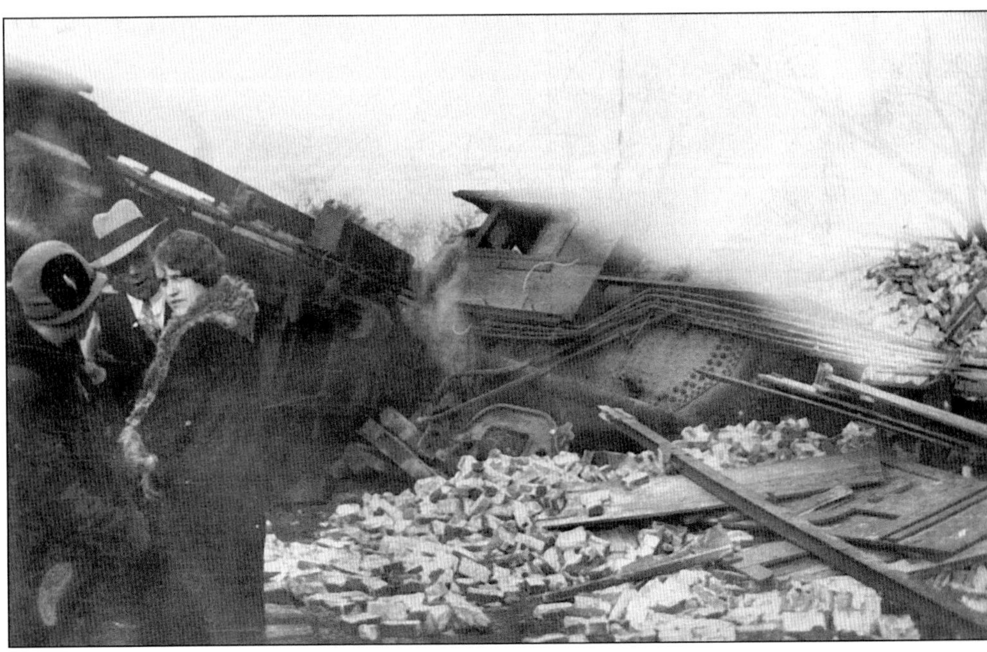

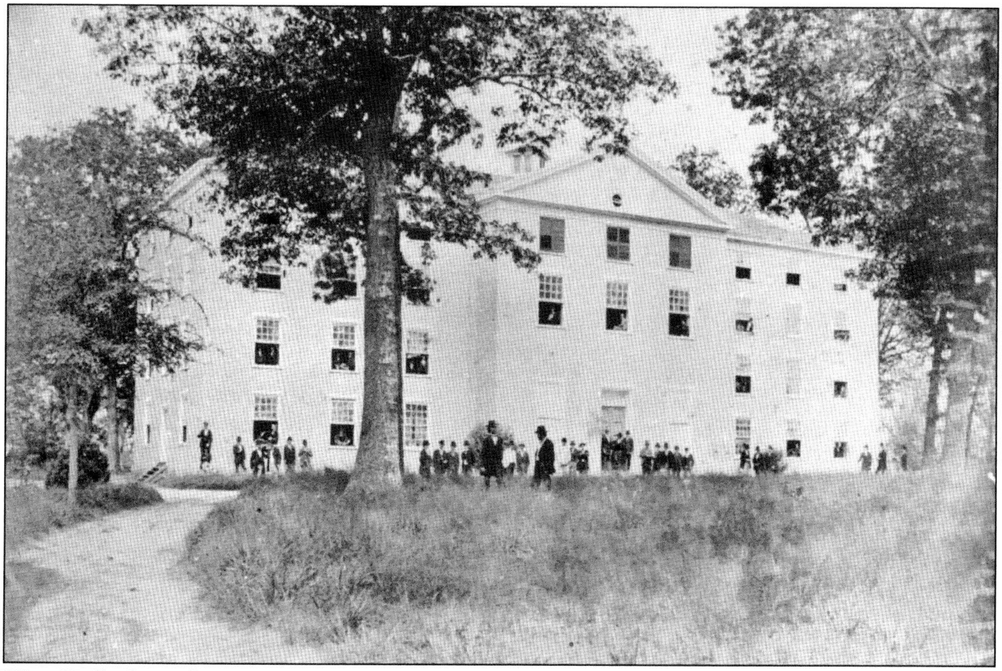

Wait Hall, the college's 98-year-old administration building, burned to the ground in the early-morning hours of May 5, 1933, kicking off a string of more than 70 unsolved arsons. Fierce investigations yielded no clues, and the "firebug" was never caught. Wait Hall, made of native clay, was a huge loss. When it burned, folks said it simply crumbled. (Courtesy of Southeastern Baptist Theological Seminary.)

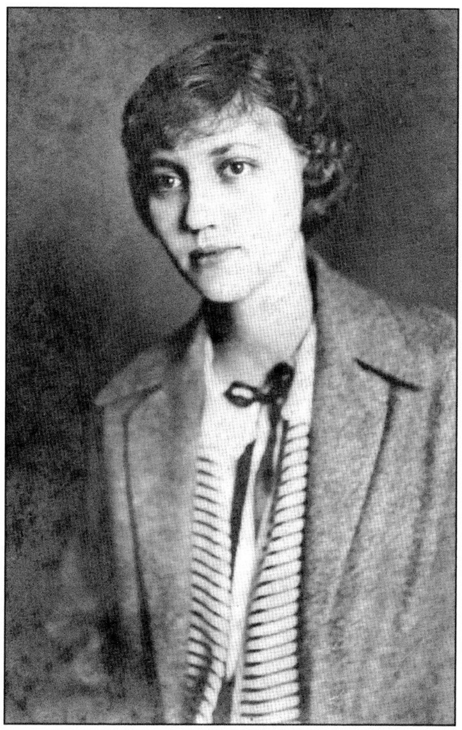

With paranoia growing on campus, gossips tagged the daughter of a beloved professor as the possible arsonist. An eccentric who once padlocked the hood of her car to prevent pranksters from meddling with the engine, she lived out her days in Wake Forest. No connection to the fires was ever established, and she has loyal defenders to this day. (Courtesy of the Wake Forest Birthplace Museum.)

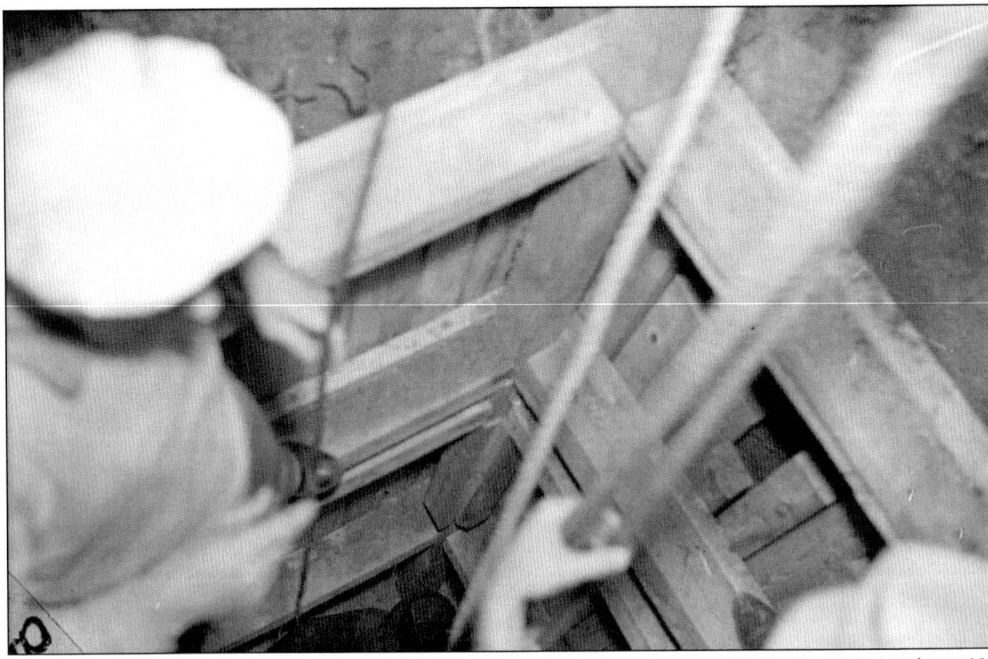

A desperate, 12-hour rescue operation failed in the nighttime hours of May 26, 1938, when 60-year-old well digger George Nelson was pulled from a collapsed shaft mere minutes after losing his courageous battle to survive beneath tons of fallen debris. Fire chief John Taylor organized the effort with volunteers working in shifts, hauling up buckets of rock while a crowd of more than 1,000 watched. Nelson died just before his legs were freed and rescuers could have lifted him to the surface, where an ambulance awaited. He lived long enough to express appreciation for the efforts to save him. (Courtesy of the *News and Observer* and North Carolina State Archives NO.38.5.68-70.)

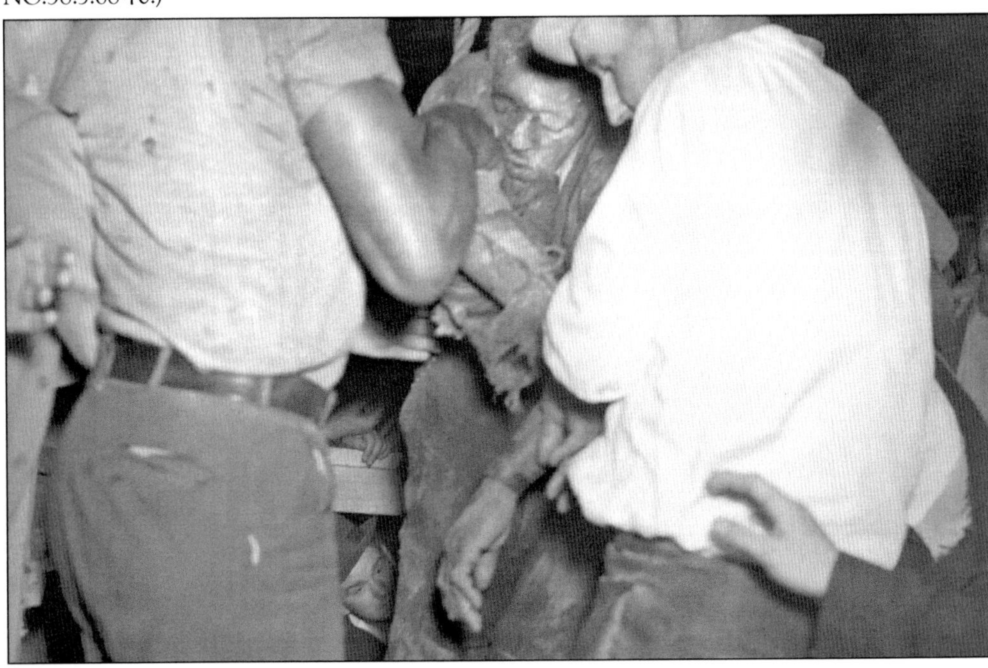

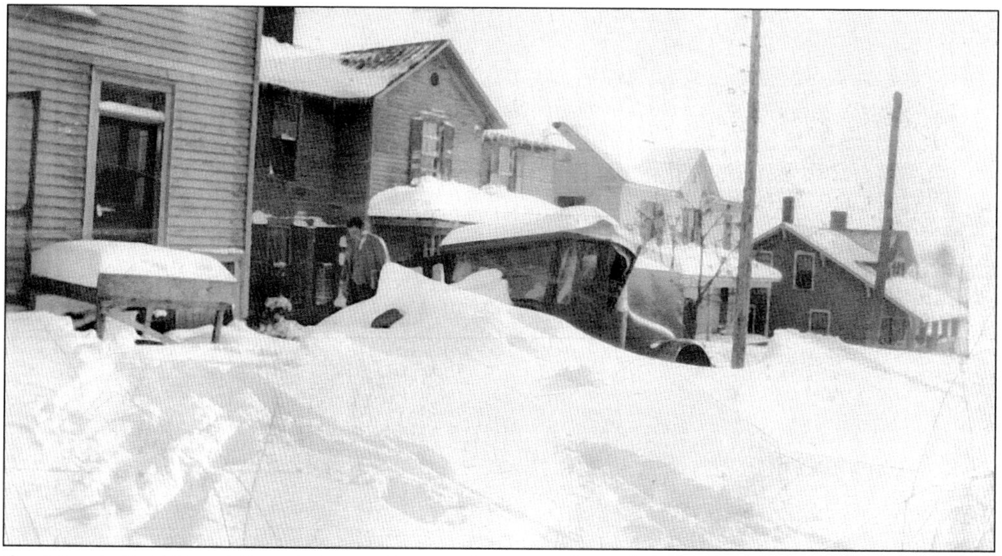

On March 2, 1929, a blizzard dumped more than two feet of snow on the town. This view is of Jones Street in downtown Wake Forest. (Courtesy of the Wake Forest Birthplace Museum.)

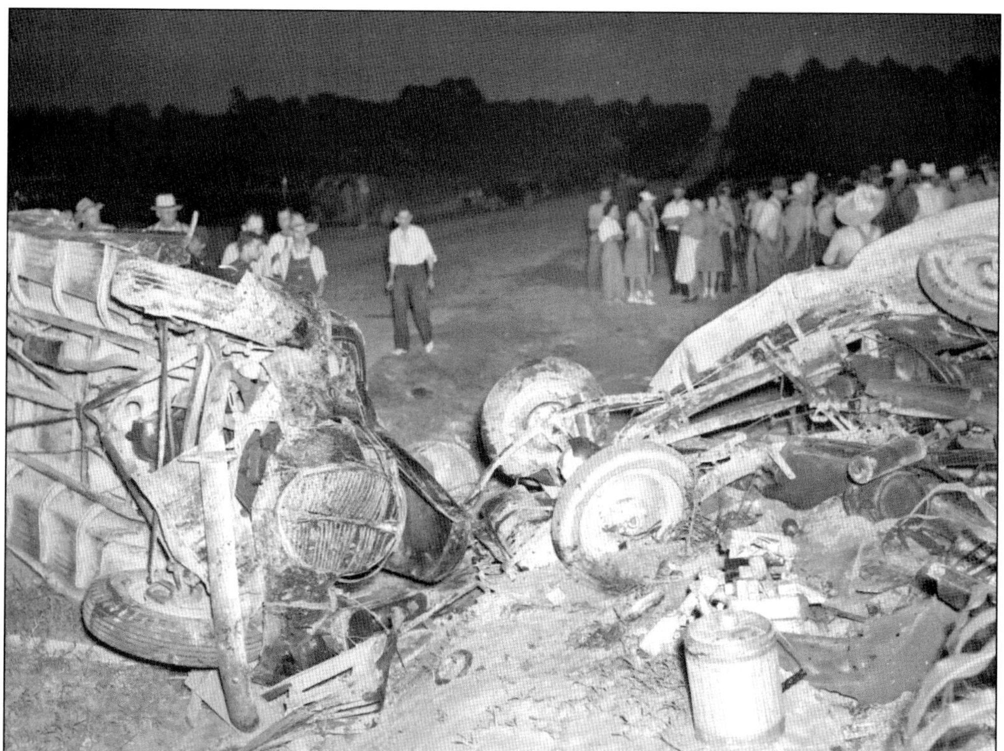

Early automobile travel was sometimes unsafe, with motorists driving at relatively high speeds on country roads unimproved from horse and buggy days. This fatal 1939 wreck on Louisburg Highway shows the tragic consequences. (Courtesy of the *News and Observer* and North Carolina State Archives NO.39.13.402, 403, and 408.)

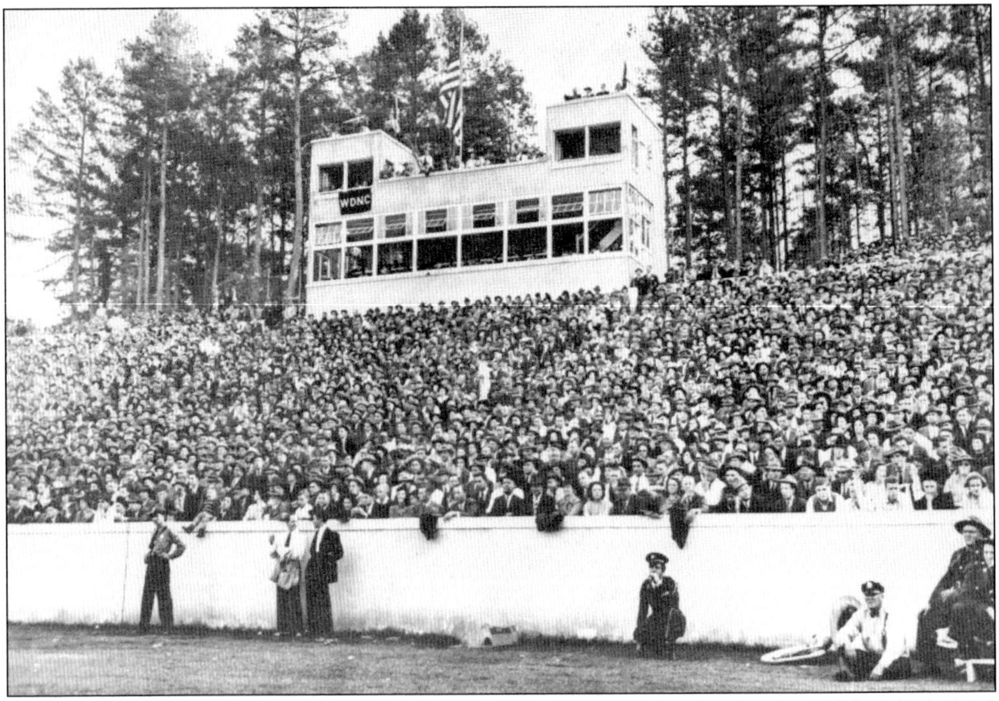

The Wake Forest College football team had strong and spirited support from townsfolk, who helped fill the stands at the big game against Duke University at Groves Stadium on October 26, 1940. This is a view of the south stands and press box. (Courtesy of the North Carolina State Archives N.95.2.42.)

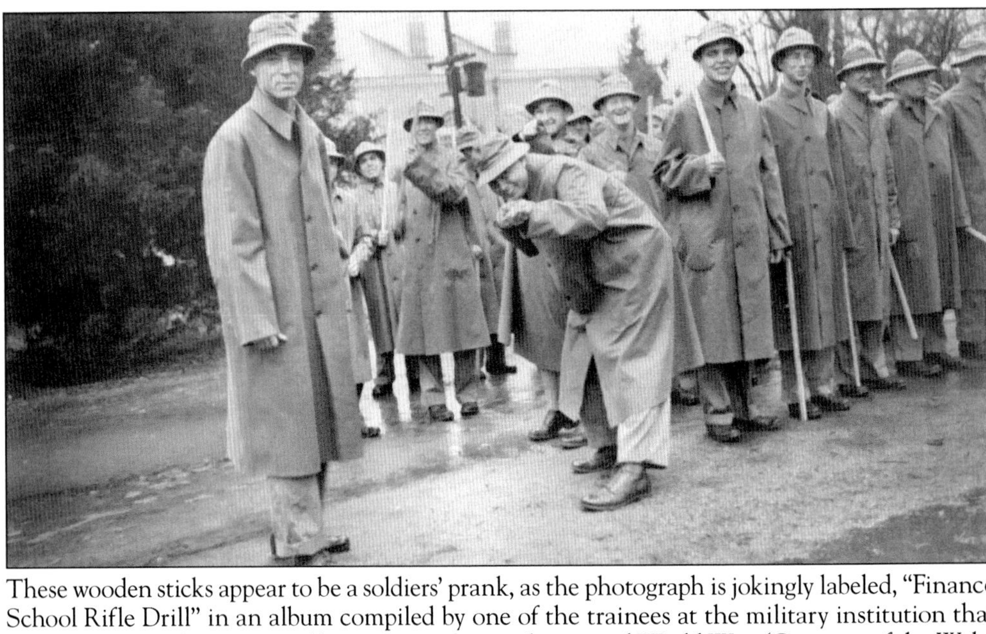

These wooden sticks appear to be a soldiers' prank, as the photograph is jokingly labeled, "Finance School Rifle Drill" in an album compiled by one of the trainees at the military institution that took over the Wake Forest College campus during the second World War. (Courtesy of the Wake Forest Birthplace Museum.)

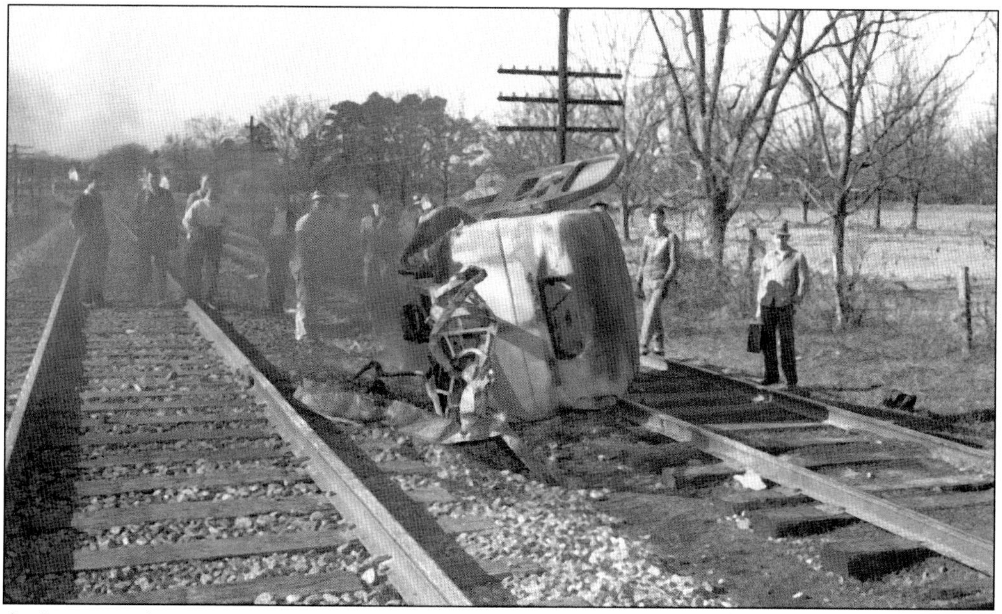

On January 15, 1942, a crack Seaboard passenger train, speeding southward at more than 50 miles per hour, slammed into a Staudt's Bakery Truck, instantly killing the driver, Merrill Reynolds. The New York–Florida Limited ripped the truck in two parts and strewed wreckage for 2,900 feet. (Courtesy of the *News and Observer* and North Carolina State Archives NO.42.1.119-133.)

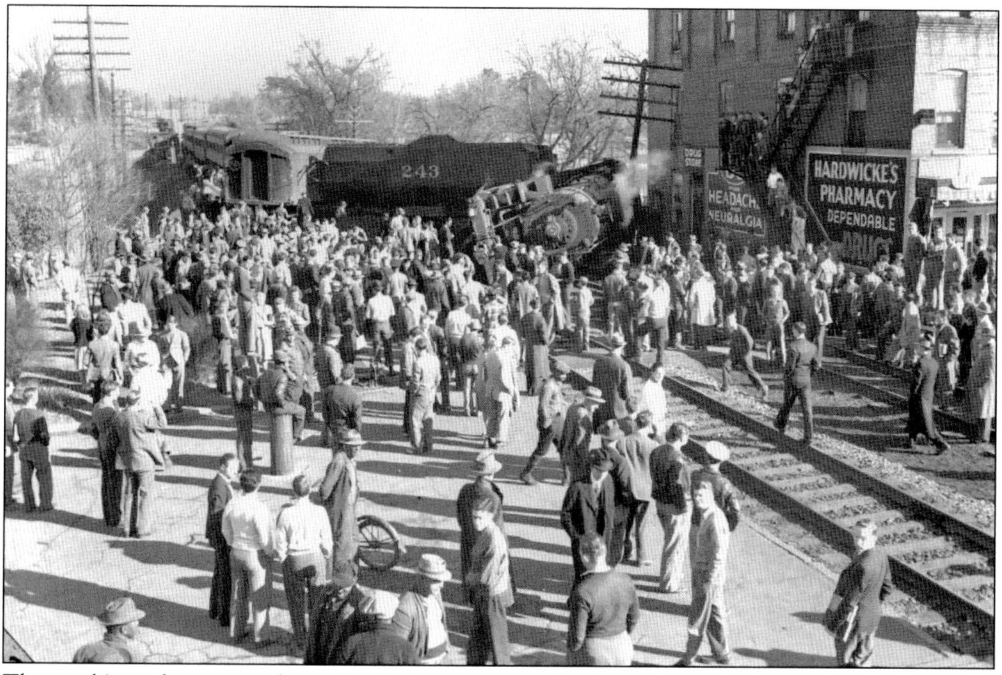

The truck's steel parts caught under the locomotive's wheels and capsized it in the middle of Wake Forest. It was the sixth grade crossing fatality near Wake Forest in a decade. The wreck caused a cessation of activity at Wake Forest College as hundreds of students and townspeople gathered to look at the derailed locomotive. (Courtesy of the *News and Observer* and North Carolina State Archives NO.42.1.119-113.)

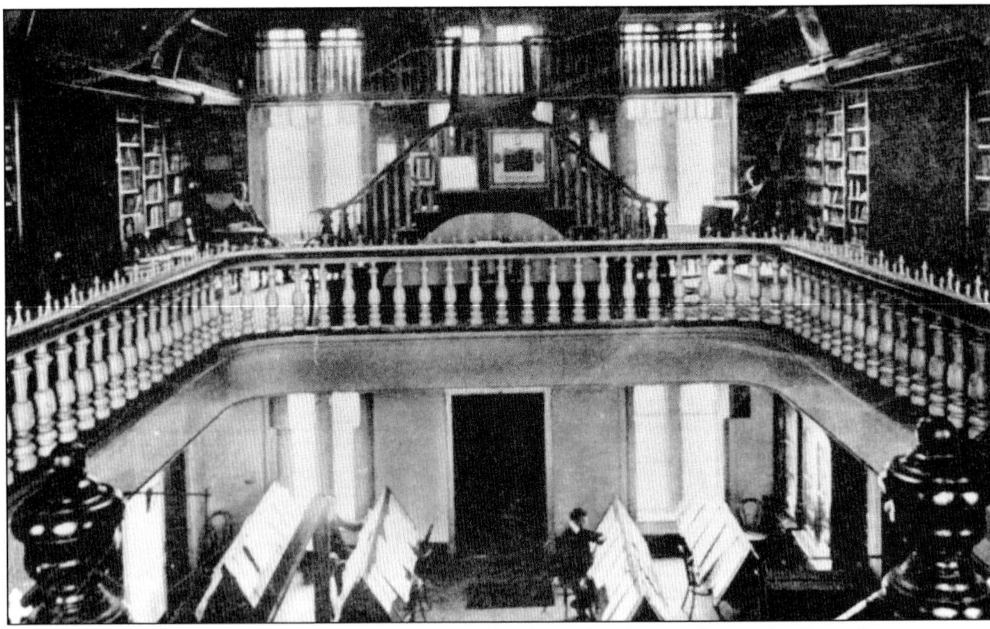

The Wake Forest College library, also home to the law school, was elegant both in the content of its collection and its eye-popping architecture. In the summer of 1940, a rare first edition of the literary classic *Paradise Lost*, purchased by a generous donor, sank to the bottom of the Atlantic Ocean when Germans bombed the ship carrying it across. (Courtesy of Southeastern Baptist Theological Seminary.)

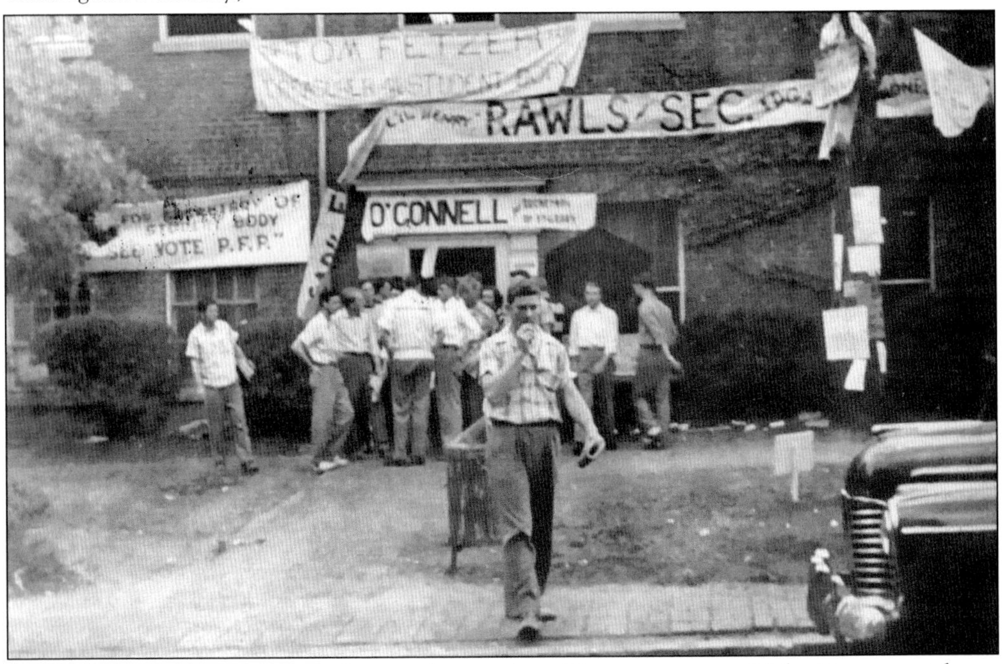

The name on this 1848 student elections banner is well known to many Wake County residents. The candidate in this Wake Forest College political race was the father of future Raleigh mayor Tom Fetzer. The younger Fetzer later went on to also graduate from Wake Forest. (Courtesy of the Wake Forest Birthplace Museum.)

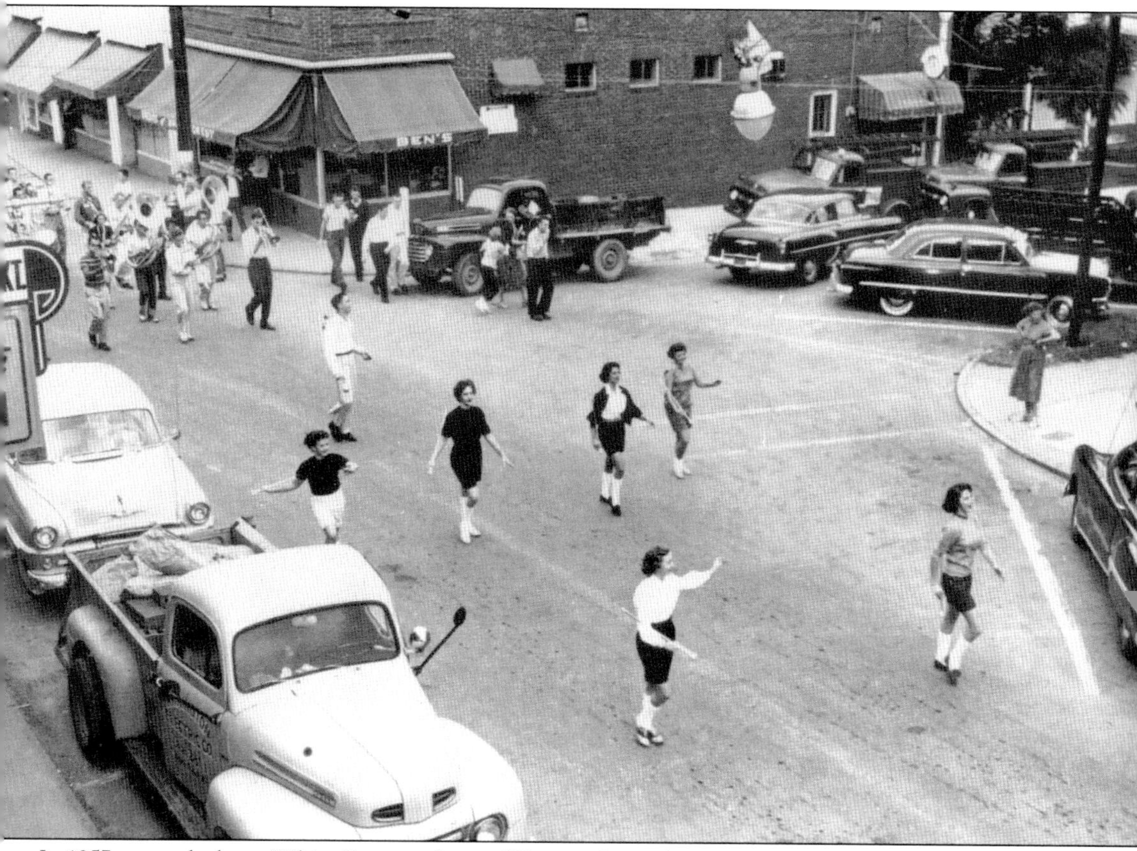

In 1957, a parade down White Street welcomed Tommy Byrne home to Wake Forest. The returning baseball hero, having enjoyed a legendary career with the New York Yankees, went on to serve more than a decade as mayor of the town where he'd gone to college and honed his skills as an athlete. Byrne first arrived in the little college town in 1937 and later said it was the quietness of the place that attracted him. "A very small, country-living place," he said, as reported in the *Wake Weekly*. It was the peacefulness of Wake Forest that called him back, a better way of life, he thought, than the bustle of big-city baseball. Byrne went on to raise his family here, ultimately spending 70 years in his adopted hometown. The town held a day in his honor in September 2007, three months before his death at age 87. (Courtesy of the Wake Forest Birthplace Museum.)

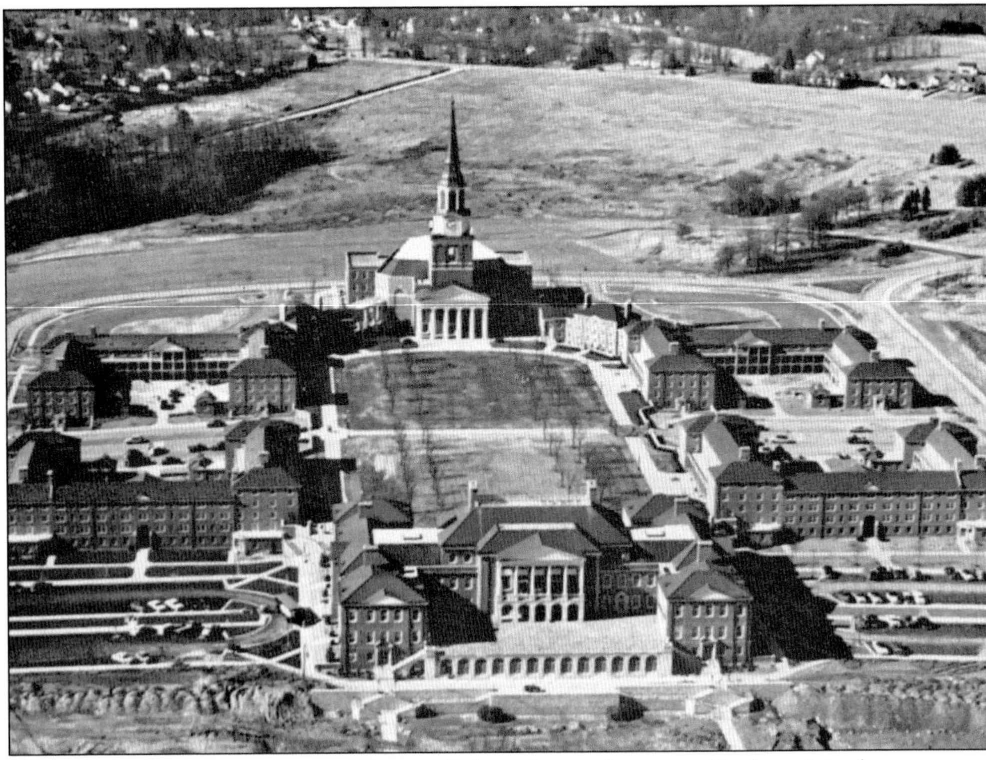

The new Wake Forest College in Winston-Salem, designed to resemble the original campus, was nearly complete in this photograph from the 1956 college yearbook. One Wake Forest resident told the *News and Observer*, "This is the saddest time I have ever known except for personal bereavements. This is a kind of bereavement for the whole town." The college moved that year. (Courtesy of the Wake Forest Birthplace Museum.)

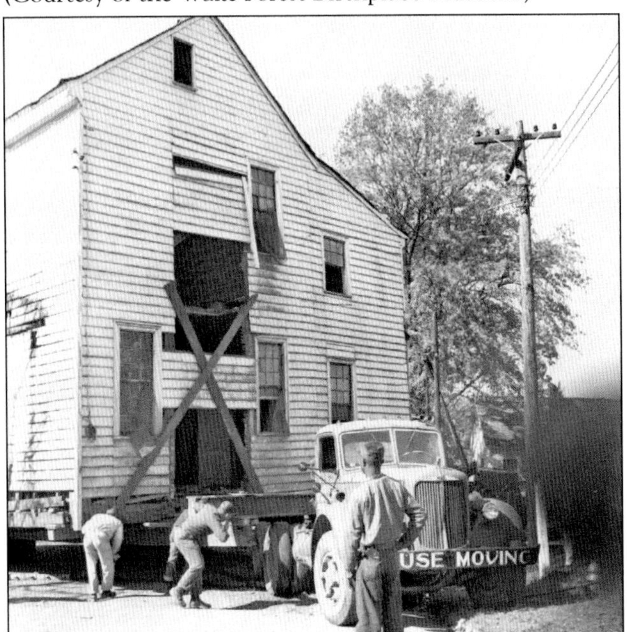

The Calvin Jones House, once home to first college president Samuel Wait, his wife, and several rooms full of boarding students, also made headlines in 1956. After two previous moves, it was relocated one last time, finding a permanent address at the former athletic field on North Main Street. This move was performed by the Crouch Brothers in 1956. (Courtesy of the North Carolina State Archives N.56.11.13.)

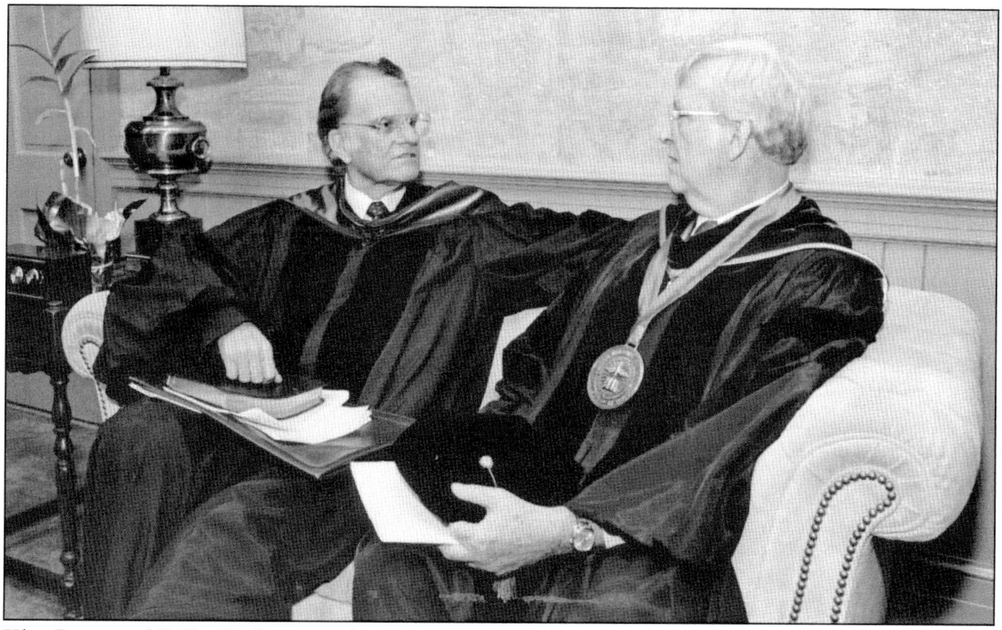

The Reverend Billy Graham made a rare visit to campus in 1988 when Dr. Lewis Drummond was sworn in as fourth president of Southeastern Baptist Theological Seminary. Dr. Graham, who'd been ill, had not planned to attend the inauguration. But Dr. Drummond held the Billy Graham Chair of Evangelism at Southern Seminary and very much wanted his mentor present at the ceremony. Dr. Graham (left) is pictured with Ray Honeycutt. (Courtesy of Southeastern Baptist Theological Seminary.)

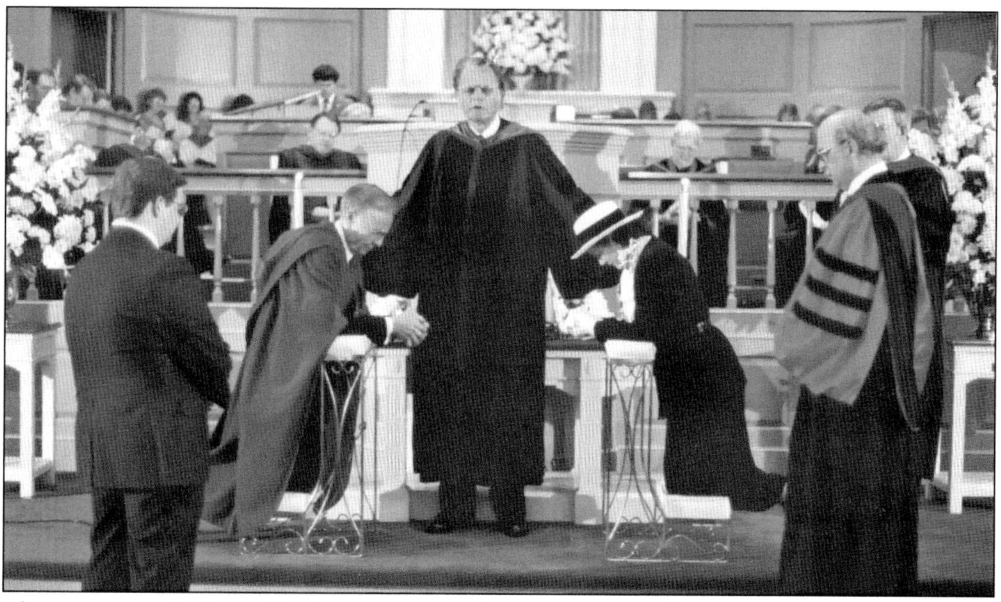

This was a time of upheaval for the seminary, marking a controversial switch to a more fundamentalist course. By 1986, the Southern Baptist Convention considered the seminary too liberal in some matters, including its training of women for the ministry. The conflict brought Dr. W. Randall Lolley's resignation as president, with Dr. Drummond replacing him. Student enrollment initially dropped but has risen steadily since. (Courtesy of Southeastern Baptist Theological Seminary.)

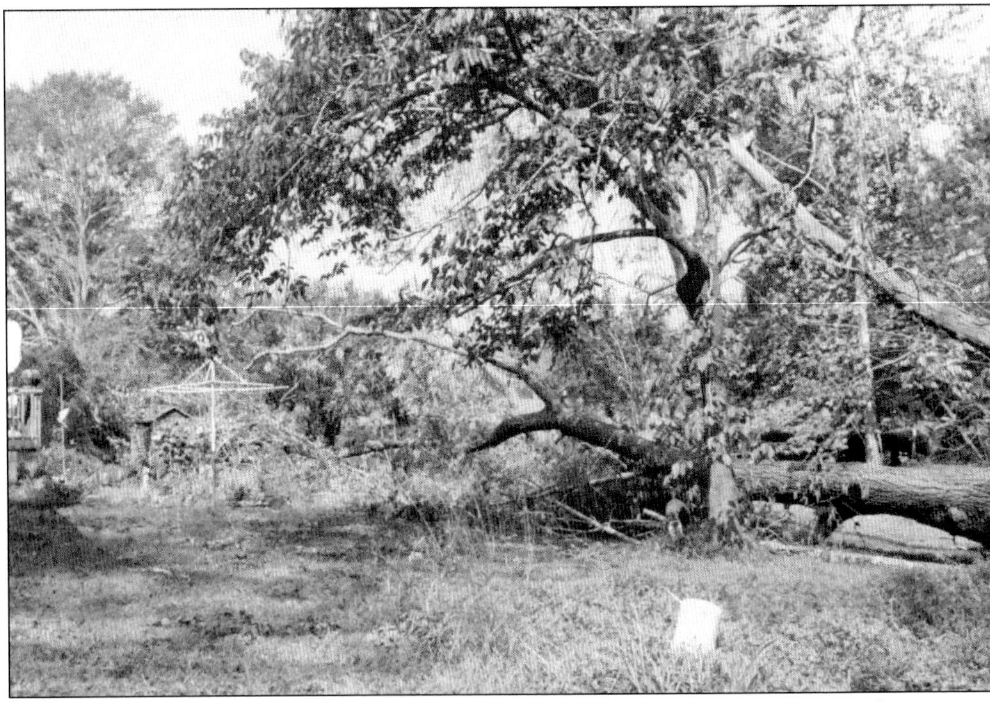

Hurricane Fran, a classic Cape Verde storm that rolled off the west African coast, was the strongest hurricane to push across North Carolina since Hazel surged ashore in 1954. Striking the Wake Forest area on the night of September 6, 1996, the storm damaged property and dropped trees, including this large one at Oakforest. (Courtesy of Speed Massenburg and family.)

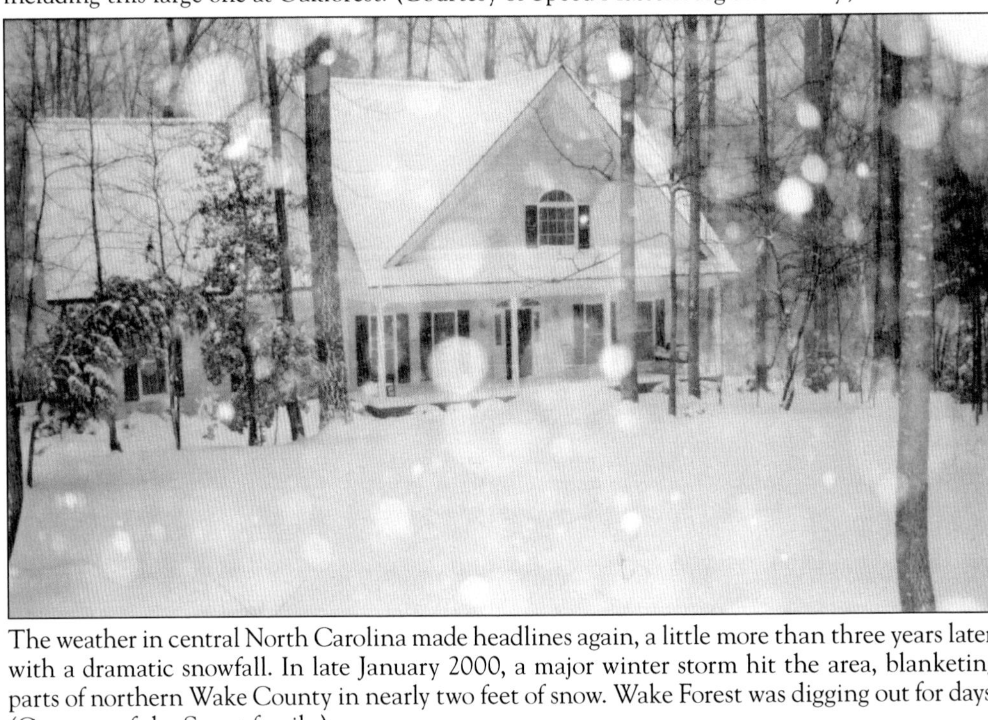

The weather in central North Carolina made headlines again, a little more than three years later, with a dramatic snowfall. In late January 2000, a major winter storm hit the area, blanketing parts of northern Wake County in nearly two feet of snow. Wake Forest was digging out for days. (Courtesy of the Smart family.)

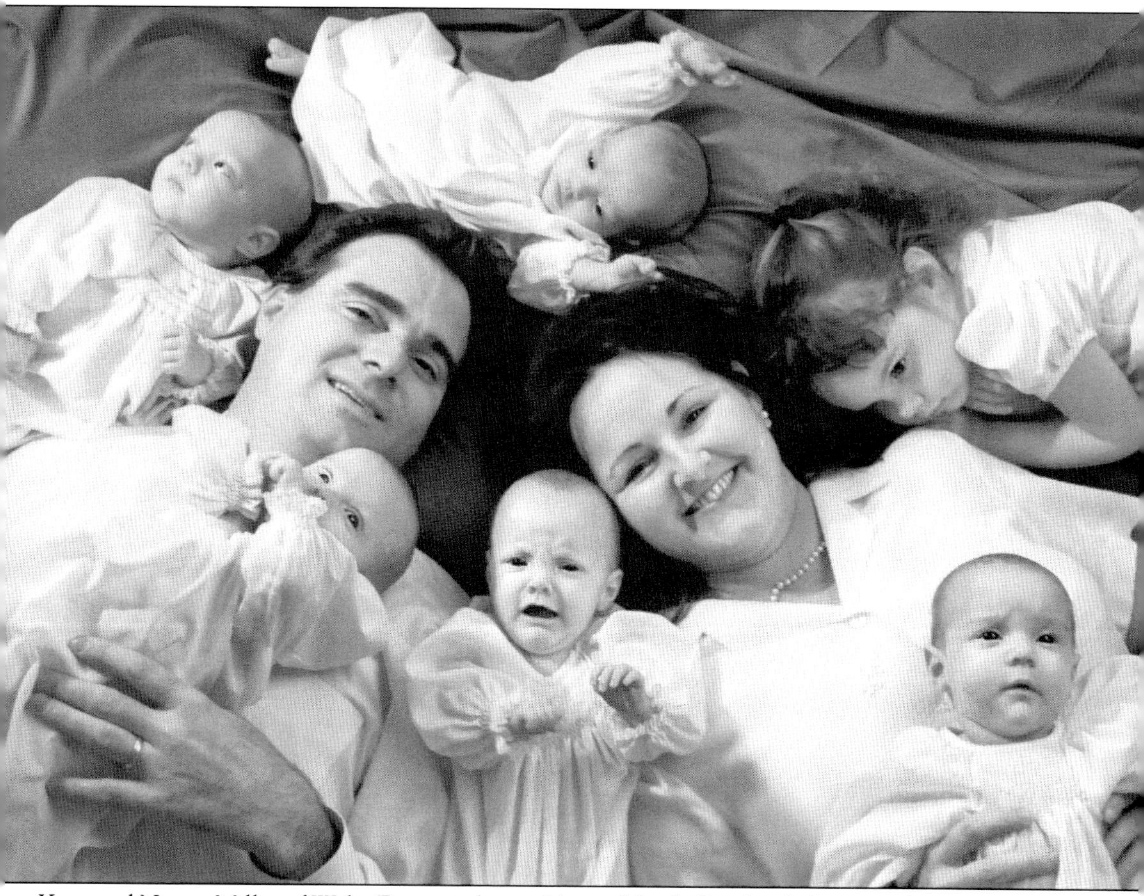

Kent and Nancy Miller of Wake Forest welcomed home North Carolina's first set of quintuplets in July 1998. After a period of fertility treatments followed by a successful multiple pregnancy consisting of months of bed rest, Nancy delivered the five healthy babies with the help of 27 doctors and nurses at UNC Hospitals in Chapel Hill. Born 10 weeks prematurely, the babies eventually transferred to Wake Medical Center in Raleigh before finally coming home to join their parents and big sister, Anna. The arrival of little Maggie, Grace, Ellie, Emery, and Martin brought intense media attention and hundreds of donations, including a "Quintathon" on radio station G-105. (Courtesy of the *News and Observer*.)

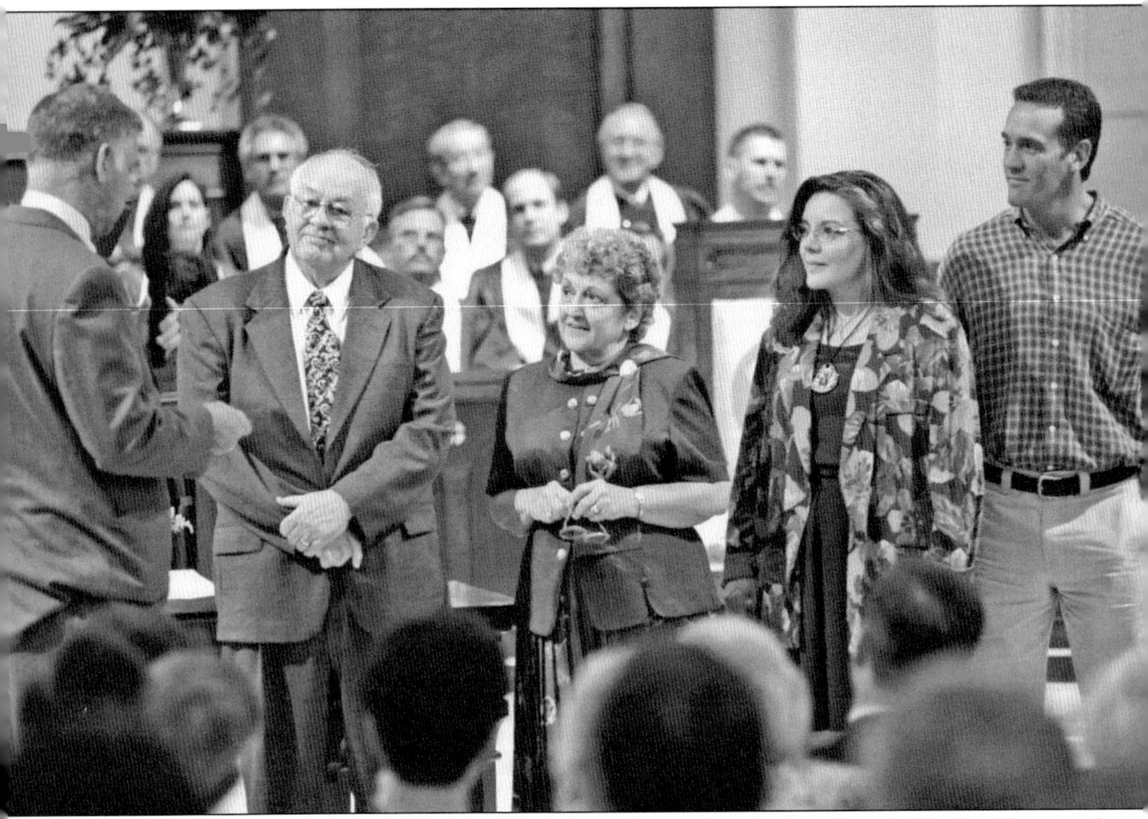

Wake Forest mayor George Mackie presented a key to the town to Rev. J. Wesley Shipp and family in 1999. The honor came 30 years after the Shipps bravely stood their ground in the face of vicious racial violence in the Stony Hill area west of Wake Forest. Daughter Karen Shipp, 16 at the time of the December 1969 incident, had been hosting an integrated house party for some teenage friends when an unknown assailant fired a shotgun through the living room window of the house. Although no one was hurt, the event sparked months of racial tension in the town, where an investigation was launched but no arrests were ever made. Reverend Shipp, a stalwart civil rights activist who refused to renounce integration or apologize for inviting African American youths into his home, immediately lost his job as pastor of an area Baptist church. "We're just shocked at the man who shot," he said at the time. "It just didn't occur to us that a human being would try to kill a group of children." (Courtesy of the *News and Observer*.)

Eight

Characters and Legends

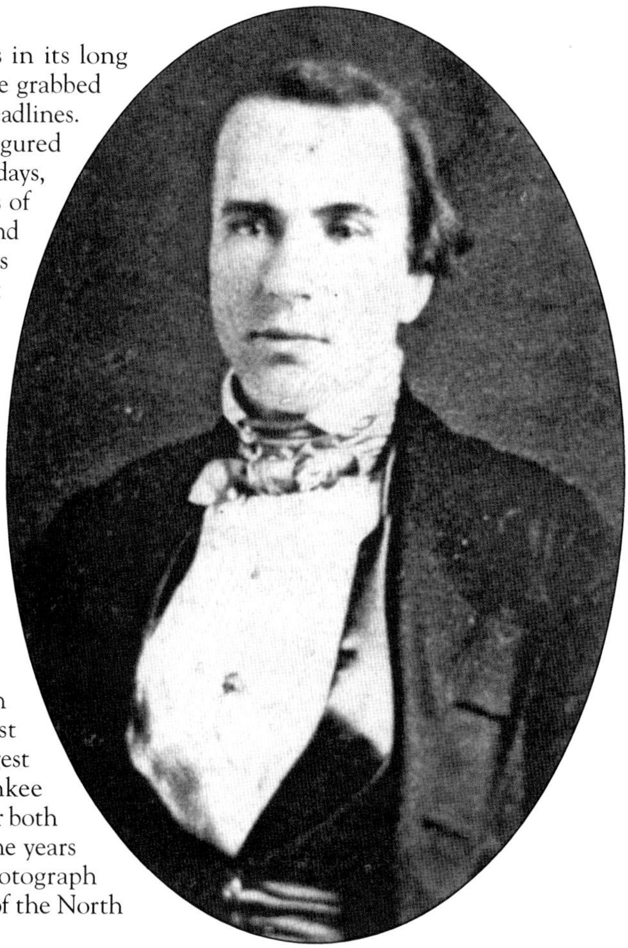

With no shortage of newsmakers in its long history, Wake Forest's citizens have grabbed their own fair share of interesting headlines. Leaders in politics and religion figured prominently in the town's earliest days, giving way in later years to heroes of education, justice, entertainment, and sports. One of the earliest notables hailed, not from Wake Forest, but from nearby Forestville. When that town was still an independent entity, the Joneses were its most famous residents. Wiley Daniel Jones (1819–1891) served in the Confederate army before becoming a leading Republican in the Reconstruction era. Called a man of force who, according to the *Raleigh State Chronicle*, "lent respectability to the Republican party" at a time when Republicans were not welcome in the South, he was a tax collector who mixed with Yankees. A resident of Oakforest plantation, historic documents suggest his influence with occupying Yankee forces secured military protection for both his homestead and the college in the years following the Civil War. This photograph was taken around 1850. (Courtesy of the North Carolina State Archives N.95.1.69.)

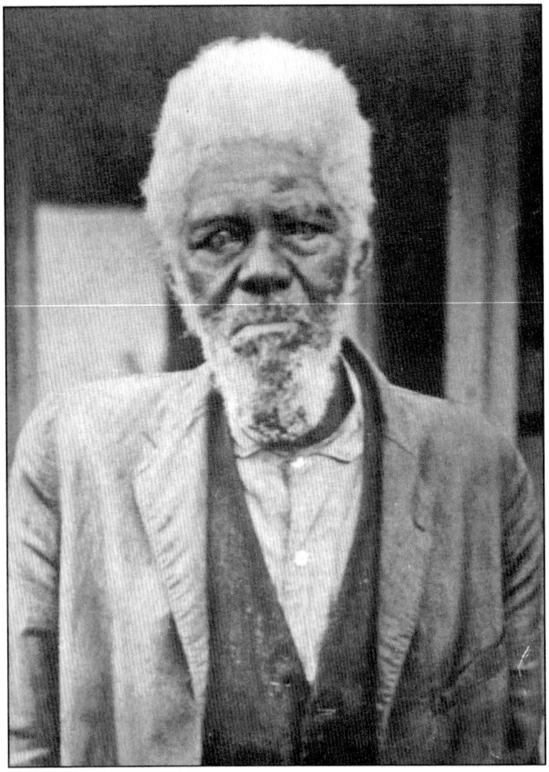

Nelson Ligon was a spiritual man who'd spent his life as a slave in the Wake Forest area. In 1866, moved by God's glory, he leapt from the balcony at Forestville Baptist Church during a service. Somewhat unnerved, the white congregation quickly decided to help establish a separate chapel for its African American worshippers. Called Friendship Chapel Baptist Church, Nelson Ligon is revered as its founding member. (Courtesy of Friendship Chapel Baptist Church.)

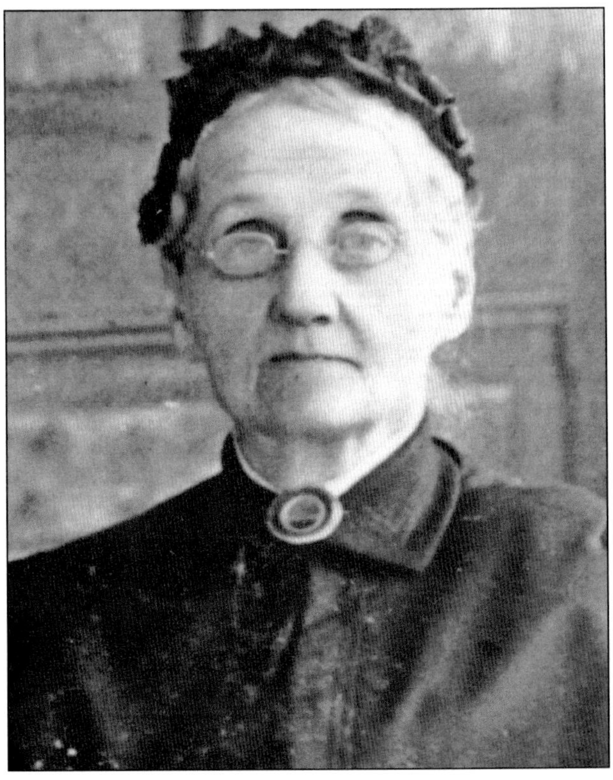

Ann Eliza Wait Brewer, the matriarch of a large family that grew to include many prominent members of Wake Forest society, was the only child of Samuel Wait, the first president of Wake Forest College. When her famous father returned to Wake Forest to live out his golden years, she lovingly cared for him until his death. (Courtesy of Hallie Arrington Hearn.)

Akiyama Konosuke, class of 1910, was from Tochigi, Japan. He was the first foreign student to attend Wake Forest College. This photograph was given to Prof. Benjamin Sledd and was handed down in the Sledd family. (Courtesy of the Wake Forest Birthplace Museum.)

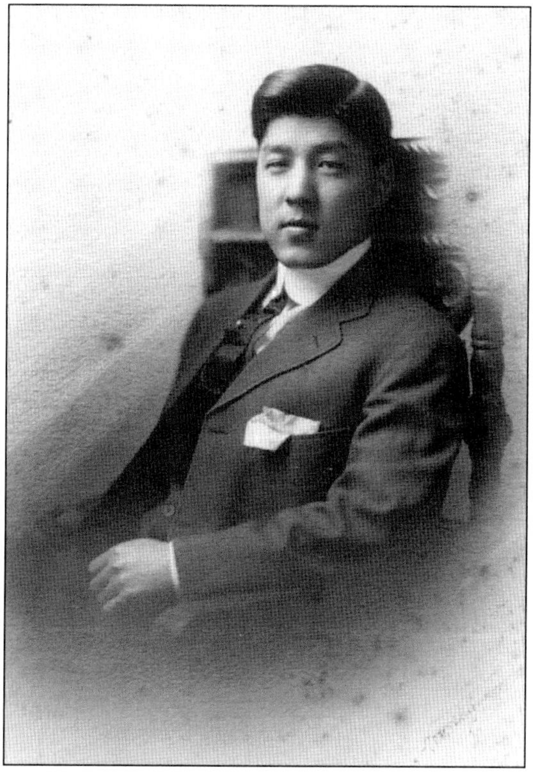

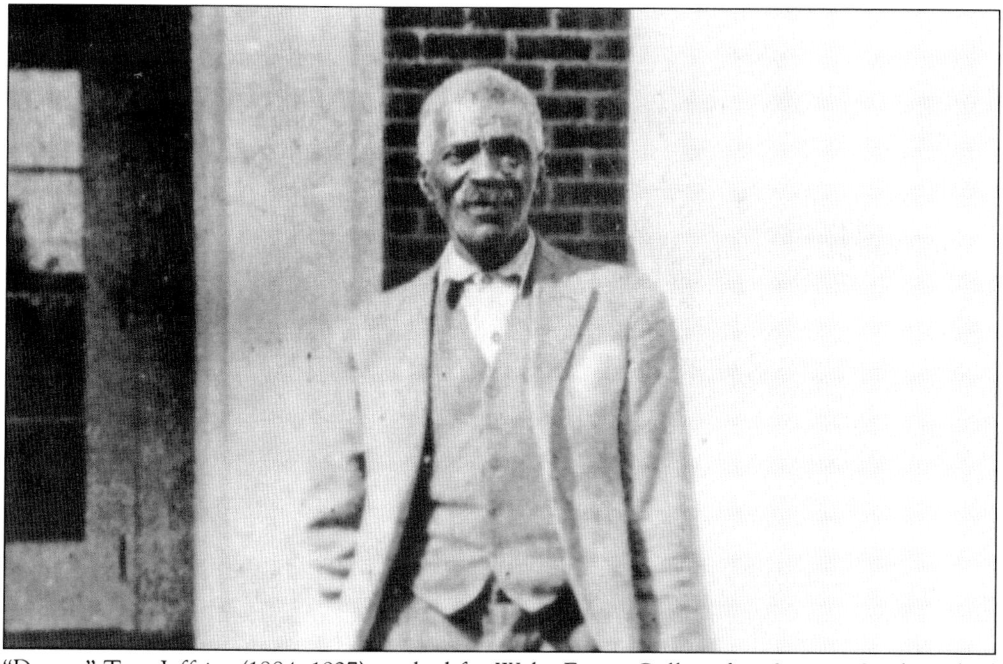

"Doctor" Tom Jeffries (1884–1927) worked for Wake Forest College for 43 years. Students had taken to calling him "Doctor" in recognition of his folksy wisdom. Jeffries is best remembered for building the amazing stone wall that surrounds campus and was responsible for planting many of the college's trees and flowering plants. (Courtesy of the Wake Forest Birthplace Museum.)

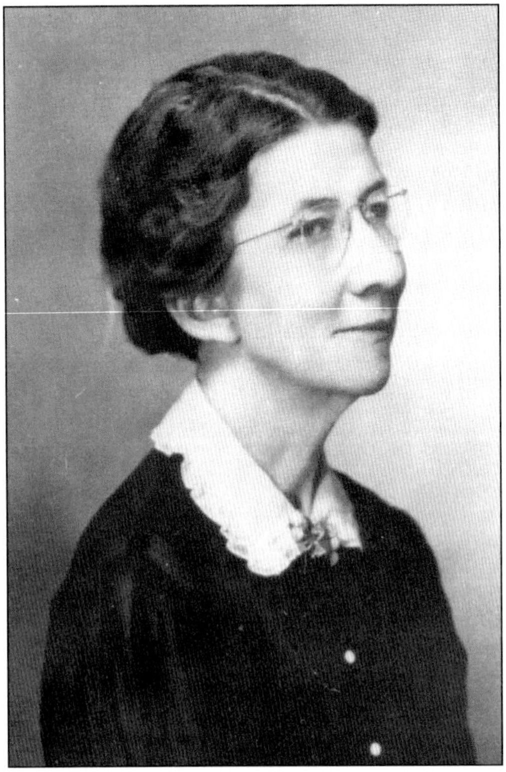

Ruby Reid, one of the town's early telephone operators, later became an astute businesswoman whose endowment helped establish the Ruby Reid Daycare Center. Reid started an insurance agency, meeting with clients in her lovely Victorian home on South White Street before selling the business to Harvey Holding in the mid-1930s. Her position as a leader in business was both unusual and impressive for a woman of her era. (Courtesy of Southeastern Baptist Theological Seminary.)

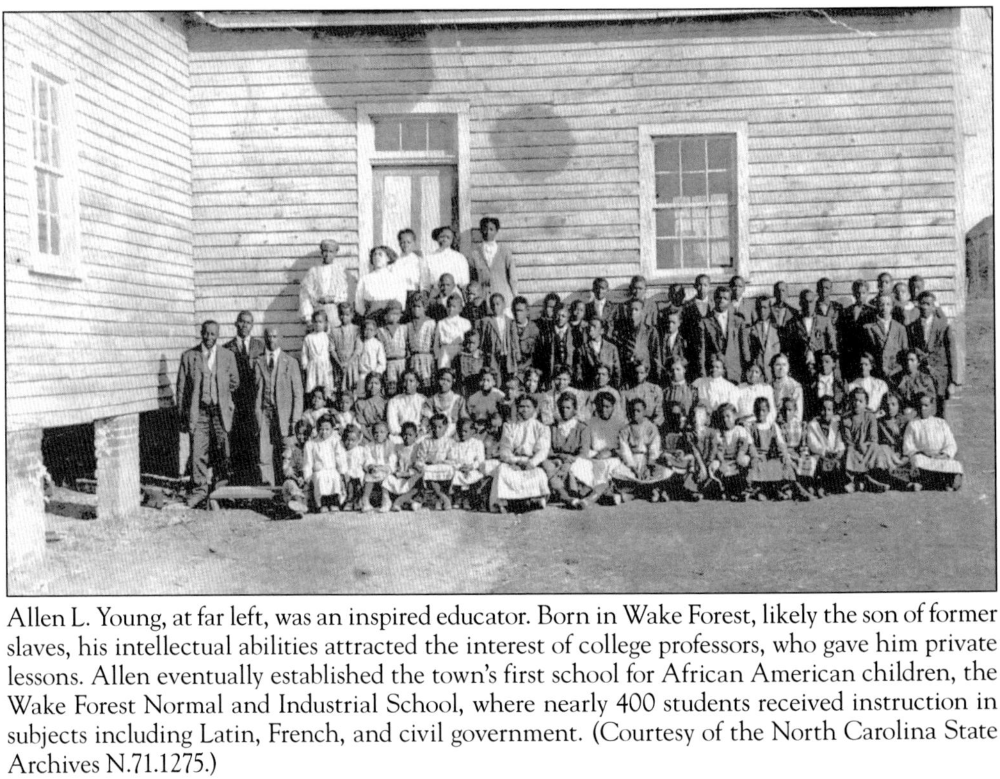

Allen L. Young, at far left, was an inspired educator. Born in Wake Forest, likely the son of former slaves, his intellectual abilities attracted the interest of college professors, who gave him private lessons. Allen eventually established the town's first school for African American children, the Wake Forest Normal and Industrial School, where nearly 400 students received instruction in subjects including Latin, French, and civil government. (Courtesy of the North Carolina State Archives N.71.1275.)

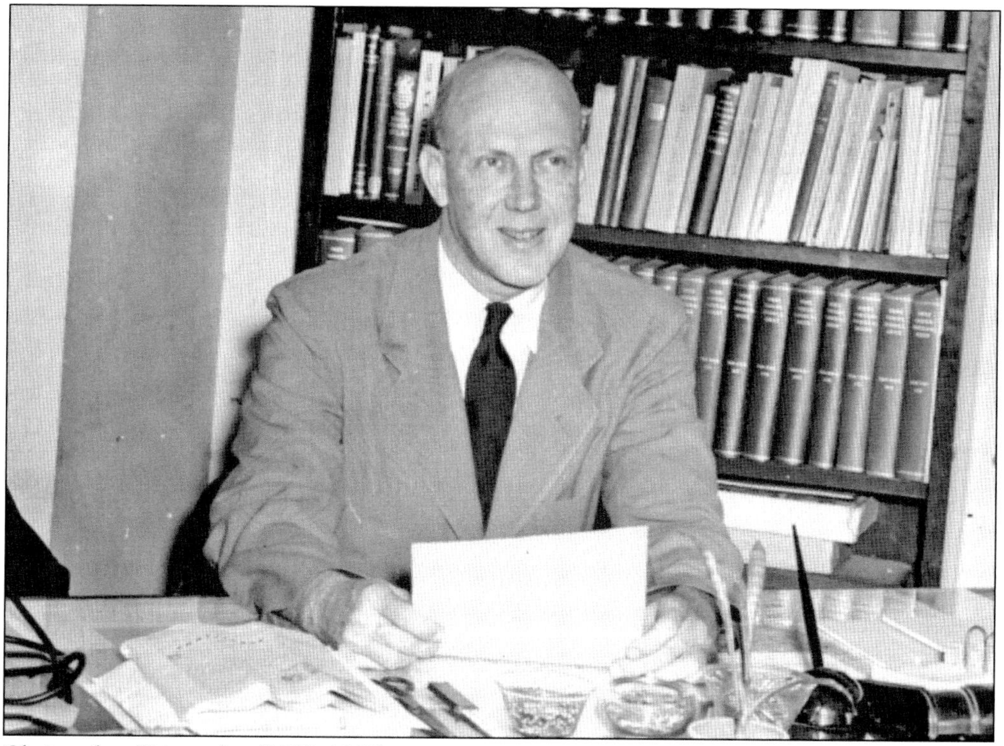

Christopher Crittenden (1902–1969), secretary of the North Carolina Historical Commission, gave the state its historical highway markers, state-owned historic sites, and modern museum and preservation programs. A town native whose parents both worked at the college, Crittenden graduated from the school before earning a doctorate from Yale University. His mission to bring history to all the people was most successfully fulfilled. (Courtesy of the North Carolina State Archives N.51.9.9-13.)

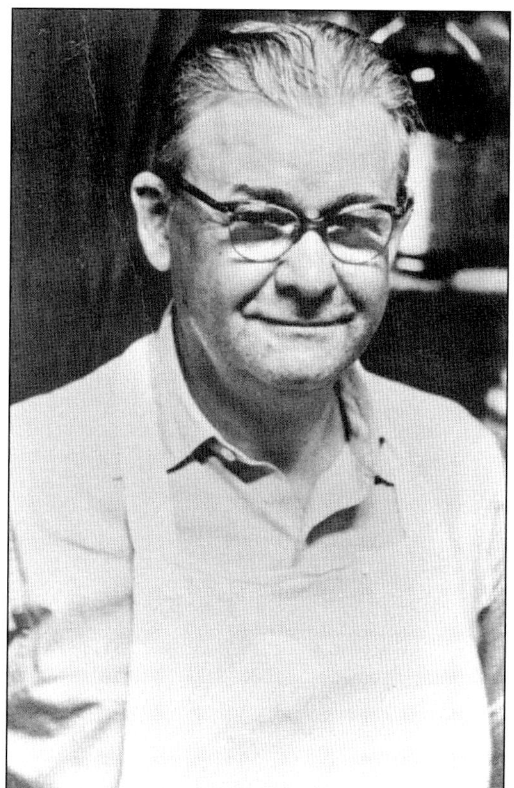

Millard "Shorty" Joyner is best known as the proprietor of Shorty's, the combination restaurant and pool hall that still occupies its familiar storefront on South White Street. Established in 1916, the place quickly became a favorite hangout for students and town residents alike. Everyone knows Shorty's hotdogs and has for generations. (Courtesy of the Wake Forest Birthplace Museum.)

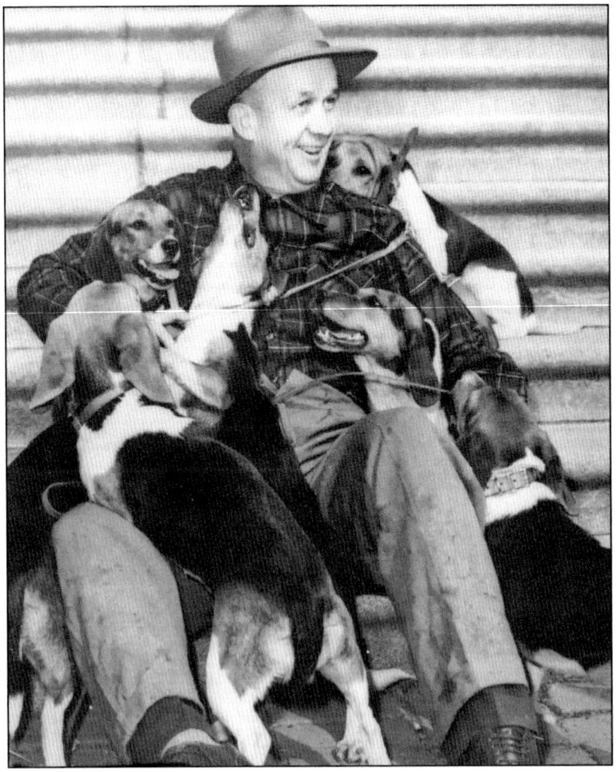

Pictured with his hunting dogs around 1945, Murray Greason coached Wake Forest basketball from 1933 to 1957. One of the college's most respected athletic leaders, an award in his memory is presented annually to the men's basketball team member who has had the greatest impact on his teammates through hard work, determination, effort, and performance. (Courtesy of the North Carolina State Archives N.95.2.41.)

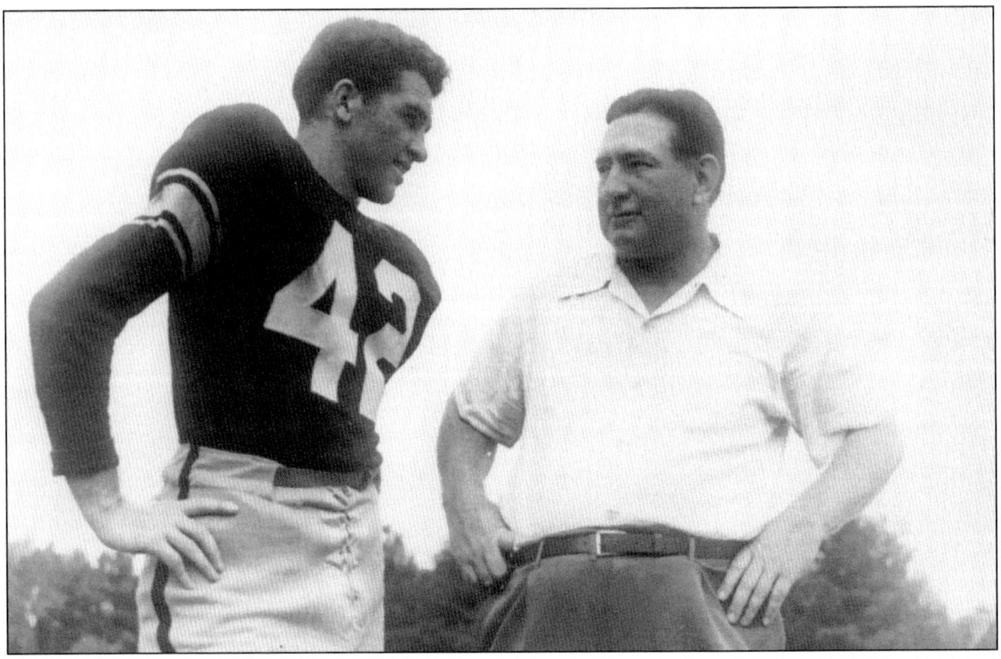

Douglas Clyde "Peahead" Walker was Wake Forest's football coach from 1937 to 1950. Establishing a brilliant career based on recruiting, technique, and discipline, he compiled a 77-51-6 record for the Demon Deacons and led the school to two bowl games, including the first ever Gator Bowl in 1946. (Courtesy of the Wake Forest Birthplace Museum.)

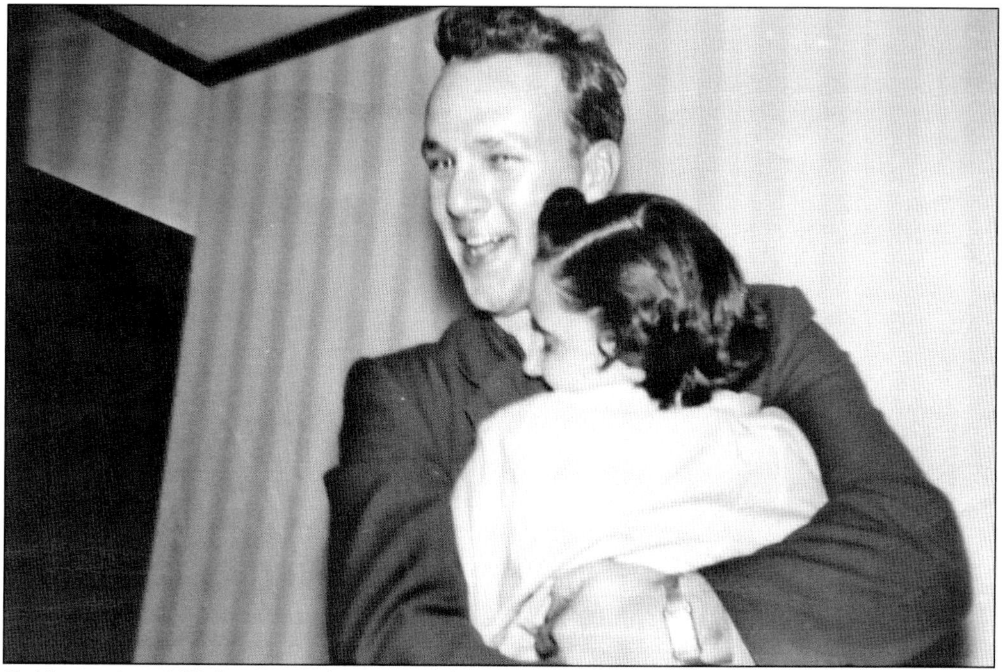

Golf great Arnold Palmer rented a room in the South Brick House while he was a student at Wake Forest College. Owned by the Johnston family, the house adjacent to campus was a good place to board and wasn't far from the golf course. In this 1952 photograph, Palmer greets 18-year-old Betty Johnston, younger sister of golf coach Johnny Johnston. (Courtesy of Betty Johnston Frankow.)

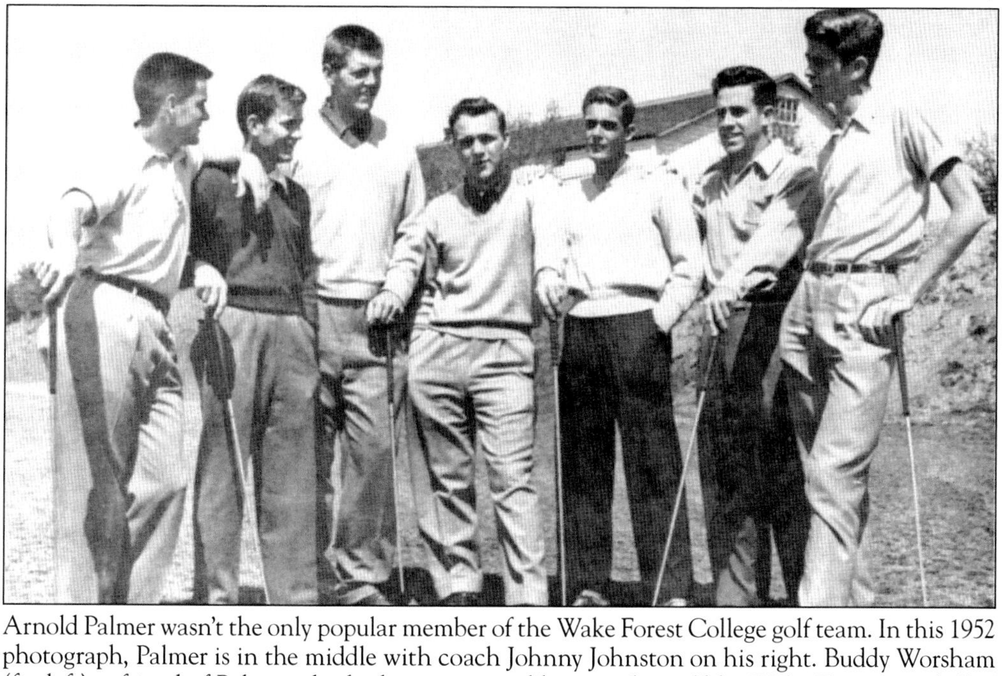

Arnold Palmer wasn't the only popular member of the Wake Forest College golf team. In this 1952 photograph, Palmer is in the middle with coach Johnny Johnston on his right. Buddy Worsham (far left), a friend of Palmer who had accompanied him to play golf for Wake Forest, was killed in a tragic car accident not long after this photograph was taken. (Courtesy of the Wake Forest Birthplace Museum.)

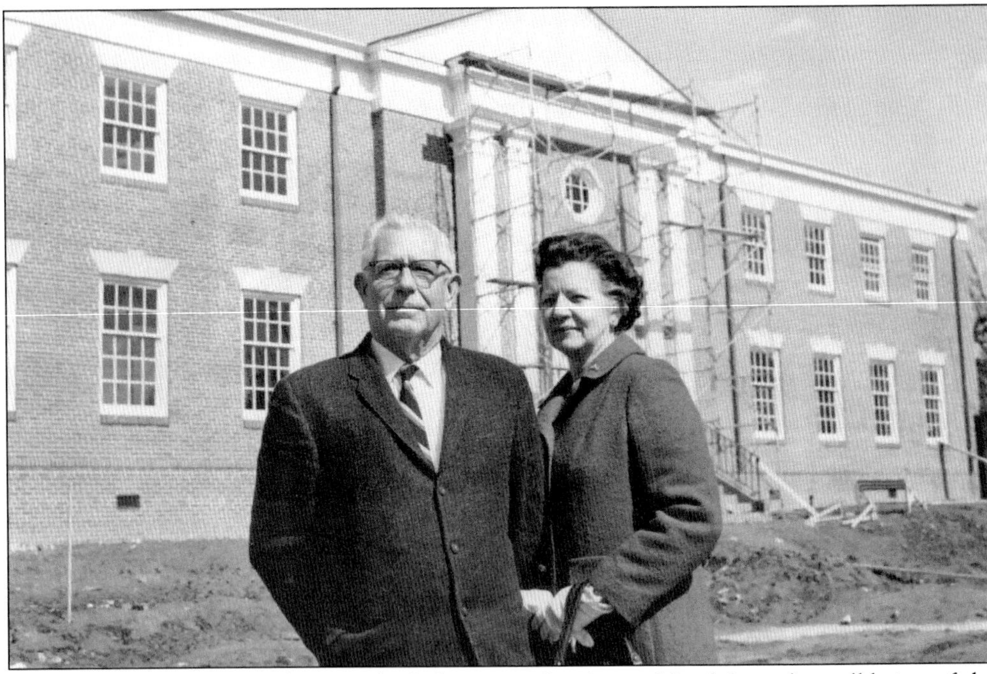

Dr. George Mackie was a distinguished physician who devoted his life to the well-being of the Wake Forest community. His wife, Kathleen, was an important member of the Wake Forest Garden Club and Wake Forest Birthplace Society, as well as a creative leader who played a major role in the beautification of the seminary campus. (Courtesy of Southeastern Baptist Theological Seminary.)

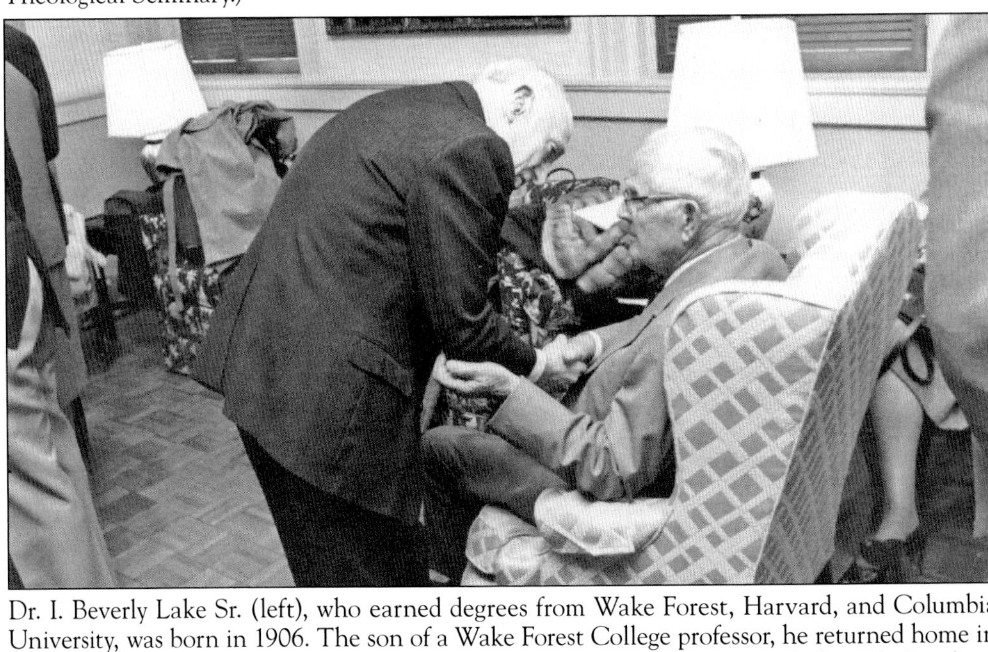

Dr. I. Beverly Lake Sr. (left), who earned degrees from Wake Forest, Harvard, and Columbia University, was born in 1906. The son of a Wake Forest College professor, he returned home in 1932 to teach at the law school. He later served as assistant attorney general of North Carolina, associate justice of the North Carolina Supreme Court, and in 1960, ran for governor. (Courtesy of Southeastern Baptist Theological Seminary.)

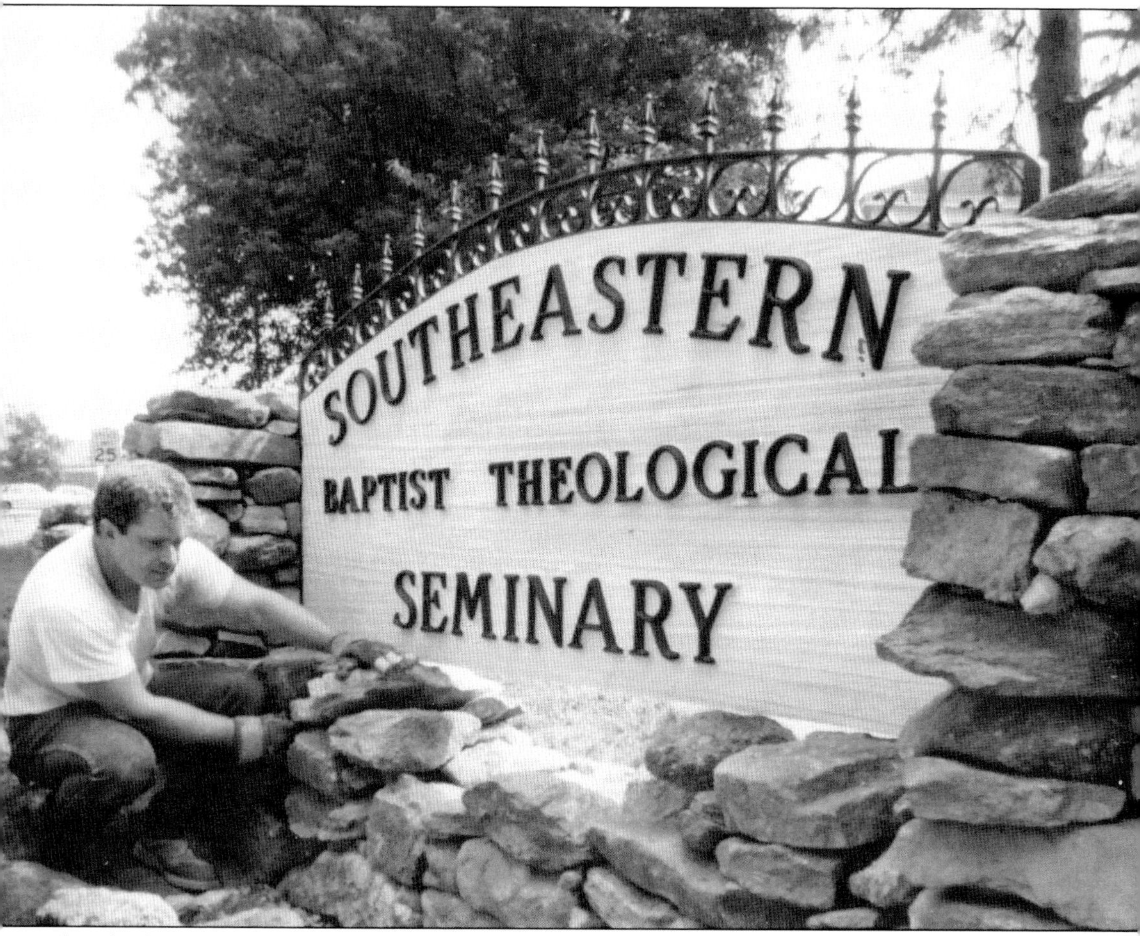

When he heard his calling, seminary student Doug Buttram felt compelled to respond. That was how he became a familiar face along the campus perimeter, as he spent the years from 1990 to 1994 systematically dismantling, cleaning, and reconstructing the rock wall that "Doctor" Tom Jeffries had built more than a century before. Wearing out a pair of leather gloves with each week of tedious work, Buttram removed the ivy covering the stones for the first time in the wall's storied history, revealing its 3,000 feet of original stonework. The project uncovered some interesting artifacts, including animal bones, pottery shards, and an antique light bulb. (Courtesy of Southeastern Baptist Theological Seminary.)

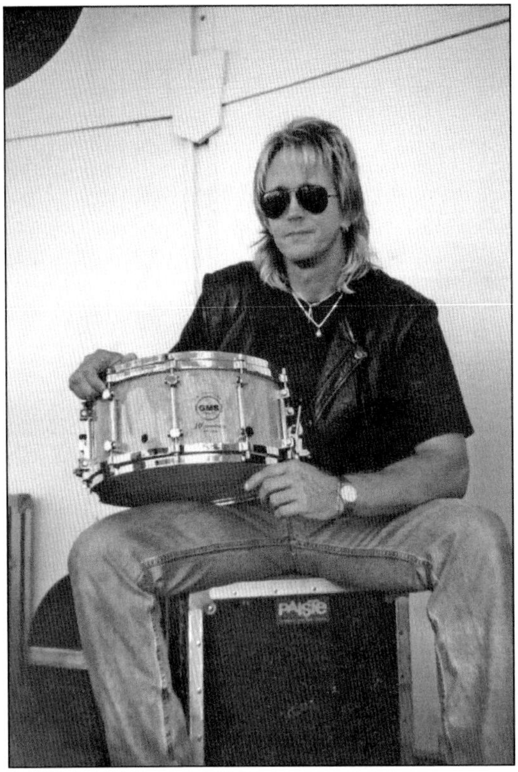

Dexter Horton, nephew of former Wake Forest golf coach Johnny Johnston, is a familiar face to generations of Wake Forest Elementary School graduates who know him as one of the school's teachers. Dexter also plays the drums for the Bill Lyerly Band, a roots-rock group that has performed with some of the most famous names in music today. (Courtesy of Betty Johnston Frankow.)

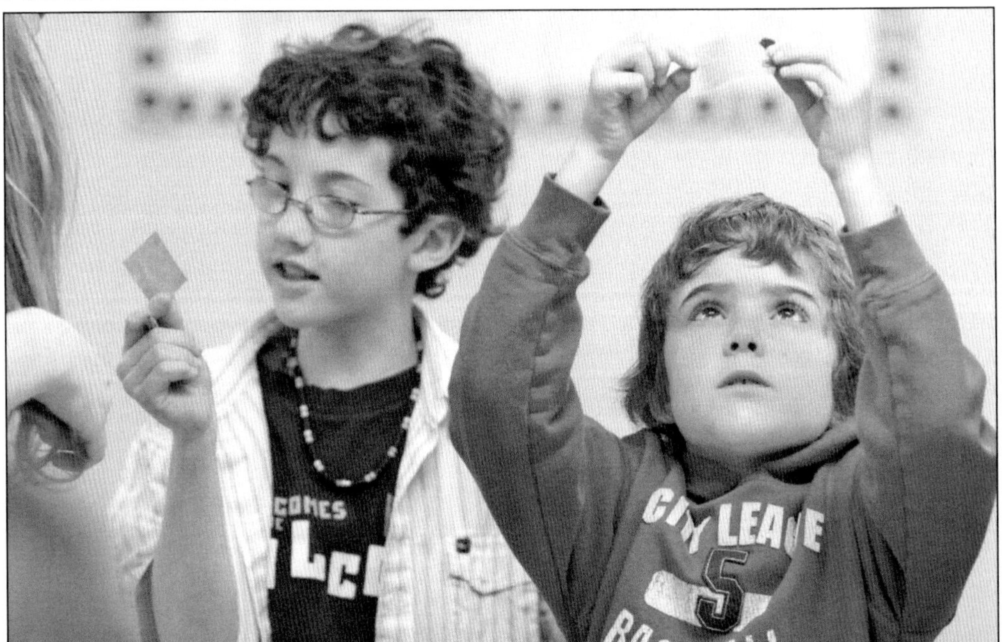

When he was cast in the CBS hit show *The New Adventures of Old Christine*, Trevor Gagnon (right) was a 10-year-old student at Wakefield Elementary School. Called "weirdly professional" by his adult costars, Trevor knows how to take his profession seriously while still being a kid. (Courtesy of the *News and Observer*.)

Nine

HISTORIC HOMES

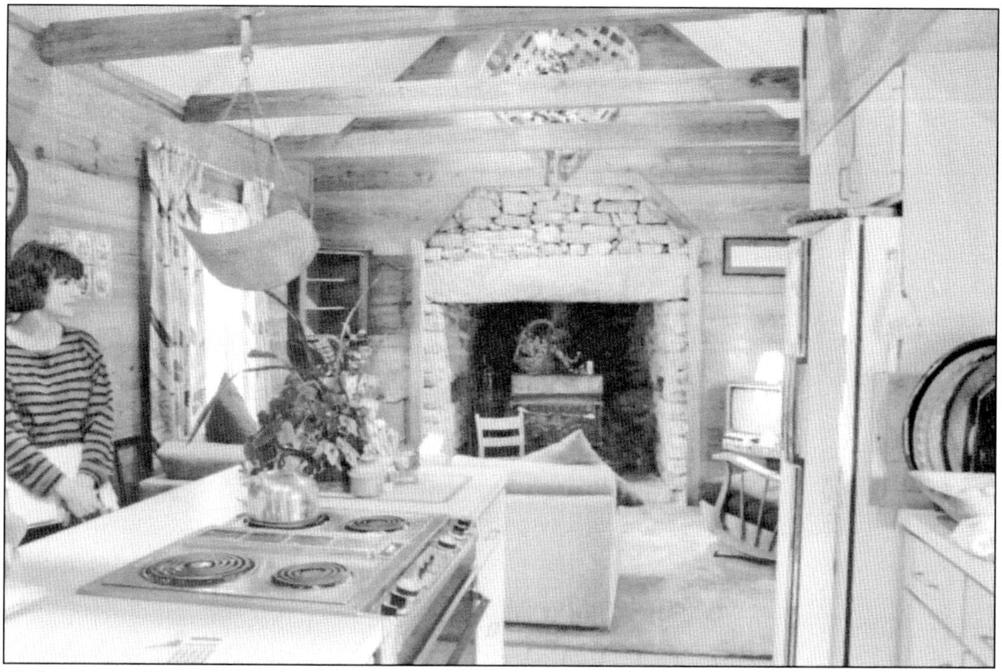

Wake Forest Township, which encompassed the town and surrounding rural areas including Rolesville, was established in 1868 and still boasts some of the county's most interesting historic architecture. Although the town of Wake Forest was always the most densely population section, significant homes are scattered throughout the township. Chief among them is the Wakefields plantation complex, north of Wake Forest along U.S. 1 and consisting of an imposing Federal–Greek Revival main house, two adjoining earlier structures, including a home and a kitchen, and an even older, original cabin dating to the 1700s. The rear portion of the main house, originally belonging to Ransom Sutherland, was a stop on the post road that went by the location. This contemporary photograph shows the gable-roofed kitchen with its massive stone chimney. Once a free-standing structure, it was eventually attached to the rest of the house. Records show the Sutherlands called their homestead "Wakefields" as early as 1807. (Courtesy of the North Carolina State Archives N.93.4.277.)

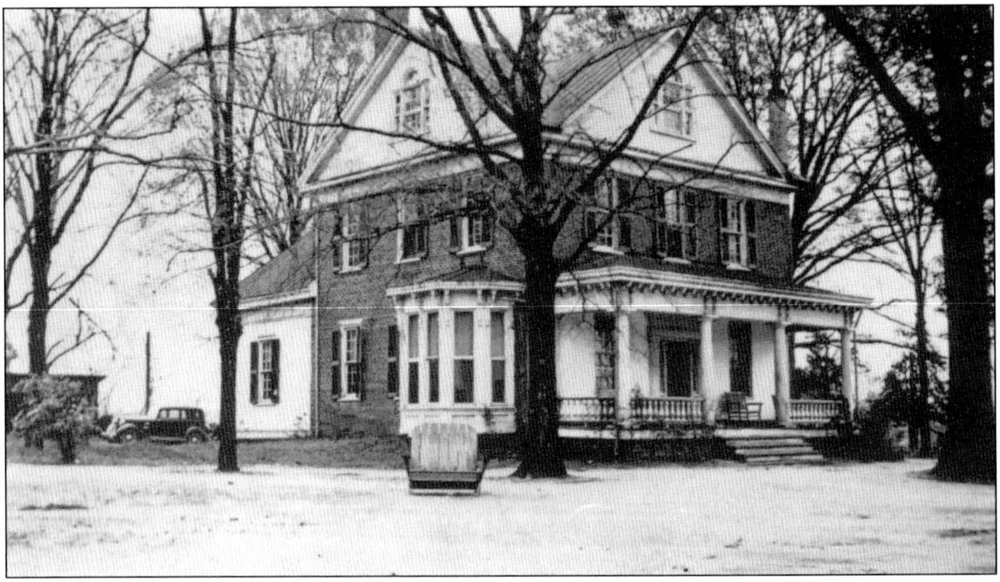

The North Brick House and South Brick House were two of three structures, the other being the original college administration building, that the Baptist State Convention commissioned for the new campus in the mid-1830s. All were built of brick made from local clay, and the homes originally housed faculty members. The administration building fell victim to the 1930s "firebug," and the North Brick is gone as well. The South Brick remains one of Wake County's two surviving antebellum brick buildings outside of Raleigh. (Courtesy of the Wake Forest Birthplace Museum and North Carolina State Archives N.72.9.292.)

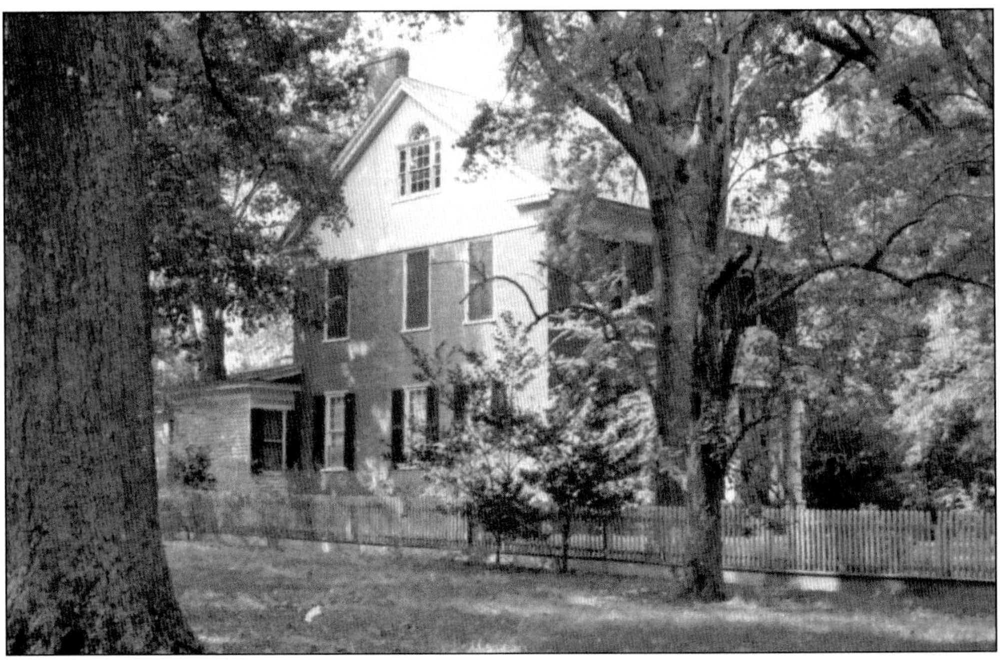

A young Harriet Brewer Powers, daughter of Ann Eliza Wait Brewer and John Marchant Brewer, was playing along the fence of her family home after the Civil War, when Sherman's soldiers straggled down Faculty Avenue. One pointed his rifle at her, and a terrified Harriet fled into the house. The soldiers killed one citizen while in Wake Forest. The college, which some feared wouldn't survive, reopened in January 1866. (Courtesy of Hallie Arrington Hearn.)

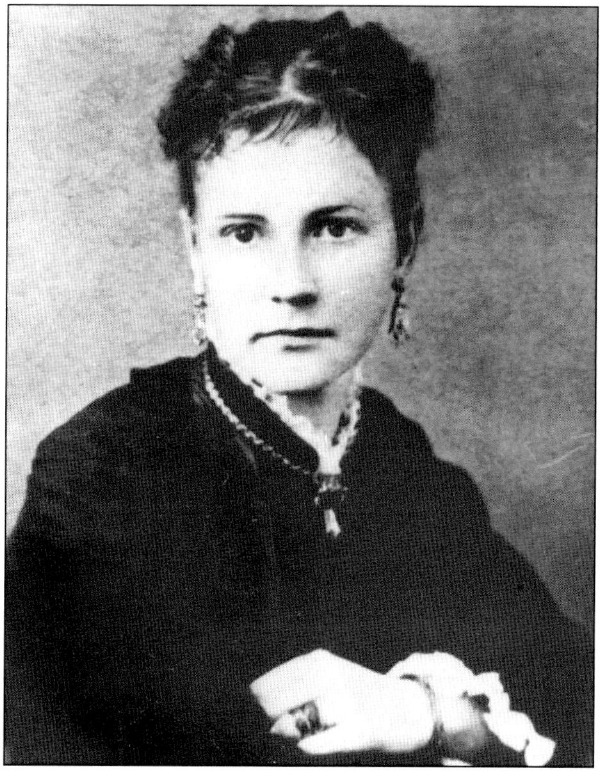

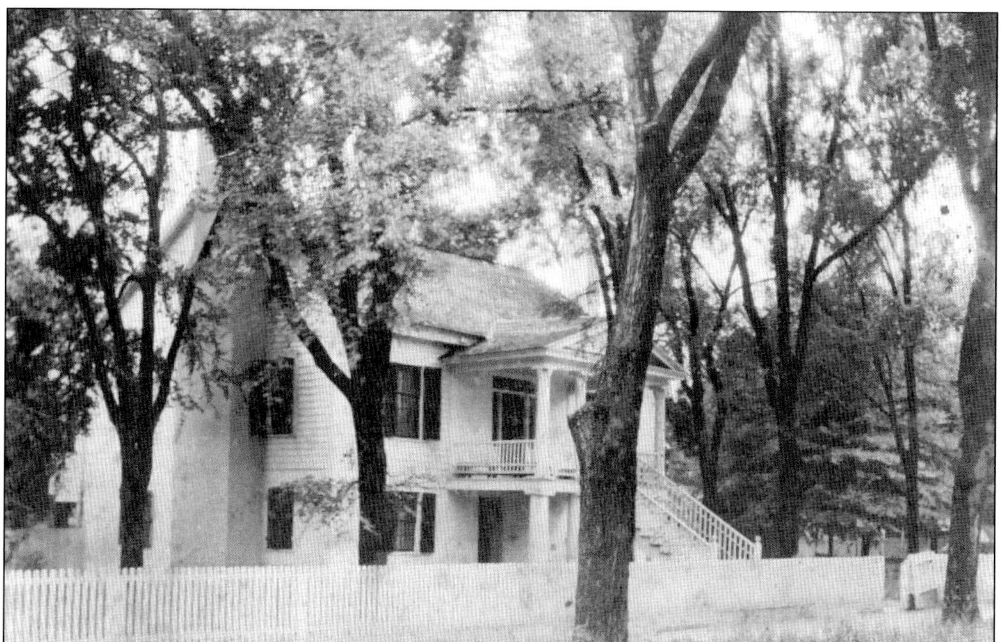

The John Brewer House, where Harriet was playing that day, was built around 1840 as a two-room log house but was given an upper floor addition during the Reconstruction era. With the original dwelling serving as an aboveground basement, a long staircase was designed to lead to the upstairs entry. (Courtesy of the Wake Forest Birthplace Museum.)

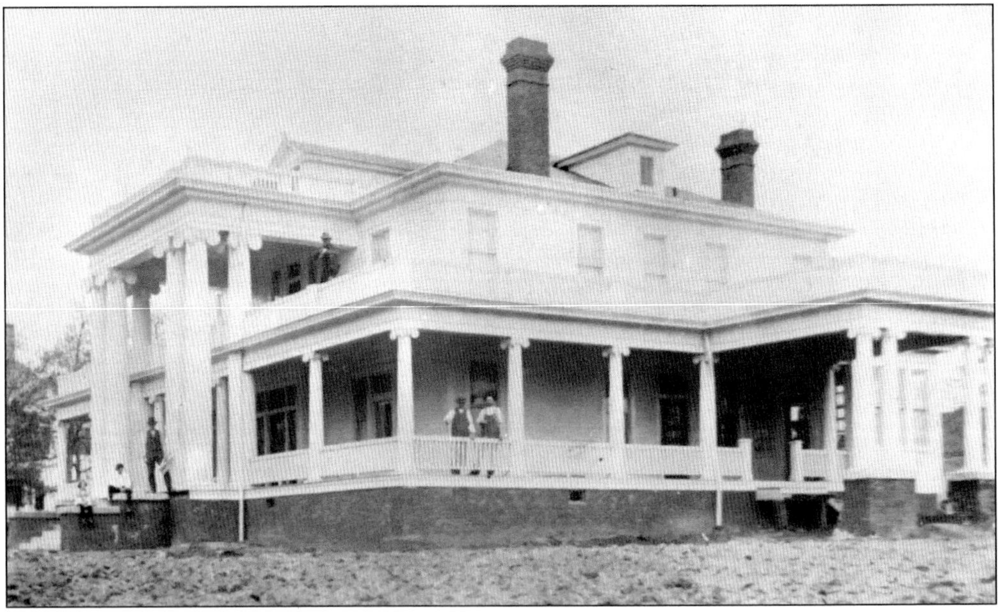

William R. Powell, of Glen Royall Cotton Mill, built this majestic home on Faculty Avenue at the beginning of the 20th century, nearly losing it to foreclosure after the mill went bankrupt in 1934. With no cash for taxes, he paid the bill with mill bonds. In later years, the house was home to the first coeds to enroll at Wake Forest College. (Courtesy of the Wake Forest Birthplace Museum.)

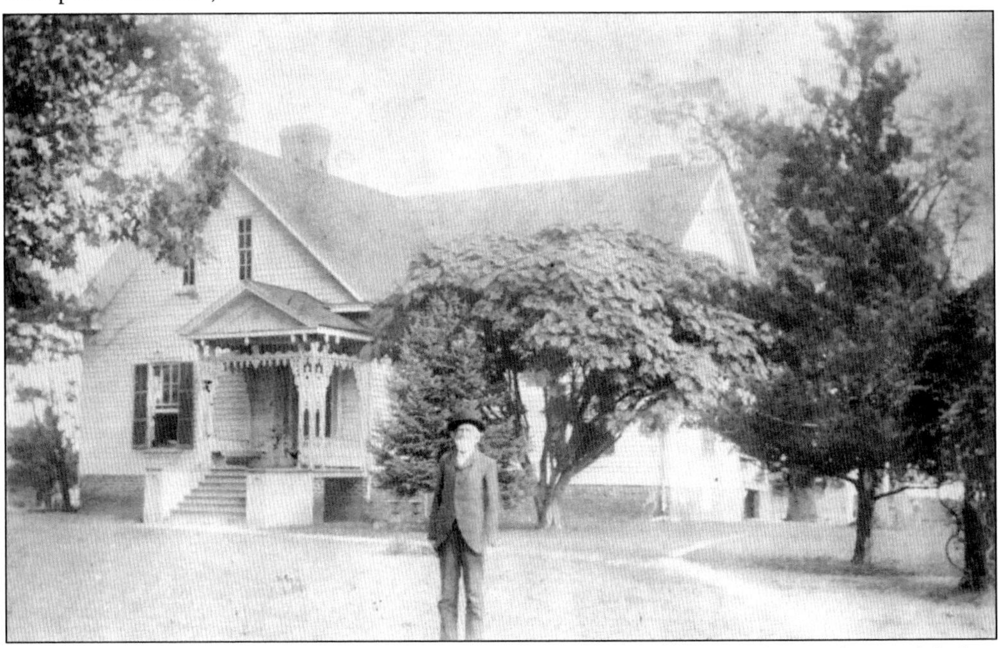

Crenshaw Hall was once a pair of small 19th-century houses put together and remodeled to form a type of center hall, Greek Revival structure. By 1860, the Crenshaw family had amassed a tobacco farming operation with 1,400 acres of land and 42 slaves. This photograph, c. 1910, was taken shortly before the current full-facade porch with its fluted Corinthian columns was added. (Courtesy of the North Carolina State Archives N.91.6.36.)

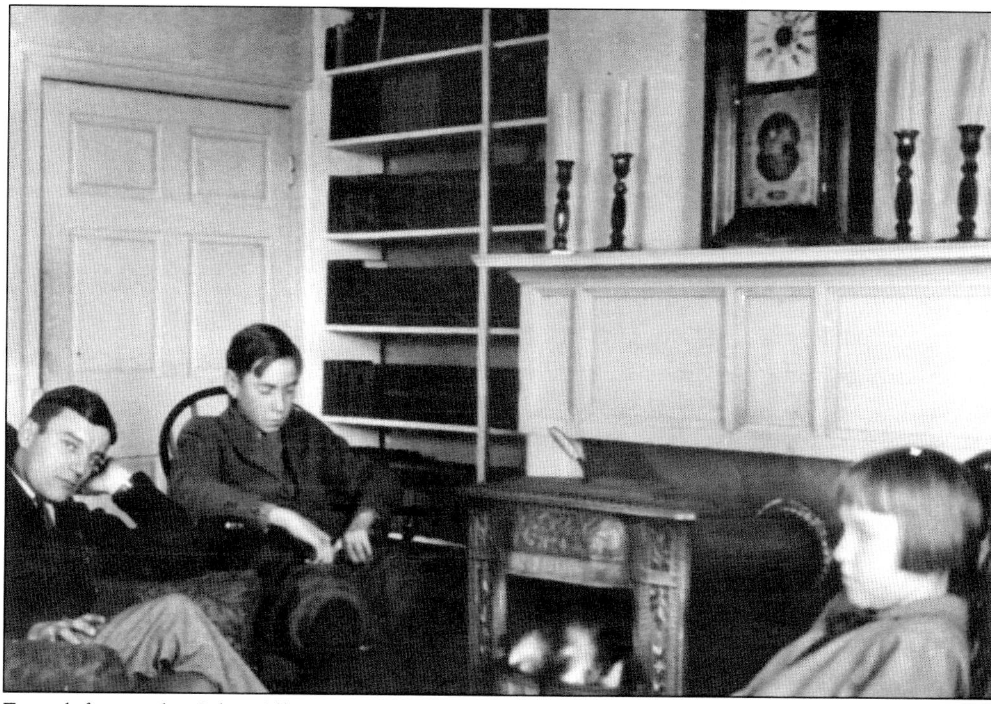

From left to right, John Allen, Kenan Seawell, and Octavia Seawell were photographed sitting in the library at Oakforest around 1925. The house, constructed in several stages, was built by John Smith beginning in 1803 on land originally acquired by his father. The home is a mix of Greek Revival and Federal styles inside and out. Boxwoods lining the front walk are thought to predate the Civil War. (Courtesy of Speed Massenburg and family.)

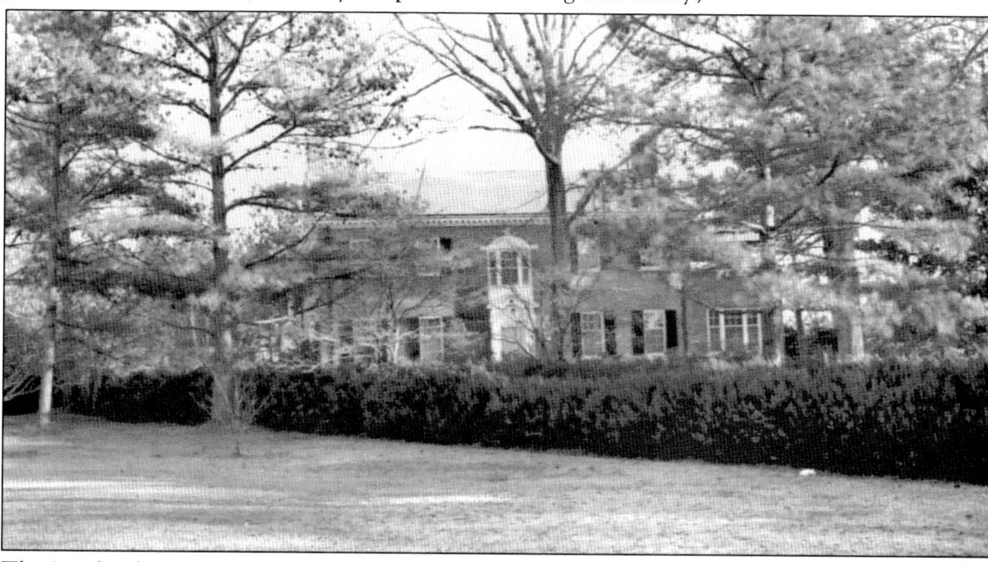

The Mackie house, built for Dr. George Mackie and his wife, Kathleen, in 1934, is a two-story brick affair designed by Raleigh architect William H. Deitrick and constructed by Durham contractor George W. Kane. The Colonial Revival home, with its large Palladian window and hedge-lined driveway, remains a North Main Street landmark. (Courtesy of the North Carolina State Archives N.79.9.1080.)

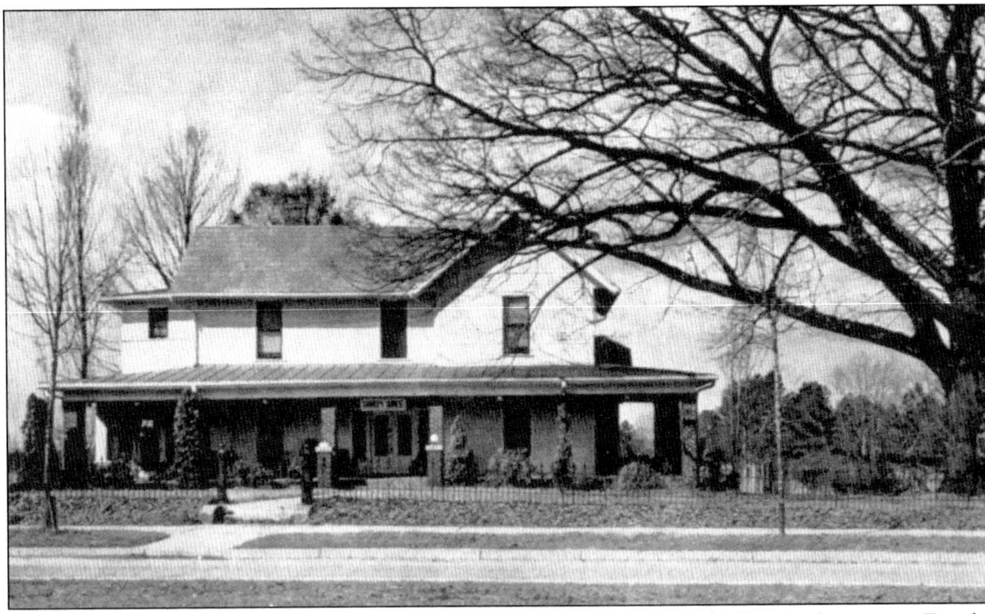

Beginning in the 1920s, motorists traveling U.S. 1 passed through Wake Forest along quiet Faculty Avenue. Some stopped for the night at the Shady Oaks Tourist Home, owned by Jack Medlin. Medlin also operated the next-door filling station until neighbors, anguished over the presence of gas pumps, brought their opposition to the North Carolina Supreme Court and won. (Courtesy of the North Carolina State Archives N.71.7.272.)

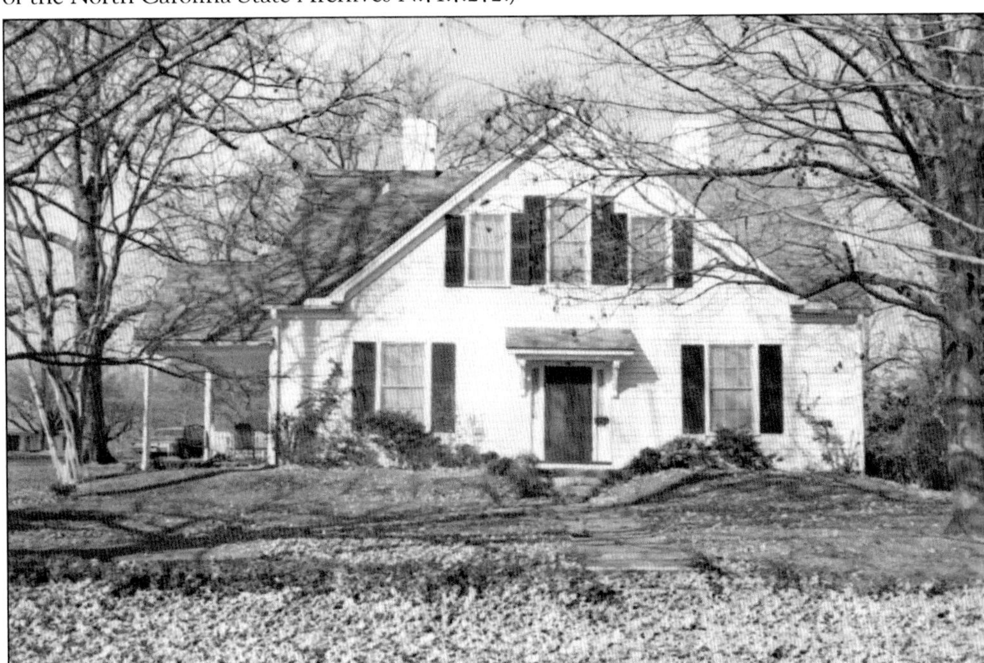

Prof. James L. Lake and his family, including son I. Beverly Lake, moved into this house at 403 North Main Street in 1915. This move was their first to a home with electric lights. I. Beverly Lake later became a Wake Forest law professor, North Carolina Supreme Court justice, and 1960 gubernatorial candidate. (Courtesy of the North Carolina State Archives N.74.1.571.)

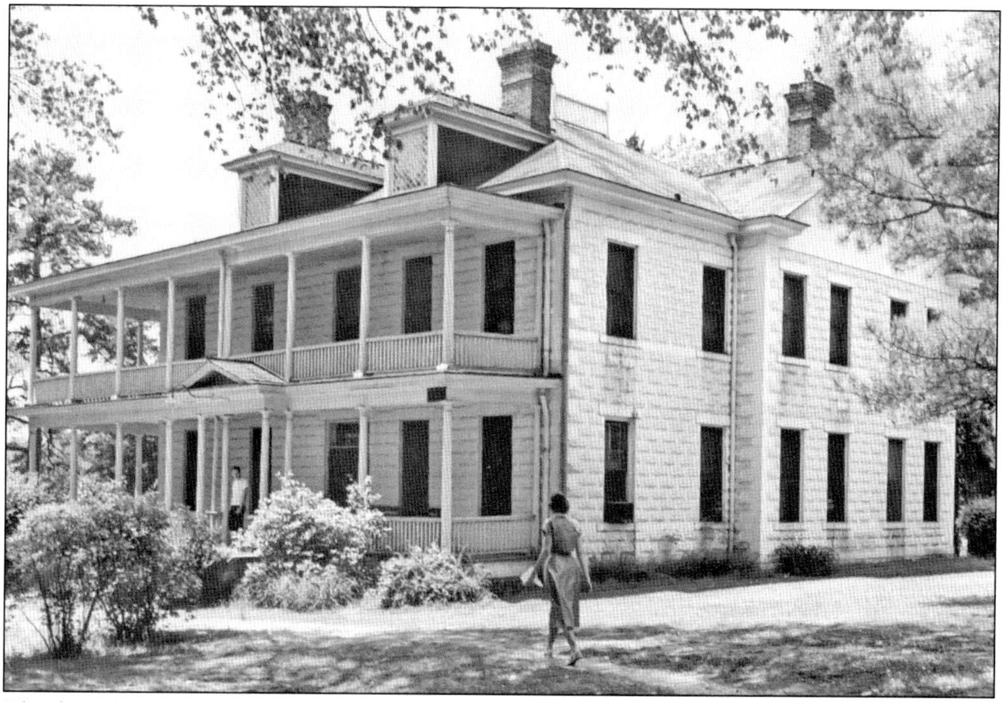

The former college infirmary, built in 1906, was located at the southwestern corner of campus where the seminary's Lolley Dormitory now stands. It served the college and town. Wake Forest medical students did their internships here, though rumor has it the young men were not permitted to provide care for expectant mothers, as it was deemed improper. (Courtesy of Southeastern Baptist Theological Seminary.)

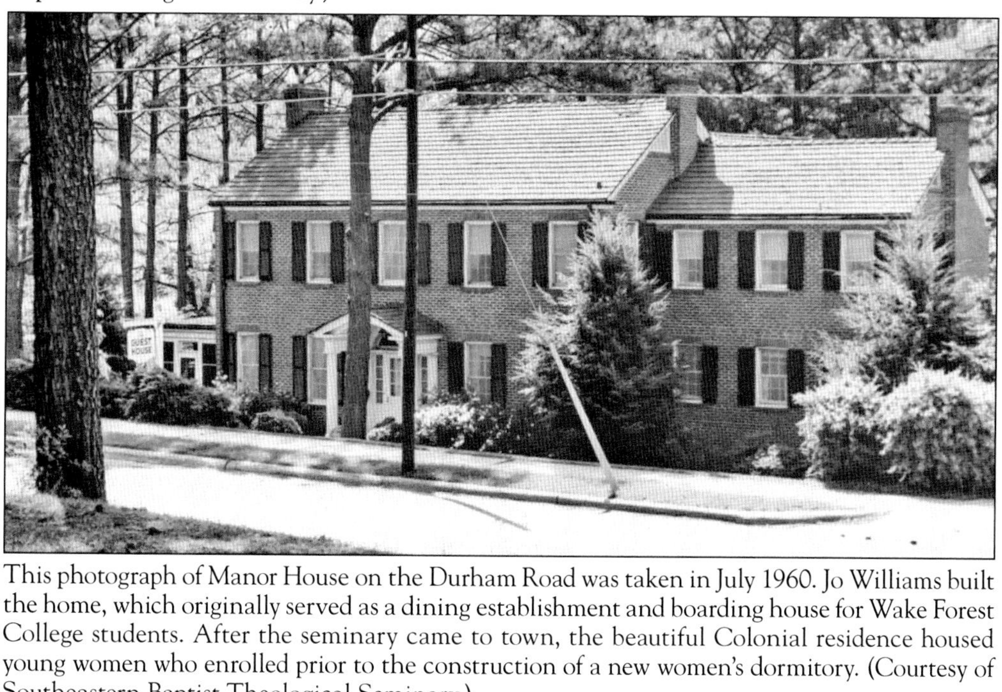

This photograph of Manor House on the Durham Road was taken in July 1960. Jo Williams built the home, which originally served as a dining establishment and boarding house for Wake Forest College students. After the seminary came to town, the beautiful Colonial residence housed young women who enrolled prior to the construction of a new women's dormitory. (Courtesy of Southeastern Baptist Theological Seminary.)

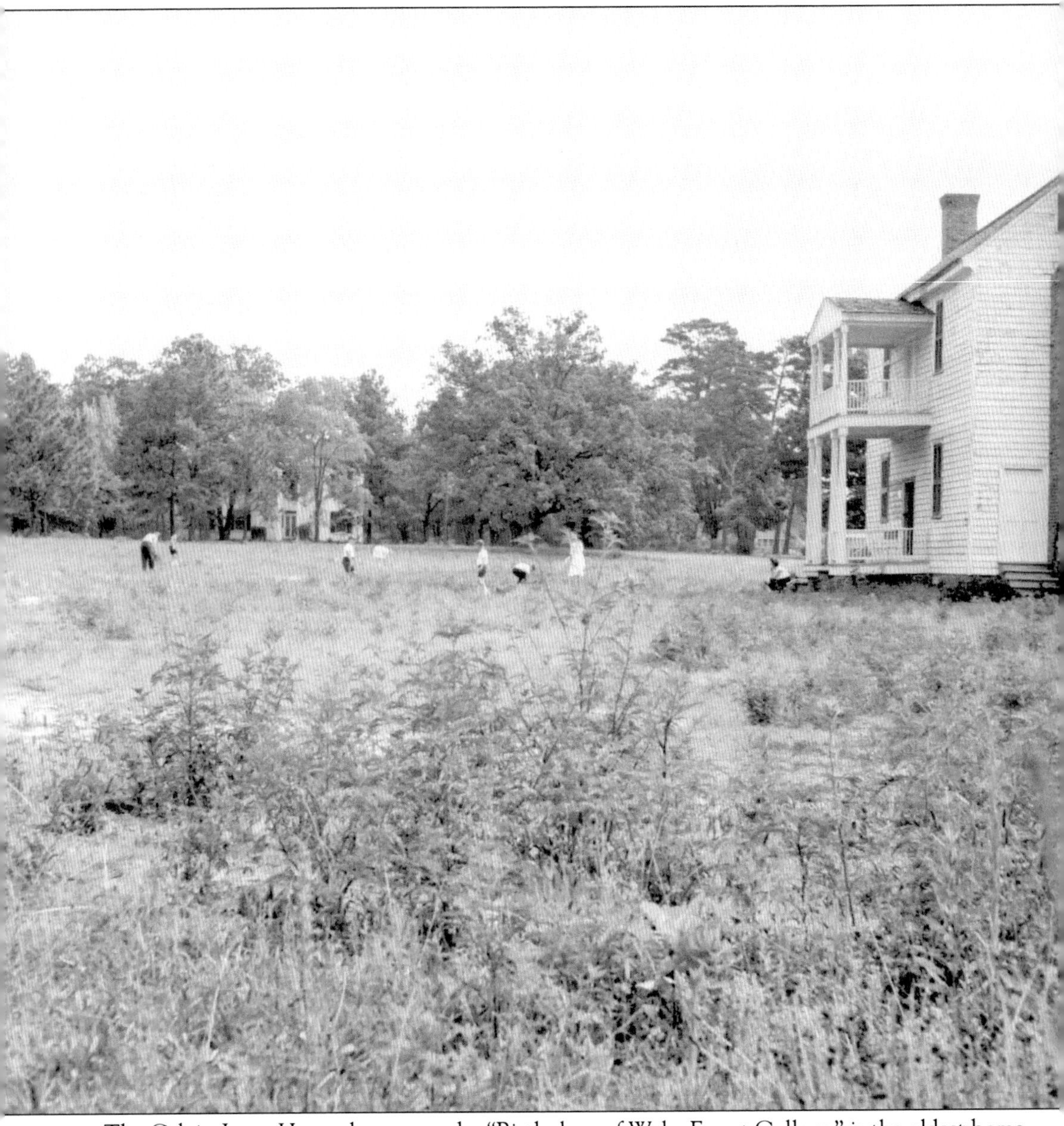

The Calvin Jones House, known as the "Birthplace of Wake Forest College," is the oldest home in Wake Forest. Begun in 1820, when Dr. Calvin Jones of New England purchased 615 acres in Wake Forest Township from Davis Battle, the home was originally built as a sturdy, two-story frame farmhouse. When John Purefoy, a Baptist minister, learned that Dr. Jones planned to sell the property, he urged the Baptist State Convention to acquire it as a training school for ministers. The Convention bought the farm for $2,000, and the school opened in February 1834. Pres. Samuel Wait taught classes in the home's comfortable rooms, where he lived with his family, while students boarded in upstairs rooms and the property's outbuildings. At that time, the farmhouse was at its original location near the center of the present-day campus. Following a pair of moves, it finally found a home on North Main Street. This photograph was taken in July 1963, when residents held a party to clear the grassy field of rocks. (Courtesy of the Wake Forest Birthplace Museum.)

Ten

COMMUNITY LIFE

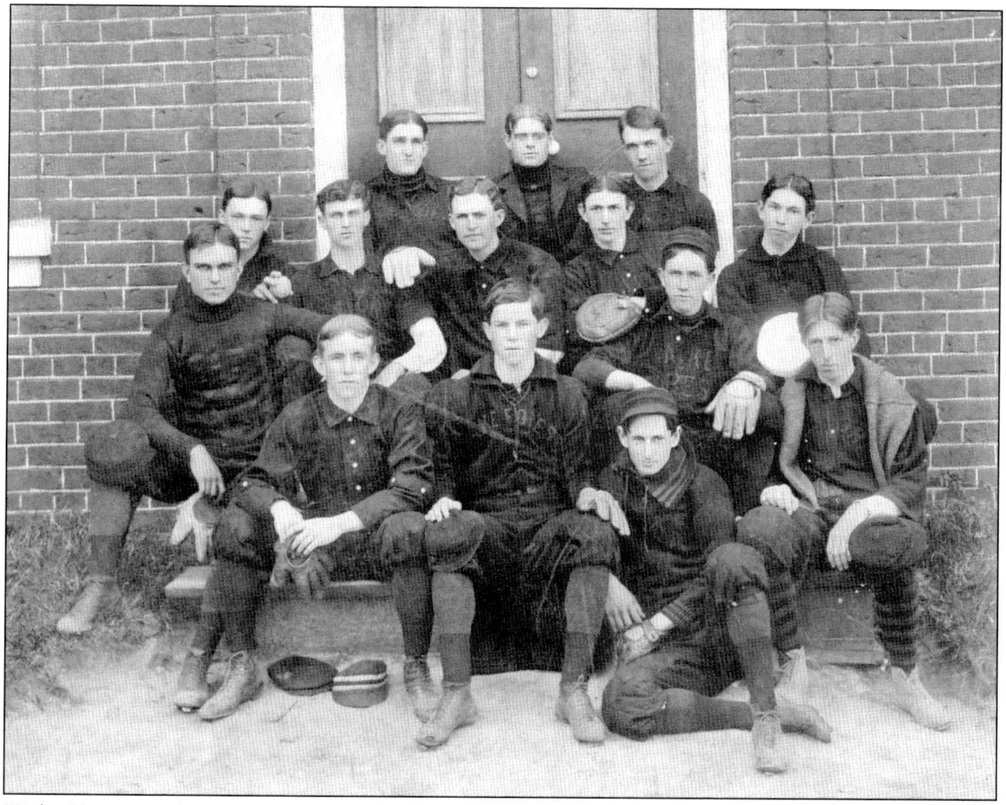

Wake Forest underwent major changes between the 19th and 20th centuries. At the end of the Civil War, the town had only 15 houses, one hotel, and one store. But the arrival of the Raleigh and Gaston train station in 1874 changed everything, providing the foundation for the social and commercial networks that formed the growing town. Electricity came in 1909. And with a population of 1,115, the community known as Wake Forest College officially changed its name to the Town of Wake Forest. But the school and its town would remain intertwined, as both enjoyed the other's company and took pride in each other's accomplishments. This early photograph of the Wake Forest College baseball team was already documenting a piece of history when it was taken; the first collegiate baseball game in the state had been played between Wake Forest and North Carolina in May 1891. Wake Forest scored three runs in the 11th inning for a 10-7 win. The game was played in Raleigh. (Wake Forest Birthplace Museum.)

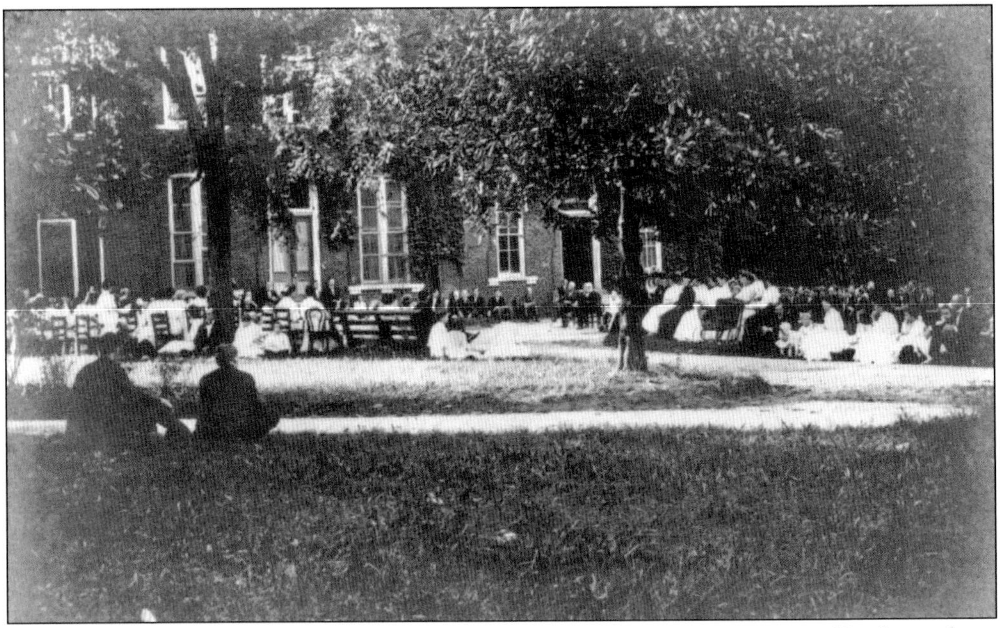

The spring commencement ceremony on the college grounds was an event enjoyed by the students and townsfolk alike. This photograph, *c.* 1910, was taken around the same time that Wake Forest and its college were beginning the exciting transition to electricity from coal oil and kerosene. (Courtesy of the Wake Forest Birthplace Museum.)

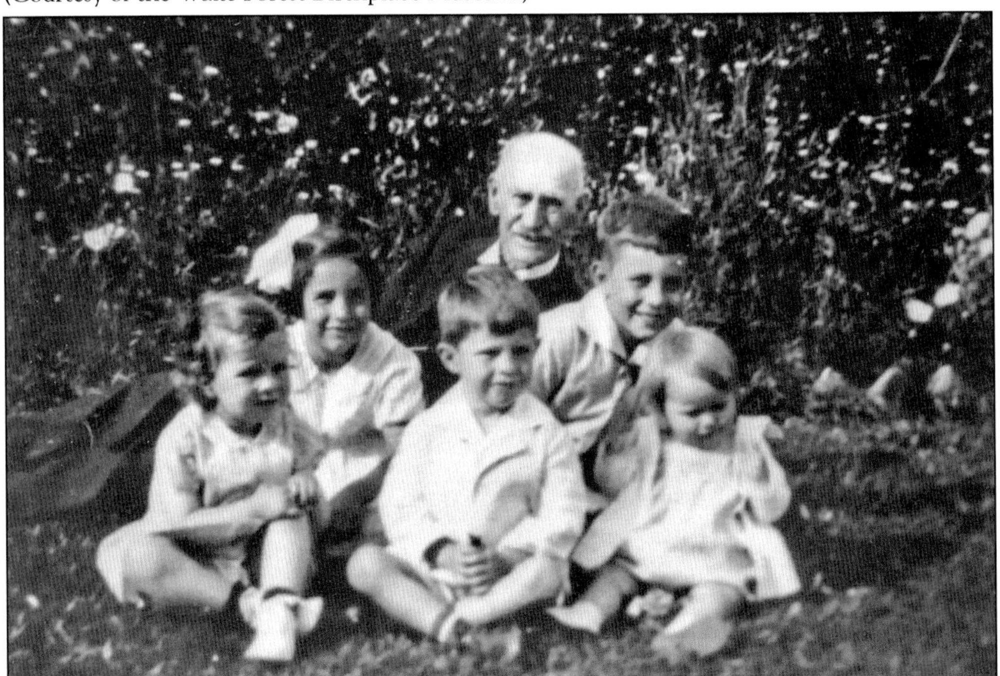

Everyone knew the Lake family. Photographed in the summer of 1937, Wake Forest College professor James L. Lake posed with 5 of his 11 grandchildren: from left to right are Virginia Lake, Bettie Marable Patterson, I. Beverly Lake Jr., Grady Patterson Jr., and Sarah Patterson. (Courtesy of the Wake Forest Birthplace Museum.)

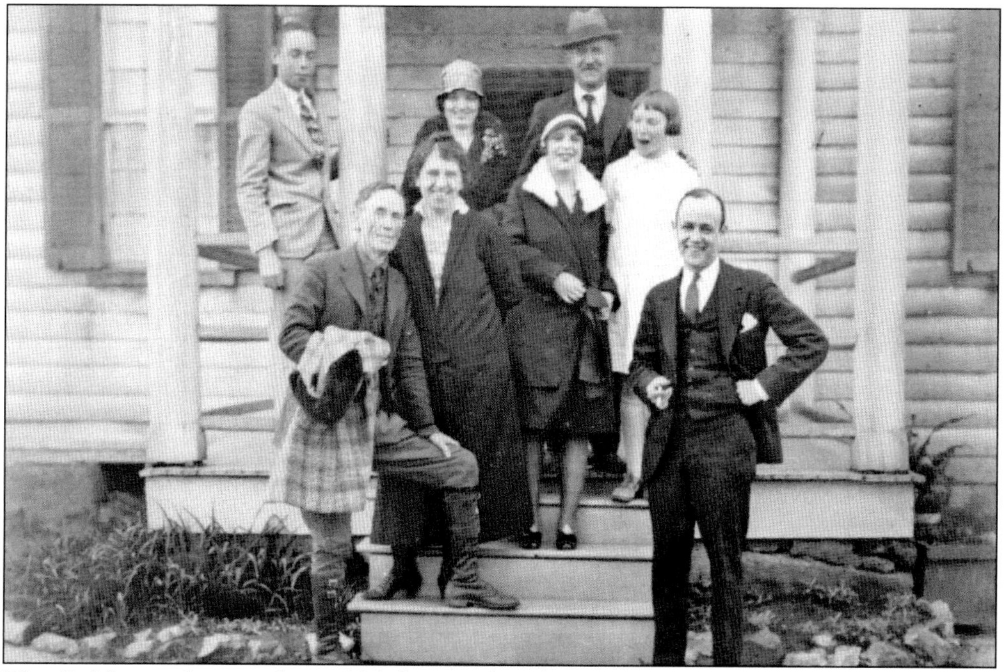

This Oakforest photograph, *c.* 1925, features friends and family from Raleigh. They are, from left to right, (first row) J. L. Seawell, Pearl Carver Seawell, Lou Hinton, Octavia Seawell, and Jack Hinton; (second row) Kenan Seawell, Mrs. James Denmark, and J. W. Jones. Visitors to Oakforest would ride the train to Forestville, disembarking on the tracks directly in front of the old plantation house. (Courtesy of the North Carolina State Archives N.93.8.63.)

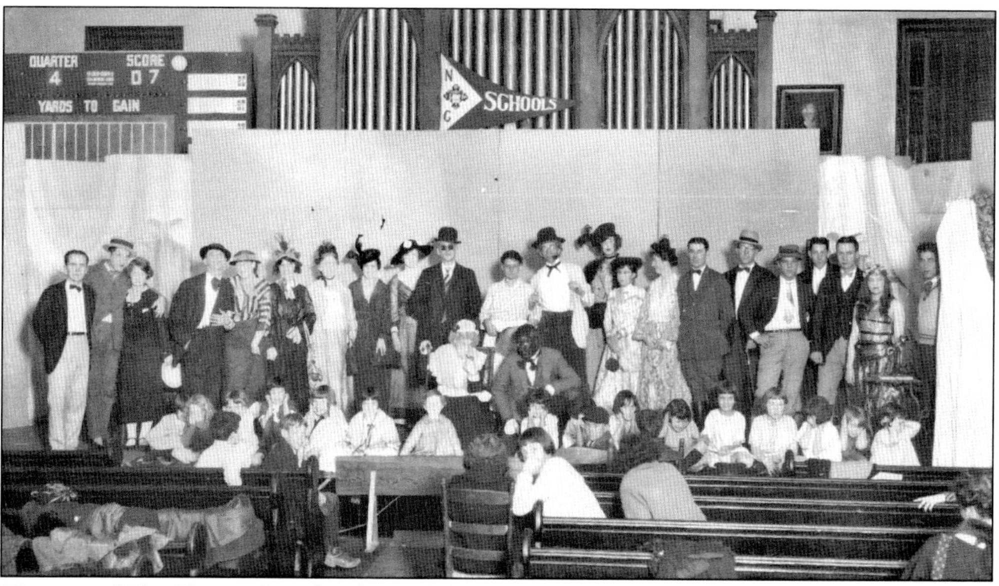

The cast of *The Flapper Grandmother* gathered for this group photograph on February 23, 1925. Their stage production, performed at Wingate Memorial Hall on the Wake Forest College campus, was directed by Thelma Richardson. The three-act musical comedy was written by Mollie Moore Godbold and Hettie Jane Dunnaway and was described as being full of pep, dash, and spirit. (Courtesy of the Wake Forest Birthplace Museum.)

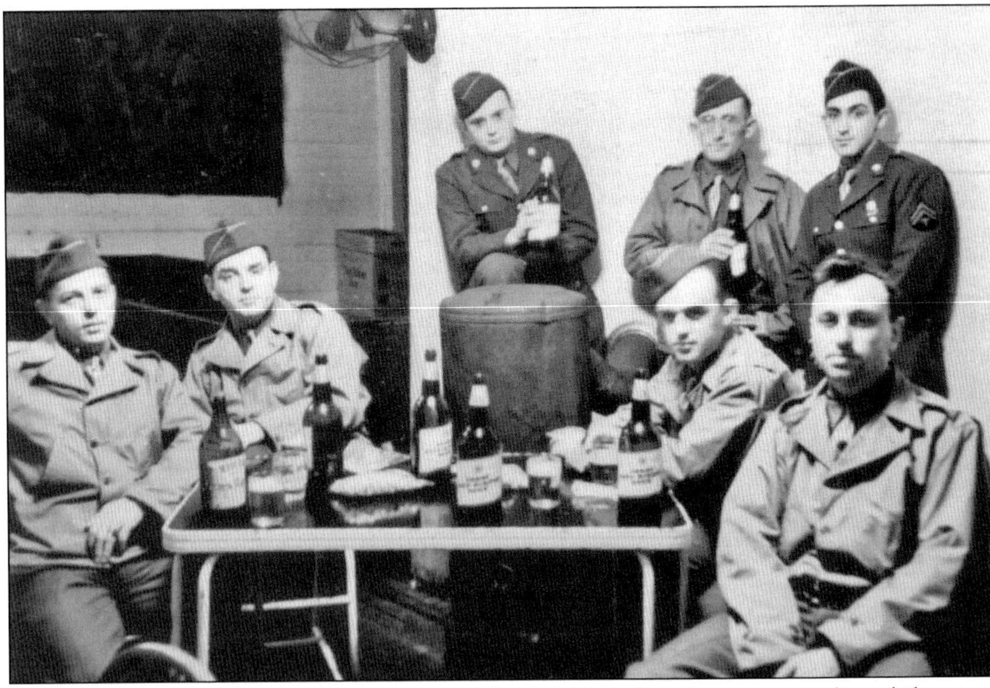

These soldiers found time to socialize while serving their country at the Army Finance School around 1942. As Grady Patterson recalled to the *Wake Forest Gazette*, the school "was moved here from Fort Benjamin Harrison in Ohio and was really the salvation of the college, which had fallen upon difficult financial times due to the war." (Courtesy of the Wake Forest Birthplace Museum.)

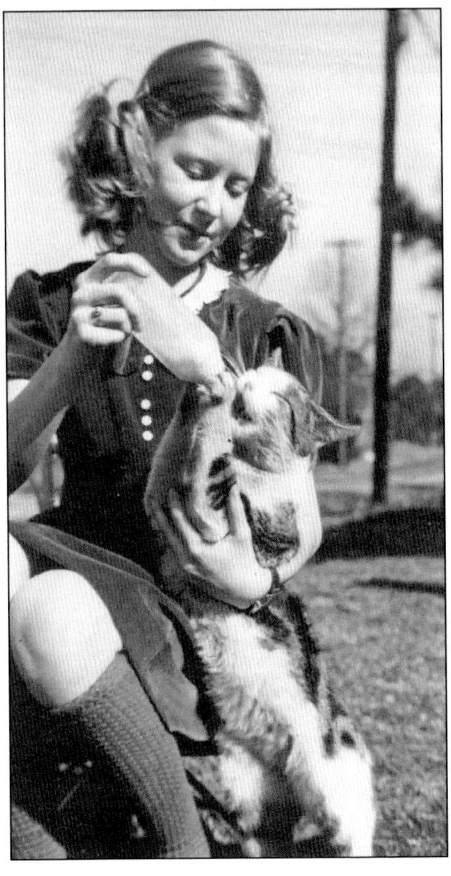

This photograph, captioned "Mary and Major—the smiling cat," was found in a wartime album compiled by a soldier at the Army Finance School. (Courtesy of the Wake Forest Birthplace Museum.)

The old well, *c.* 1935, was likely dug by the Wilson Artesian Company. Records suggest it was 101 feet deep, 70 feet through solid rock. The well was eventually moved to the Wake Forest Birthplace Museum on North Main Street, where it was honored with a dedication ceremony from devoted alumni and townsfolk on April 21, 2001. (Courtesy of the Wake Forest Birthplace Museum.)

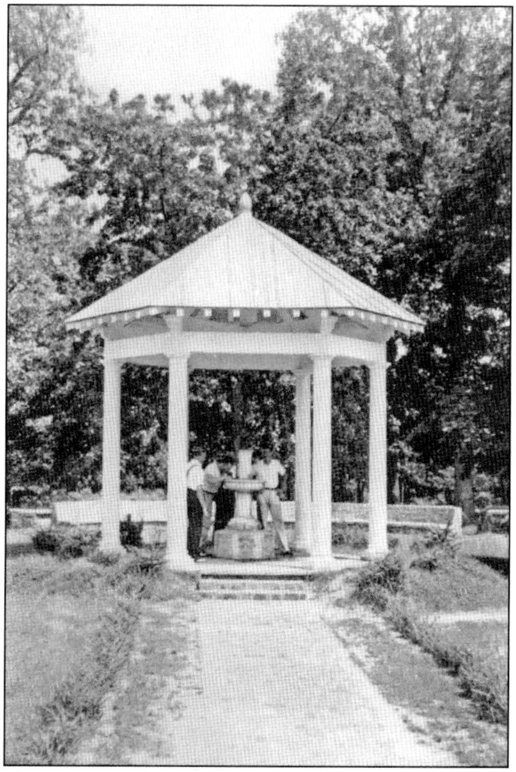

The Magnolia Festival was an annual event staged each spring by the Physical Education Department of Wake Forest College. Pageants, dances, skits, and music were included in a program organized for town and gown audiences. The highlight was the presentation of the Festival Queen and her court. This photograph of a dance routine was taken during the festival's heyday in the early 1950s. (Courtesy of the Wake Forest Birthplace Museum.)

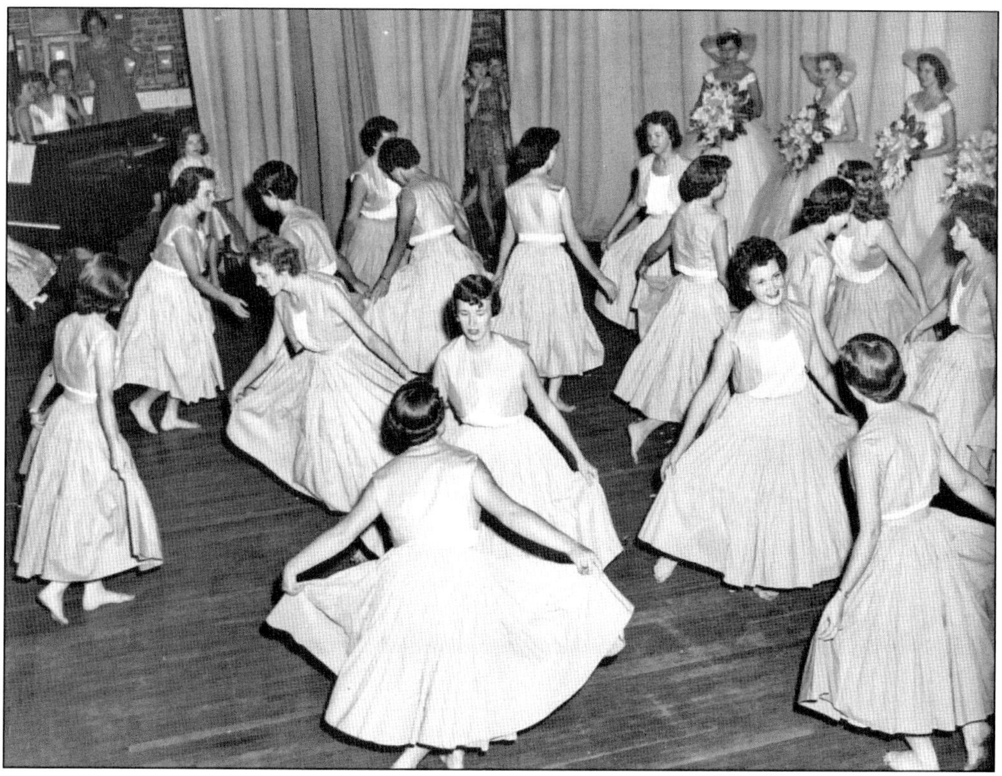

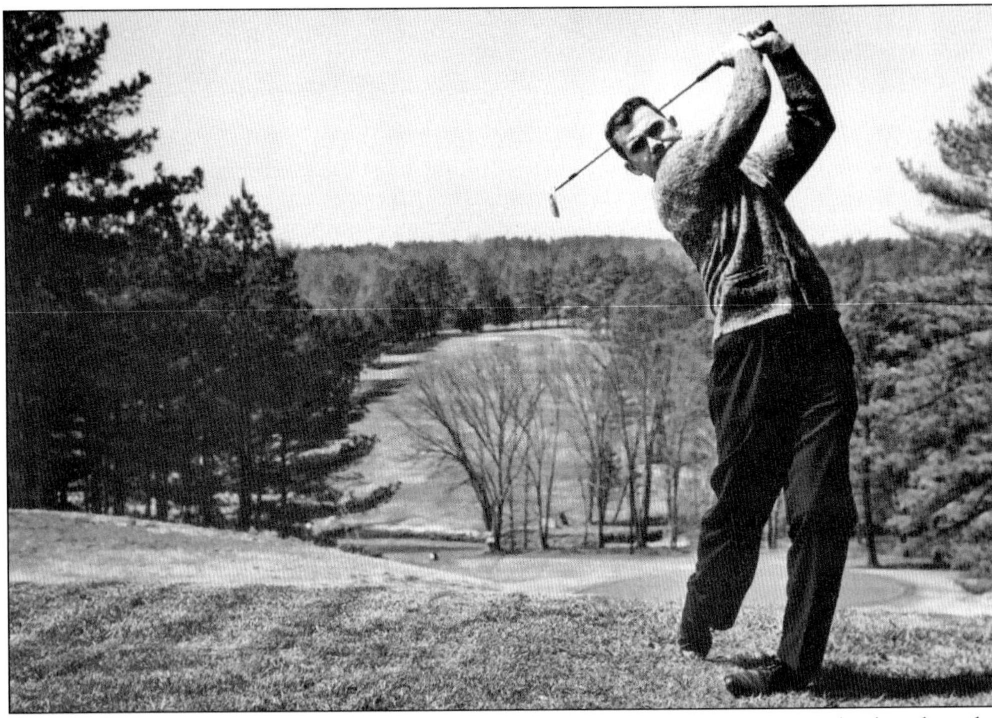

Jack Wilson of Warrenton, North Carolina, a golf champ in 1965–1966, frequently played on the Paschal Golf Course. The nine-hole course was built shortly after the college purchased the 155-acre tract in 1915. When Durham Road was built in 1930, some of the greens lay in its right of way and had to be relocated onto land loaned by Dr. George Paschal. (Courtesy of Southeastern Baptist Theological Seminary.)

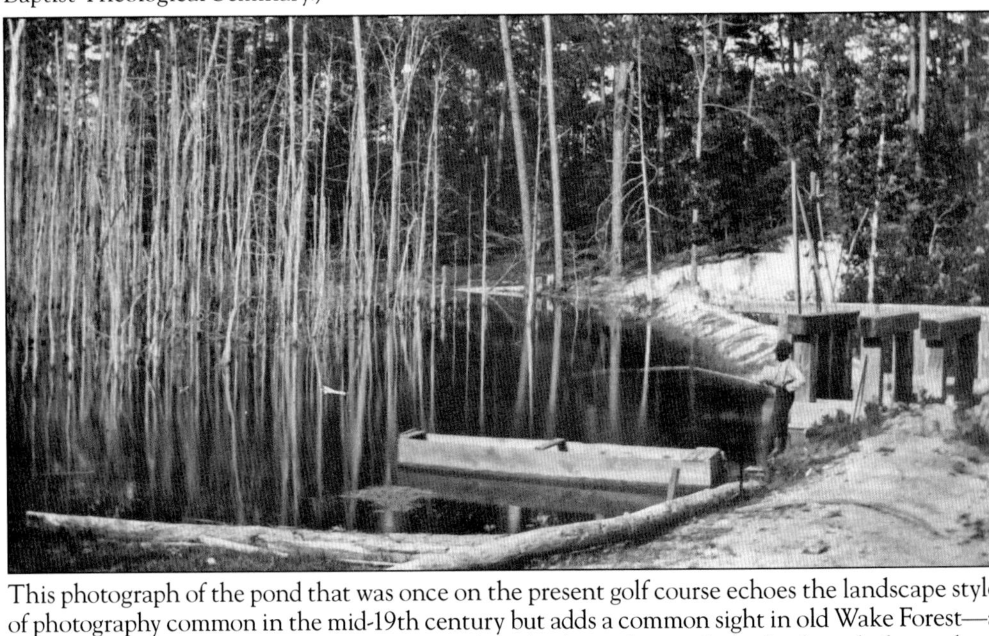

This photograph of the pond that was once on the present golf course echoes the landscape style of photography common in the mid-19th century but adds a common sight in old Wake Forest—a young man fishing beside a wooden boat. It is thought this is the pond which, cleared of trees, later became the town's first swimming pool. (Courtesy of the Wake Forest Birthplace Museum.)

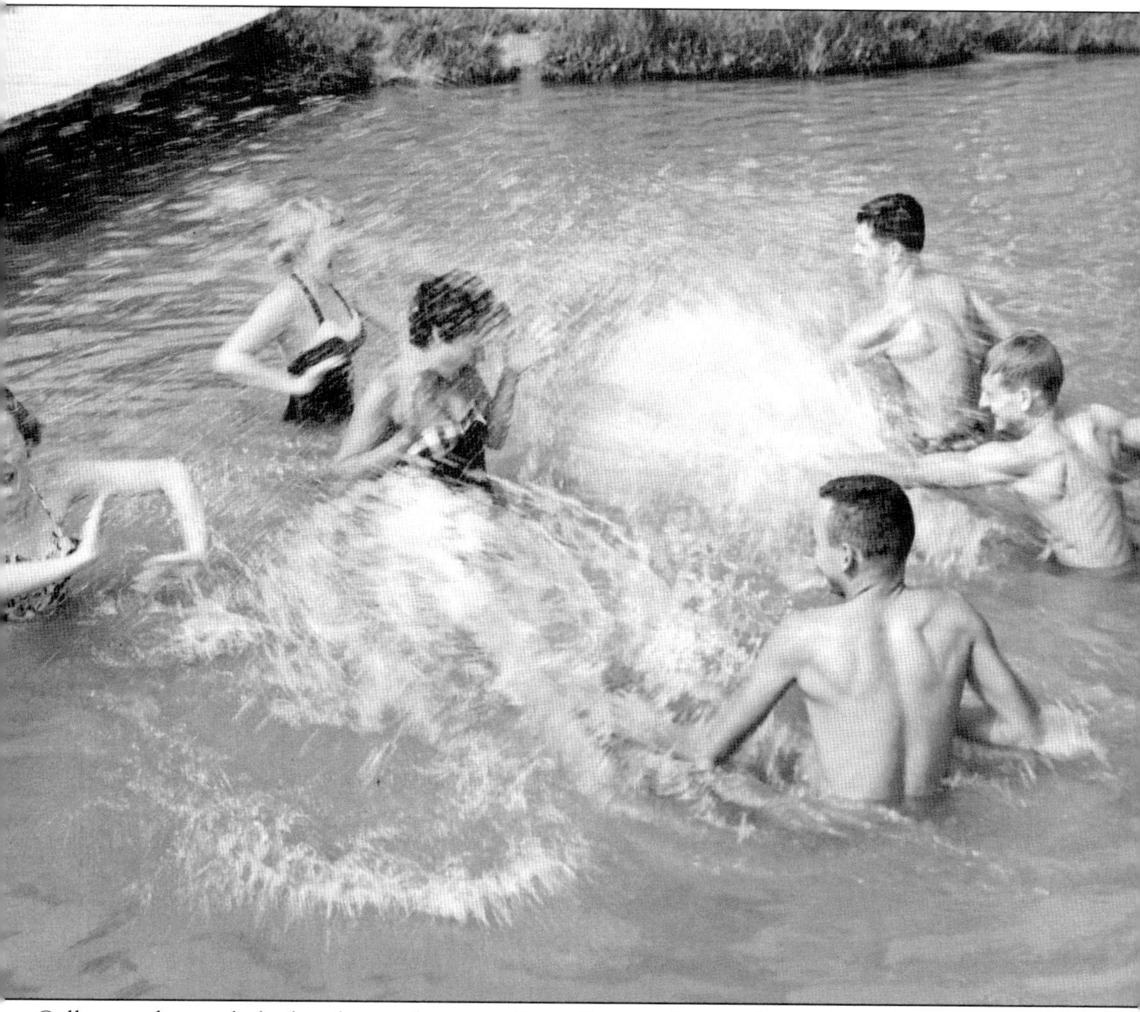

College students splashed in the pond water at Camp Kanata, the wooded outdoor YMCA facility set on 150 rolling acres just west of Wake Forest along the Durham Road. (Courtesy of the Wake Forest Birthplace Museum.)

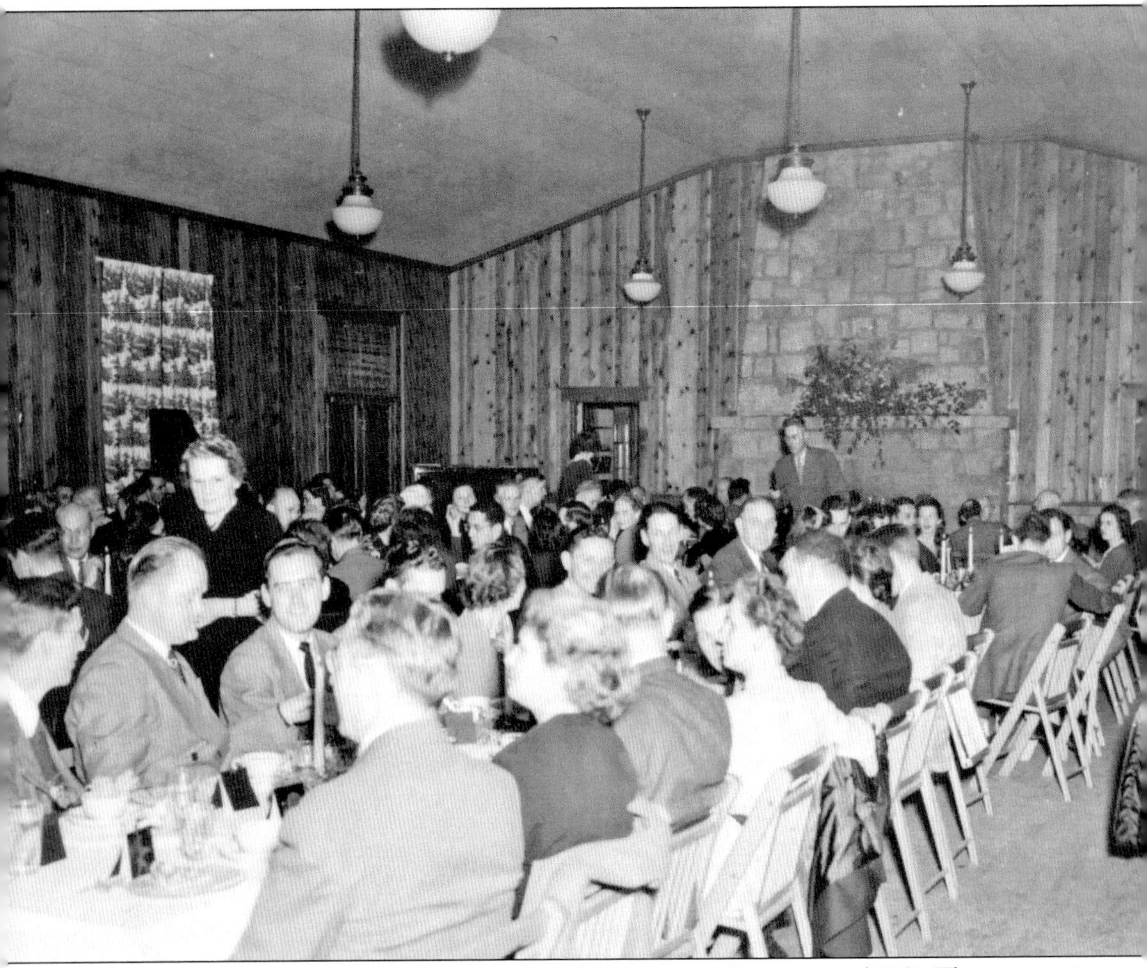

College faculty members enjoyed a dinner at the community house around 1950. The community house was another project funded by Pres. Franklin Delano Roosevelt's Works Progress Administration. In 1940, the town purchased the property from Dr. Solomon Holding, and the WPA spent $67,117 building the house. (Courtesy of the Wake Forest Birthplace Museum.)

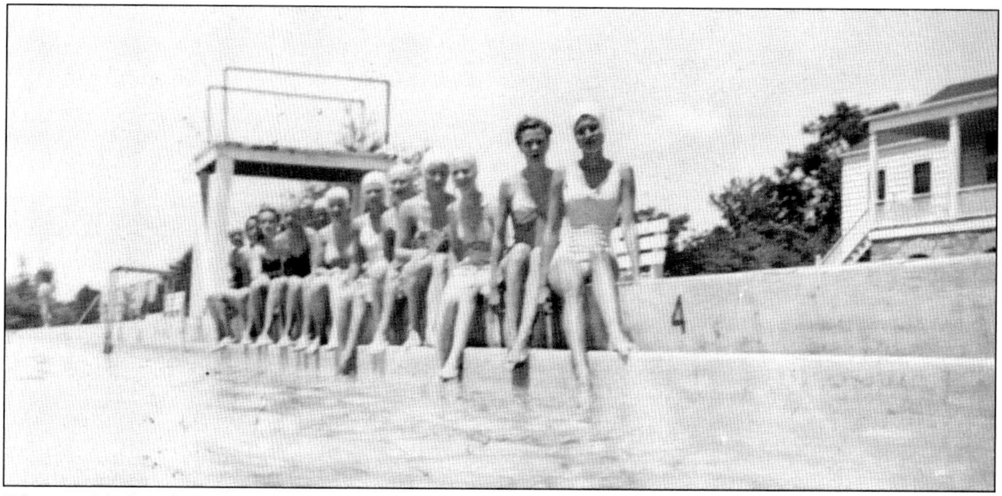

The pool behind the community house was built in 1921, predating the WPA community house project by two decades. The Wake Forest Women's Health Club put the location to good use, swimming for exercise in the middle part of the 20th century. (Courtesy of the Wake Forest Birthplace Museum.)

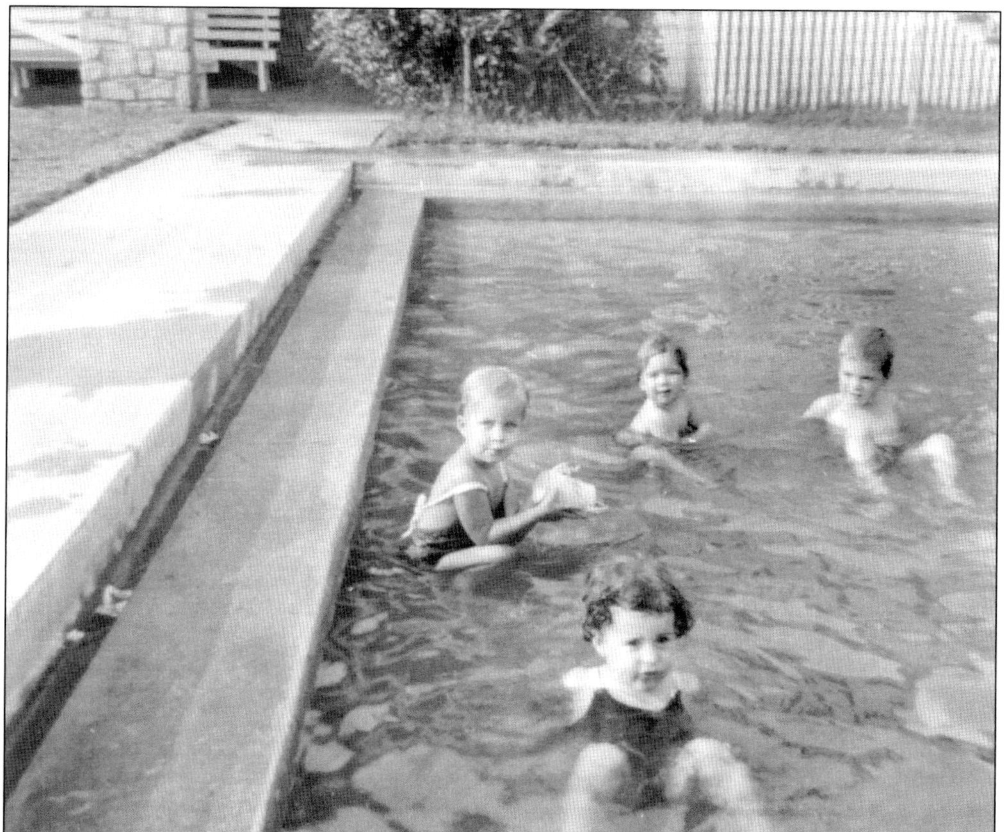

Back in those days, residents recall, the community house also had a smaller children's pool. These toddlers, basking on a summer day, appear to be relaxing in its shallow water. (Courtesy of the Wake Forest Birthplace Museum.)

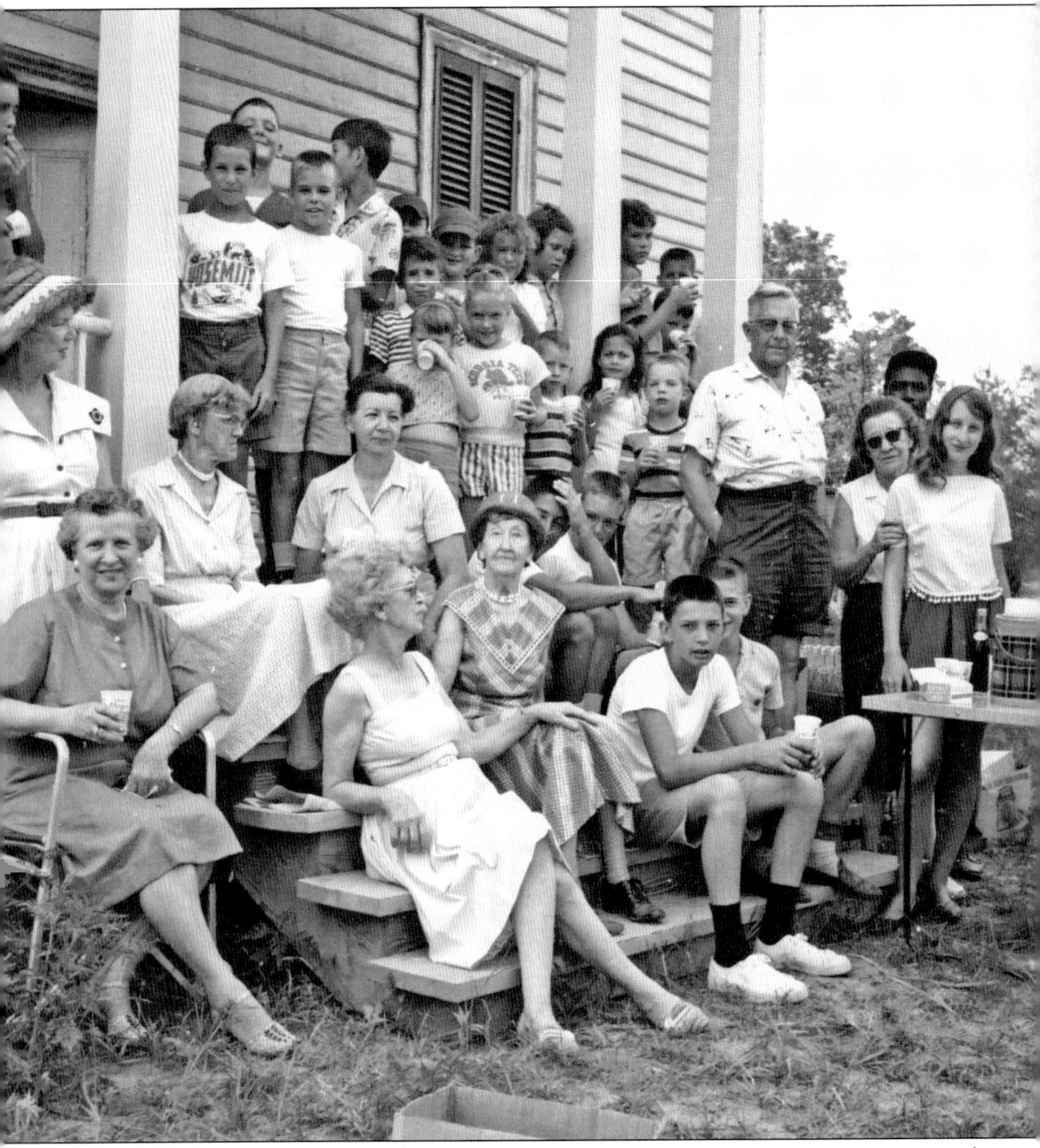

The Wake Forest Garden Club, the town's oldest existing civic organization, was instrumental in moving and preserving the Calvin Jones House. In this 1963 photograph, ladies of the club pose with volunteers on the steps of the house. Seated in the center, with dark hair and a short-sleeved white shirt, is Kathleen Mackie. Ethel Crittenden, daughter of former Wake Forest College president Dr. Charles Taylor and mother of Christopher Crittenden, sits to her left. This social event, called the Rock Party, was intended to help rid the field surrounding the historic home of excess rocks and was one of many countless efforts the Garden Club has sponsored over the years. Members have also planted grass and trees on parkways, crepe myrtles and Lombardy poplars along the road to the cemetery, and put shrubs at the community house, around school buildings, and in the downtown area. (Courtesy of the North Carolina State Archives N.64.7.119-120.)

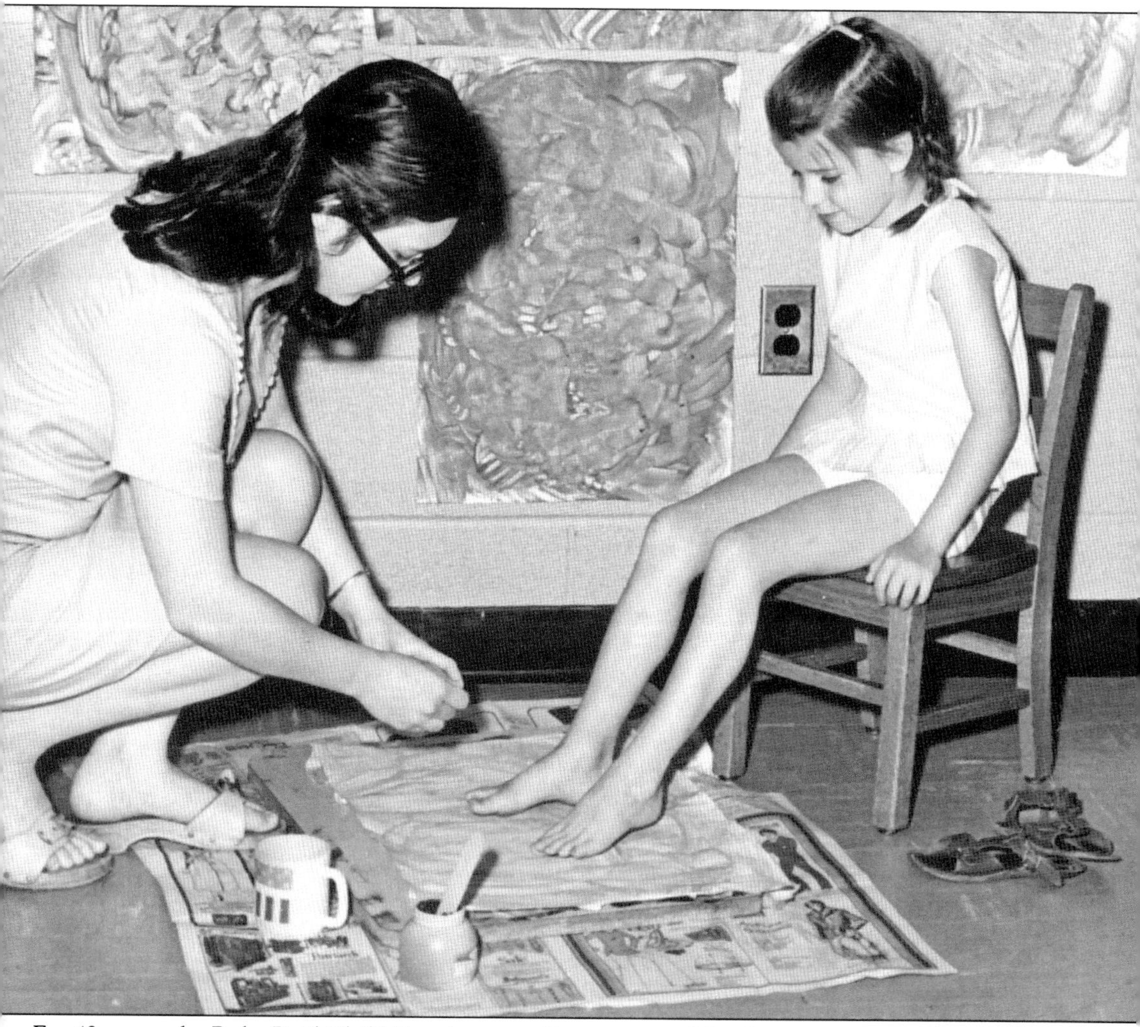

For 42 years, the Ruby Reid Child Development Center, named for the pioneering Wake Forest businesswoman whose funding helped finance the facility, provided top-ranked daycare for children on the seminary grounds. This *c.* 1970 photograph illustrates the excellent care provided as the seminary fulfilled its mission to care for and assist children in the Wake Forest community. So when it was announced the daycare would close in 2001, parents were in an uproar. Seminary president Paige Patterson said the controversial decision was both functional, as childcare was no longer viewed as part of the school's mission, and ideological. "Recent discoveries regarding children reared in child-care centers have only escalated our convictions that the child that is most likely to have a happy and useful life is a child reared in the home with the parents, not in a child-care center," he said. Parents, determined to save the beloved institution, moved it to a new location and kept it running as a non-profit corporation. (Courtesy of Southeastern Baptist Theological Seminary.)

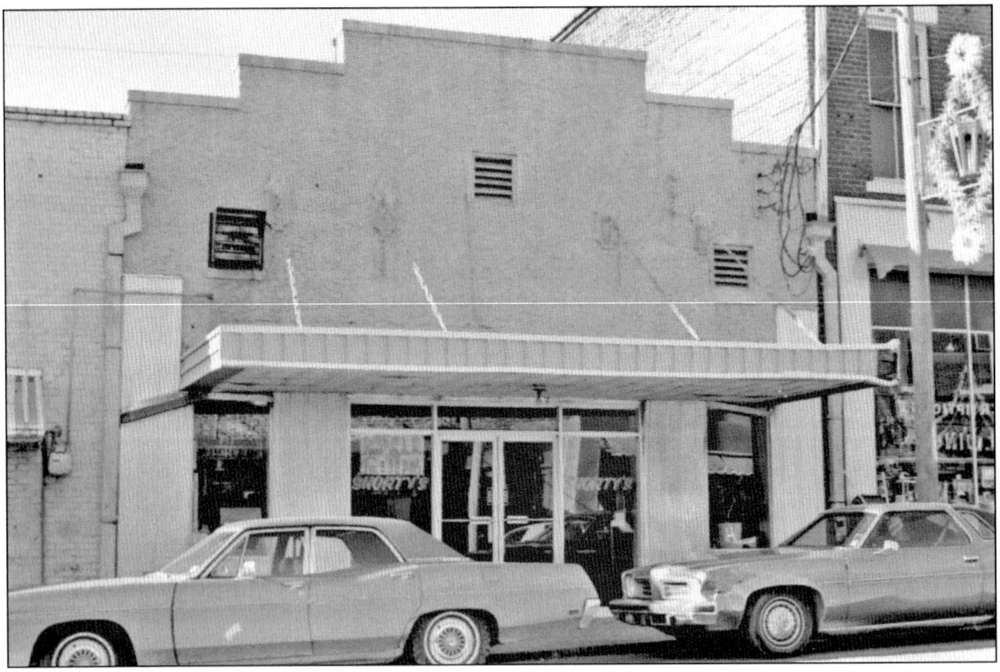

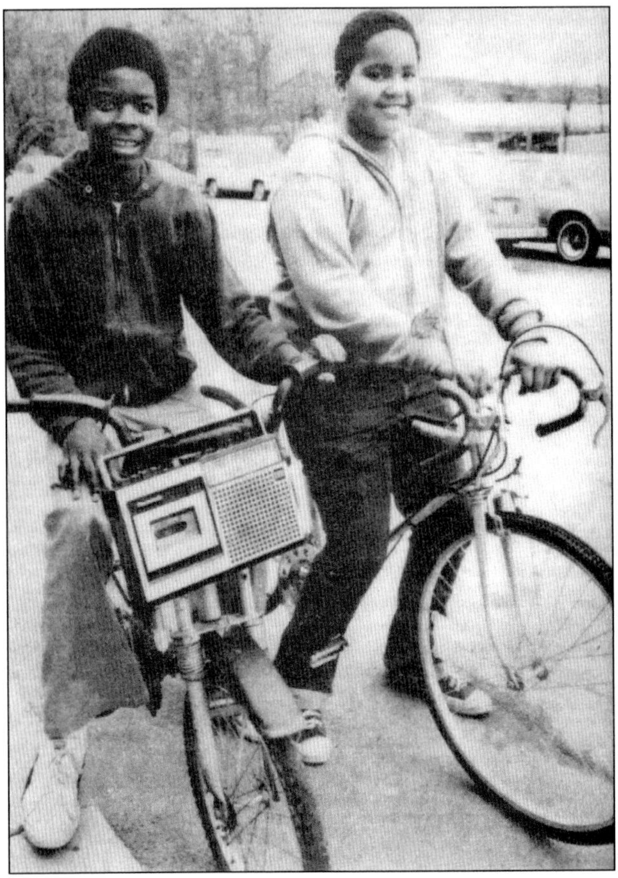

Serving customers since 1916, Shorty's is one of the oldest hot dog shops in the country. One of the few businesses to survive the college's departure, it attracted a new clientele with the arrival of the seminary and influx of new residents. As a tribute, a coffee shop called Shorty's on the Winston-Salem campus displays a photograph of past proprietor Millard Joyner. (Courtesy of the North Carolina State Archives N.79.9.893.)

This photograph, printed in the *Wake Weekly* on January 4, 1979, shows a young Calvin Feggins (on left) bicycling with a friend. Calvin is now well known throughout town as the owner of Feggins and Feggins Funeral Home on North White Street. (Courtesy of National Alumni Association DuBois School.)

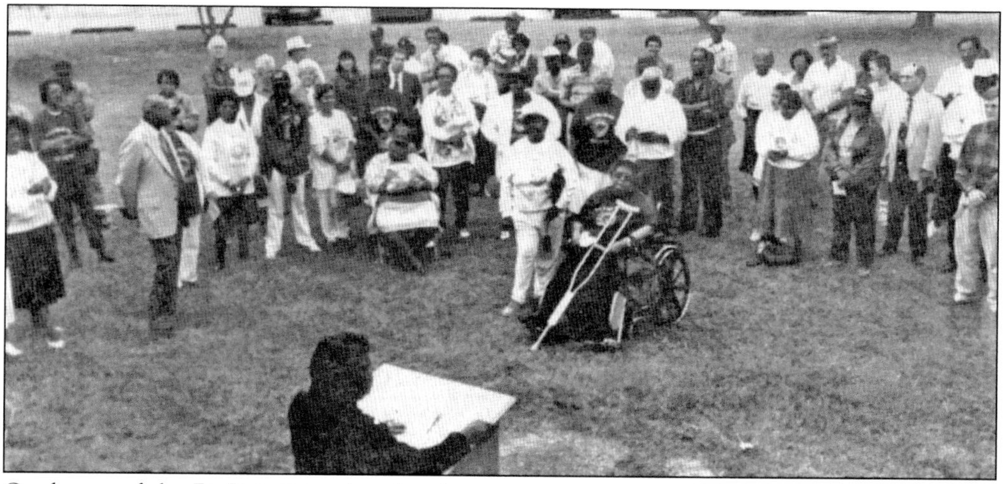

Graduates of the DuBois School gather for a reunion around 1995. Alumni and community members are now working to preserve the buildings of the original school and officially record its history. (Courtesy of National Alumni Association DuBois School.)

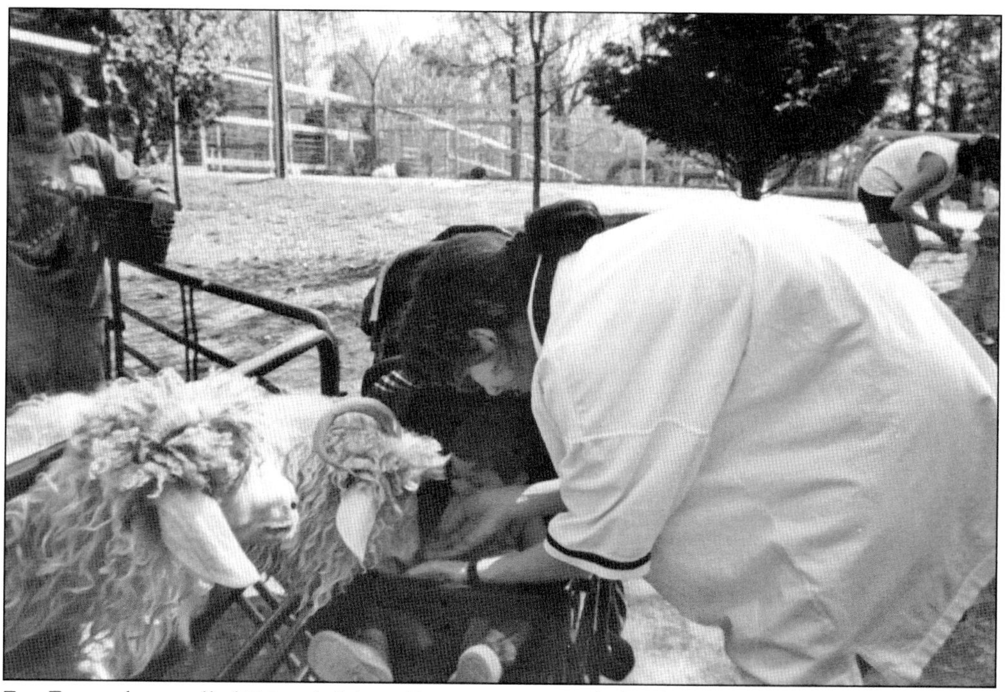

Zoo Fauna, later called Triangle Metro Zoo, was a privately funded zoo located on a large tract of land north of Wake Forest. Established by an expert animal breeder and displaying 83 varieties of exotic and domestic animals, the zoo opened to the public in September 1998. In its eight years of operation, it hosted countless visitors and school groups, and its petting barn was a popular destination for area families. (Courtesy of the Smart family.)

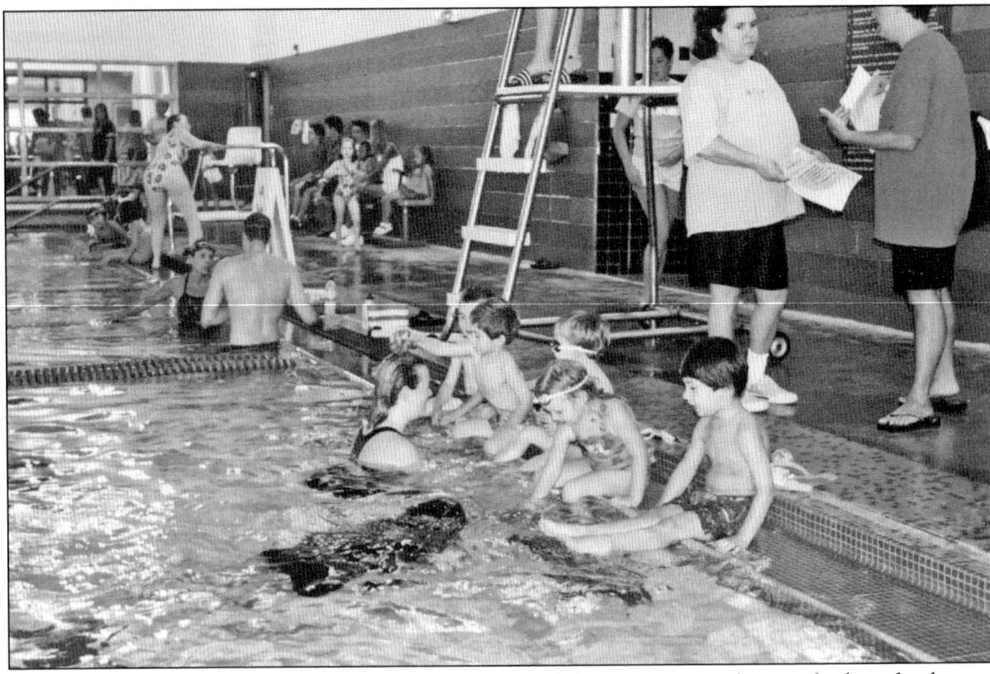

When Wakefield Plantation, a 2,200-acre country club community that ranked as the largest single residential and commercial development ever built in North Carolina, arrived on the scene, so did the Banks Kerr YMCA. The state-of-the-art athletic facility has made life more fit and fun for Wake Forest residents with countless soccer and basketball games, day camps, workouts, and swim lessons for little ones. (Courtesy of the Smart family.)

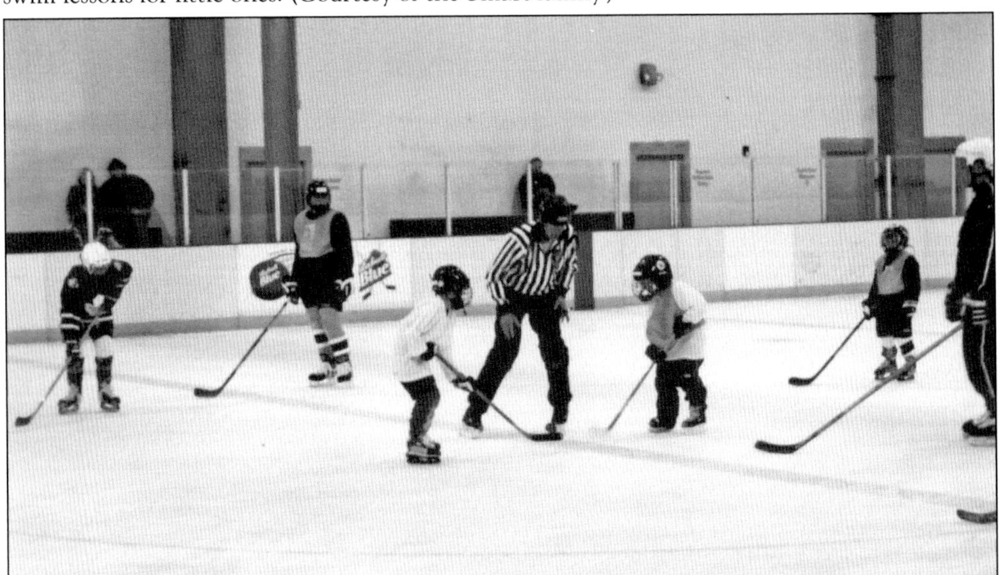

Developer Jeff Ammons had fitness in mind—as well as food, shopping, and entertainment—when he bought the 220,000-square-foot Athey plant in 2003. Called the Factory, his vision eventually included indoor soccer, karate, dance, and music instruction, as well as restaurants, shopping, and a pair of ice rinks that brought hockey and figure skating to Wake Forest. (Courtesy of the Smart family.)

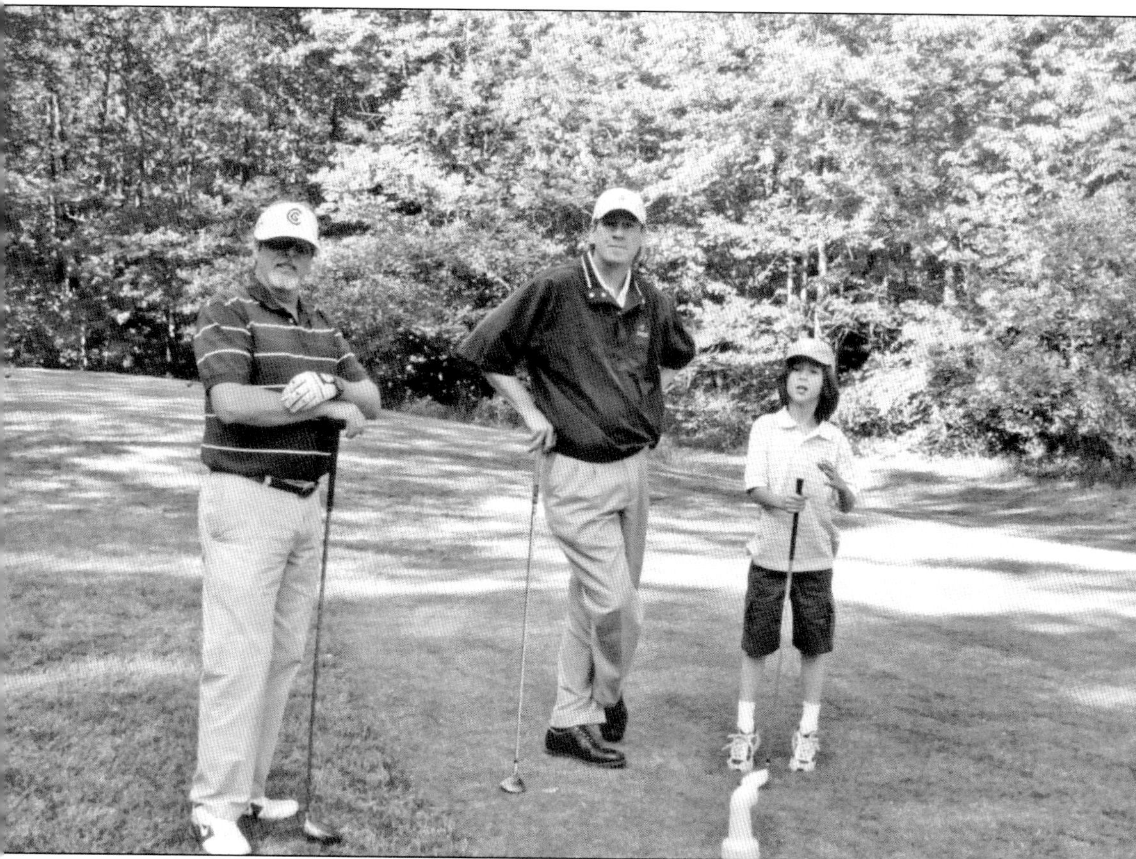

Gone are the days when the charming Wake Forest Golf Club and the nine-hole Paschal Golf Course were the only game in town. Wake Forest University graduate and golf-course architect Bob Moore (center) swung into the new millennium by designing the Heritage Golf Course, voted North Carolina's Best New Course in 2002. The award-winning, 6,929-yard, par-72 course spreads out over 200 acres of beautiful rolling hills on what was once the Marshall-Stroud Dairy Farm. The much heralded Tom Fazio course at Hasentree is the diamond in the crown of a resort development that's turning the rocky area once known as "the Harricane" into the region's most exclusive and expensive golf club community. And Wakefield Plantation's Tournament Players Club, designed by three-time U.S. Open Champion Hale Irwin, is a championship golf course that's attracted the spotlight of national competition. Together these courses and the affluent neighborhoods surrounding them are adding another chapter to the changing history of Wake Forest. (Courtesy of the Smart family.)

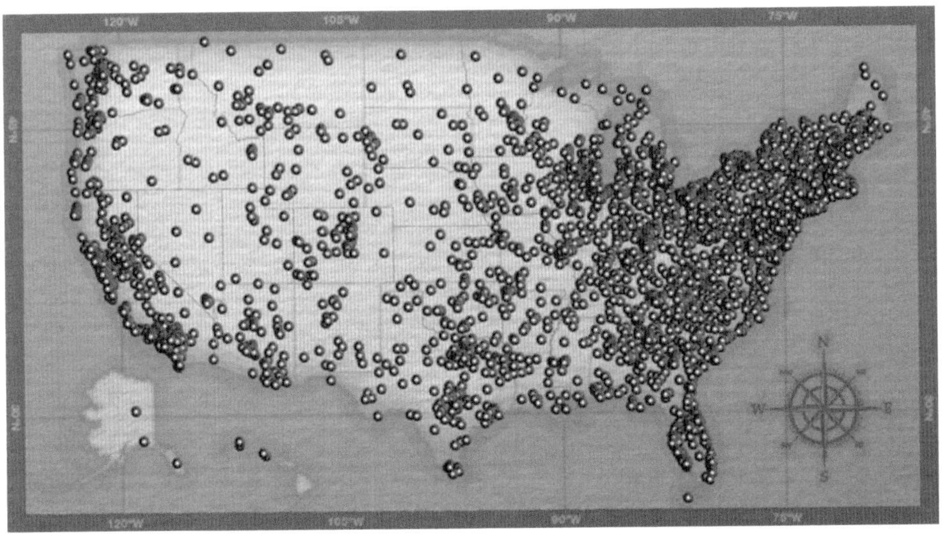